"Commentaries on Col⟨ ⟩pply. Few, however, balance the careful exegesis and pastoral sensitivity of this volume. Akin and Pace have done pastors a great service!"

Miguel Echevarria, assistant professor of New Testament and Greek, and director of Hispanic leadership development at Southeastern Baptist Theological Seminary

"Commentaries serve pastors by bringing trusted friends into your study to help you better understand God's Word. The *Exalting Jesus in Colossians and Philemon* commentary avoids the unrelatable ivory tower by offering biblically faithful, relevant, and pastoral insights that can transform the lives of God's people. I'm thankful to have this series in my library."

J. Garrett Kell, pastor, Del Ray Baptist Church, Alexandria, VA

"Pace and Akin perform a great service for the busy pastor by helpfully distilling some of the best resources on these two important letters of Paul. They skillfully demonstrate how the most essential truths of each text can be packaged into sound expository messages that exalt Christ and proclaim the great doctrines of the Christian faith. This entire series offers a rare opportunity to see Christ-centered exposition modeled by some of the most gifted preachers of our generation."

Charles Quarles, research professor of New Testament and biblical theology and Charles Page Chair of Biblical Theology at Southeastern Baptist Theological Seminary

"In ten studies on Colossians and four on Philemon, this book elevates Christ throughout. The authors display skill as exegetes, gifts as communicators, zeal as evangelists, and wisdom as pastoral leaders to shed fresh light on epistles that are critical for the church's Christological understanding, moral character, leadership methods, and social practice. Readers will discover an enjoyable manual for understanding and a suggestive model for conveying the rich implications of these storied sibling Pauline letters."

Robert W. Yarbrough, professor of New Testament, Covenant Theological Seminary, St. Louis, MO

CHRIST-CENTERED
Exposition

NT / COMMENTARY   FEATURING

AUTHORS R. Scott Pace and Daniel L. Akin

SERIES EDITORS David Platt, Daniel L. Akin, and Tony Merida

CHRIST-CENTERED

Exposition

EXALTING JESUS IN

COLOSSIANS AND PHILEMON

HOLMAN®
REFERENCE
NASHVILLE, TENNESSEE

Christ-Centered Exposition Commentary: Exalting Jesus in Colossians, Philemon
© Copyright 2021 by Daniel L. Akin and R. Scott Pace

B&H Publishing Group
Brentwood, Tennessee
All rights reserved.

ISBN: 978-0-8054-9810-3

Dewey Decimal Classification: 220.7
Subject Heading: BIBLE. N.T. COLOSSIANS—N.T. PHILEMON—
COMMENTARIES \ JESUS CHRIST

Printed in the United States of America
3 4 5 6 7 8 9 10 • 27 26 25 24 23

SERIES DEDICATION

Dedicated to Adrian Rogers and John Piper. They have taught us to love the gospel of Jesus Christ, to preach the Bible as the inerrant Word of God, to pastor the church for which our Savior died, and to have a passion to see all nations gladly worship the Lamb.

—David Platt, Tony Merida, and Danny Akin
March 2013

AUTHORS' DEDICATIONS

To modern day Bereans—
those who receive the Word with eagerness
and devote themselves
to examining the Scriptures

—R. Scott Pace

To my dear friend and brother James Merritt.
No one has blessed and encouraged me more in my life and ministry
than this wonderful servant of our Lord Jesus Christ.

—Daniel L. Akin

TABLE OF CONTENTS

ACKNOWLEDGMENTS

My mentor in the ministry, Dr. Bill Bennett, used to describe the insatiable desire for God's Word by likening Scripture to salt water: "The more you drink, the thirstier you get!" I've found this spiritual reality to be true in my own life, and nothing is more like guzzling God's Word than the rich and rewarding study to write a commentary. It has been refreshing to my soul, and it has deepened my desire to drink even more deeply from the nourishing riches of the sacred Scriptures. I pray that others will benefit in similar ways as they listen to the voice of God's Spirit through his Word.

I'm overwhelmed with gratitude for the honor to contribute to this series. I'm thankful for Danny Akin and his continued investment in my life and ministry. Through various roles—my PhD mentor, coauthor of *Pastoral Theology*, president, colleague, and friend—his leadership and influence continue to deepen my love for Christ, his church, his word, and the nations. I'm also thankful for my friends and co-laborers at Southeastern Baptist Theological Seminary who cultivate an environment of academic excellence and spiritual growth that makes writing projects like this possible. The privilege of serving our students, especially those in the College at Southeastern, also made this project worthwhile, as their sincere heart for our Savior continually inspires me to be a faithful steward of God's truth.

This project was also developed in part as a preaching series during my service as interim pastor of Beach Road Baptist Church in Southport, NC. The joy of seeing these truths impact their lives, and their kind affirmation of the Colossians series in particular, will forever be linked in my heart to these glorious texts.

I'm also indebted to the capable and professional team at B&H who have provided the guidance and support necessary to sharpen this project and make it exponentially better. My research assistant and PhD student, Ryan Ross, also deserves my hearty appreciation for his helpful suggestions and contributions along the way.

To my wife, Dana, my thanks could never fully capture the depth of my appreciation for your constant love and encouragement. I'm amazed at the strength and stamina that you exhibit in your tireless care for our family and the unwavering support you lovingly provide for me. To our children—Gracelyn, Tyler, Tessa, and Cassie—I pray that you would be captivated by the glory of Christ and "walk in him, being rooted and built up in him and established in the faith, just as you were taught, and overflowing with gratitude" (Col 2:6).

To my beloved Savior and exalted King, Jesus Christ, may you receive the honor and glory for any fruit born by this labor of love given as an offering to you!

— R. Scott Pace

Thank you Kim Humphrey, Mary Jo Haselton, and Shane Shaddix for your invaluable assistance in producing this volume. Each of you is a personal gift from God to me.

—Daniel L. Akin

SERIES INTRODUCTION

Augustine said, "Where Scripture speaks, God speaks." The editors of the Christ-Centered Exposition Commentary series believe that where God speaks, the pastor must speak. God speaks through His written Word. We must speak from that Word. We believe the Bible is God breathed, authoritative, inerrant, sufficient, understandable, necessary, and timeless. We also affirm that the Bible is a Christ-centered book; that is, it contains a unified story of redemptive history of which Jesus is the hero. Because of this Christ-centered trajectory that runs from Genesis 1 through Revelation 22, we believe the Bible has a corresponding global-missions thrust. From beginning to end, we see God's mission as one of making worshipers of Christ from every tribe and tongue worked out through this redemptive drama in Scripture. To that end we must preach the Word.

In addition to these distinct convictions, the Christ-Centered Exposition Commentary series has some distinguishing characteristics. First, this series seeks to display exegetical accuracy. What the Bible says is what we want to say. While not every volume in the series will be a verse-by-verse commentary, we nevertheless desire to handle the text carefully and explain it rightly. Those who teach and preach bear the heavy responsibility of saying what God has said in His Word and declaring what God has done in Christ. We desire to handle God's Word faithfully, knowing that we must give an account for how we have fulfilled this holy calling (Jas 3:1).

Second, the Christ-Centered Exposition Commentary series has pastors in view. While we hope others will read this series, such as parents, teachers, small-group leaders, and student ministers, we desire to provide a commentary busy pastors will use for weekly preparation of biblically faithful and gospel-saturated sermons. This series is not academic in nature. Our aim is to present a readable and pastoral style of commentaries. We believe this aim will serve the church of the Lord Jesus Christ.

Third, we want the Christ-Centered Exposition Commentary series to be known for the inclusion of helpful illustrations and theologically driven applications. Many commentaries offer no help in illustrations, and few offer any kind of help in application. Often those that do offer illustrative material and application unfortunately give little serious attention to the text. While giving ourselves primarily to explanation, we also hope to serve readers by providing inspiring and illuminating illustrations coupled with timely and timeless application.

Finally, as the name suggests, the editors seek to exalt Jesus from every book of the Bible. In saying this, we are not commending wild allegory or fanciful typology. We certainly believe we must be constrained to the meaning intended by the divine Author himself, the Holy Spirit of God. However, we also believe the Bible has a messianic focus, and our hope is that the individual authors will exalt Christ from particular texts. Luke 24:25-27,44-47 and John 5:39,46 inform both our hermeneutics and our homiletics. Not every author will do this the same way or have the same degree of Christ-centered emphasis. That is fine with us. We believe faithful exposition that is Christ centered is not monolithic. We do believe, however, that we must read the whole Bible as Christian Scripture. Therefore, our aim is both to honor the historical particularity of each biblical passage and to highlight its intrinsic connection to the Redeemer.

The editors are indebted to the contributors of each volume. The reader will detect a unique style from each writer, and we celebrate these unique gifts and traits. While distinctive in their approaches, the authors share a common characteristic in that they are pastoral theologians. They love the church, and they regularly preach and teach God's Word to God's people. Further, many of these contributors are younger voices. We think these new, fresh voices can serve the church well, especially among a rising generation that has the task of proclaiming the Word of Christ and the Christ of the Word to the lost world.

We hope and pray this series will serve the body of Christ well in these ways until our Savior returns in glory. If it does, we will have succeeded in our assignment.

David Platt
Daniel L. Akin
Tony Merida
Series Editors
February 2013

Colossians

Welcome to the Family!

COLOSSIANS 1:1-8

Main Idea: As believers in Jesus Christ, we are adopted as members into God's family to share in the divine privileges of salvation and to participate in the mission of the gospel.

I. **As Members of God's Family, We Have Reasons to Be Glad (1:1-2).**
    A. We should celebrate our personal callings (1:1).
    B. We should celebrate our spiritual community (1:2).

II. **As Members of God's Family, We Have Reasons to Be Grateful (1:3-5a).**
    A. We give thanks for our saving faith (1:3-4a).
    B. We give thanks for our sincere love (1:4b).
    C. We give thanks for our secure hope (1:5a).

III. **As Members of God's Family, We Have Reasons to Be Going (1:5b-8).**
    A. The truth of God is the gospel message (1:5b-6).
    B. The truth of God is a global message (1:6-8).

The personalized approach Paul takes in each of his letters emphasizes the importance of his greeting and its contents. Since the apostle was not responsible for planting the church at Colossae, his lack of personal rapport and familiarity required a more affirming disposition (2:1-2). The tone of Paul's letter to the Colossians was one of encouraging exhortation, and his epistolary greeting and expression of thanksgiving typify his demeanor toward them. Although his goal was ultimately corrective, and the Christological issues facing the church were of the highest doctrinal significance, he did not use a stern rebuke and confrontational approach as he did with the Galatians (Gal 1:6-9; 3:1). Instead, he chose a more personable and winsome tone that reflected his genuine enthusiasm for the Colossians' faith, and he lovingly urged them to progress further in their understanding and devotion to Christ.

In the early 1990s, one of the most famous advertising slogans was, "Membership has its privileges." This well-known mantra was promoted by American Express in an effort to elevate the perceived status of its cardholders and to invite those who could qualify to benefit from its exclusive rewards. Their advertisement piqued the interest of those who were unfamiliar with their program and celebrated the status of those who were already involved.

While they may have coined that particular phrase in their campaign, the concept itself was nothing new. In fact, the apostle Paul had described the same reality centuries before credit cards or country clubs even existed. But the membership he described was not to a financial entity; it was membership in a family. This membership is not reserved for those with elite status, it cannot be earned based on merit, and its rewards are not calculated by an earthly standard. But it does come with immeasurable benefits.

The opening section in this letter describes the ultimate membership offer that God extends to all of us. In its original context, Paul's greeting served to welcome the Colossians to the family of faith, to celebrate the divine privileges they now shared, and to inspire their faithful service in the gospel mission. For followers of Jesus Christ, the opening to Colossians provides the same contemporary purpose, as it reminds us of three important spiritual truths.

As Members of God's Family, We Have Reasons to Be Glad
COLOSSIANS 1:1-2

Paul's personal introduction to the church at Colossae follows the form of a typical epistolary greeting. He announces himself, along with Timothy, as the author, states his credentials, identifies the recipients, and extends a personal salutation. The broader audience of "the saints in Christ" indicates the public nature of the letter and Paul's intention to address the church as a whole (v. 2, cf. 4:16). But in speaking to God's family of faith, he strategically uses the standard elements of his greeting to encourage them with realities we all can celebrate.

We Should Celebrate Our Personal Callings (1:1)

Paul introduces himself as "an apostle of Christ Jesus." This parallels many of his other letters (Rom 1:1; 1 Cor 1:1; 2 Cor 1:1; Gal 1:1; Eph 1:1; Col 1:1; 1 Tim 1:1; 2 Tim 1:1; Titus 1:1), but it is of particular importance for the Colossians for two related reasons: their lack of personal familiarity with Paul (2:1) and the crucial nature of the doctrinal issues he planned to address. His authority as an apostle—one who had encountered the resurrected Lord (Acts 1:21-22; cf. 1 Cor 15:7-9), one who received his message directly from Christ (Gal 1:15-17), and one who was recognized among the authorized church leaders (Gal 2:6-9; cf. Acts 9:27-28)—serves as the basis by which he will assertively declare the doctrinal truth regarding Christ and will convincingly refute the false teachers.

While Paul is establishing his authority and exerting influence, he is not boasting of his prominence and exhibiting arrogance. The modifying phrases for his identity as an apostle, "of Christ Jesus" and "by God's will," emphasize Christ's ultimate authority over his life and God's grace in his appointment (cf. 1 Cor 15:9-10; 1 Tim 1:12-15). The apostle also humbly includes "Timothy our brother" as a co-sender of the letter.[1] Similarly, later he elevates the status of Epaphras, "our dearly loved fellow servant," as a "faithful minister of Christ" despite his lack of any formal position (1:7).

Through Paul's introductory testimony we are reminded that God has a plan for each of us. Though your position may not have an official title or status, the Lord calls each one of us to serve according to his will for our lives. As a follower of Christ and participant in his kingdom, every believer has significance and purpose because each has been called by God individually. Whether as pastors, schoolteachers, public servants, or dedicated employees, we members of his kingdom family can celebrate our personal callings!

We Should Celebrate Our Spiritual Community (1:2)

Although our individual callings can be celebrated, Paul's greeting also emphasizes the communal nature of our salvation and the joy it should produce. He addresses the believers "at Colossae" as "saints in Christ" and as "faithful brothers and sisters" (v. 2). Paul uses the

---

[1] Timothy accompanied Paul on his missionary journeys (Acts 16:1-5; 17:14; 18:5), was one of his helpers (Acts 19:22), and is mentioned in other epistolary greetings (2 Cor 1:1; Phil 1:1; Col 1:1; 1 Thess 1:1; 2 Thess 1:1). He also assumed the prominent role of leadership in the church at Ephesus where Paul addressed two pastoral letters of instruction to him (1 and 2 Tim). In the original, the plural pronoun "our" is absent, but it includes the definite article, "the brother" (cf. 2 Cor 1:1; Phlm 1), signifying Timothy's important role in God's work despite not being an apostle (Melick, *Philippians, Colossians, Philemon*, 189). This is accentuated even more with the church at Colossae, since there is no record of it being established by an apostle or person of public prominence.

term *saints* to speak of their positional status "in Christ" as God's holy ones (cf. 1:4,12,26) who are distinguished from the world and literally set apart. He also refers to them as "faithful brothers and sisters," highlighting the familial relationship they share "in Christ" and their persevering devotion.[2]

Paul extends his customary greeting, "grace . . . and peace," to them, which further defines their identity through their relationship with "God" as "our Father." As recipients of God's grace, they now enjoy peace with God and stand in right relationship with him (Rom 5:1-2). Therefore, Paul commends these ongoing, sacred gifts as a prayerful greeting and reminder of the gospel basis that unites them as God's people.

One of the most glorious truths about our salvation is the reality of our acceptance into God's family. Because of his great love for us (1 John 3:1), and through our personal faith in Jesus (John 1:12), we are adopted as his children (Rom 8:15; Gal 4:4-7) and enjoy a special relationship with God as our heavenly Father. Our common faith in Christ also unites us together as "brothers and sisters," as a family who loves and supports one another. Additionally, as members of God's spiritual family, we are joined together as members of Christ's body (Col 1:18,24; cf. Eph 4:4-6) who collectively serve Christ and strengthen one another (Col 3:12-17; cf. Eph 4:15-16).

Paul's greeting in his sister letter to the Ephesians relishes the countless blessings that our adoption entitles every believer to receive (Eph 1:3-14). This same tone of celebration marks the apostle's opening remarks to the Colossians. The familial language throughout these two introductory verses stresses the spiritual community that the believers in Colossae now constitute and the eternal community to which they now belong. As contemporary Christians and members of God's eternal family, we share these same blessings and should relish our spiritual community as we encourage one another to fulfill our spiritual calling. We certainly have reasons to be glad!

---

[2] Some scholars have argued that grammatically the descriptive phrase of Paul's recipients should translate the terms as parallel adjectives "holy and faithful" brothers (see Thomas B. Slater, "Translating ἅγιος"). However, others note that the use of the terms is best understood and translated as, "To the saints at Colossae, [that is,] the faithful brothers in Christ" (Pao, *Colossians and Philemon*, 48).

As Members of God's Family, We Have Reasons to Be Grateful

COLOSSIANS 1:3-5A

In addition to having reasons to be glad, we also have reasons to be grateful. Paul transitions from his introductory greeting to an intercessory prayer. His prayer for the Colossians is twofold; it focuses on praising God for their salvation (vv. 3-8) and petitioning God for their sanctification (vv. 9-14). Paul's appeal on their behalf also serves a dual purpose for his readers as it is both instructive and informative.

By way of example, his prayer instructs us how we should pray for others. The frequency of his prayers for the Colossians is implied by the participial phrase, "when we pray for you," and by the modifying adverb, "always." These terms imply a regular pattern of intercession that consistently includes thanksgiving on their behalf (cf. Eph 5:20). The focus of Paul's prayers[3] for the church is the one to whom he directs his gratitude: "God, the Father of our Lord Jesus Christ." This phrase is of particular importance as it establishes a baseline for the Christology of the entire letter.[4] Paul directs thanksgiving to God the Father (cf. 1:12; 3:17) while asserting the lordship of Jesus Christ who reveals the Father (1:15) and in whom "the entire fullness of God's nature dwells bodily" (2:9; cf. 1:19).

By way of expression, his prayer informs our understanding of redemption and provokes our heartfelt gratitude to God. Thanksgiving is a consistent theme throughout Paul's letter to the Colossians. It is mentioned numerous times—at least once in every chapter (1:3,12; 2:7;

---

[3] Paul's use of the plural pronoun "we," as opposed to the singular "I," has received considerable scholarly attention, especially since he shifts to the use of singular verbs in 1:23 (Melick, *Philippians, Colossians, Philemon*, 193). The plural pronoun could simply be a reference to Paul and Timothy as co-senders of the letter (O'Brien, *Colossians, Philemon*, 9). Some contend that this is the use of an "epistolary plural" that simply refers to himself with plural language (see Moule, *The Epistles*, 48). It seems preferable to interpret it as representative of those who were with Paul, including Timothy, corporately praying on behalf of the church at Colossae, since Paul uses the singular pronoun in other letters even when others are listed as co-senders (cf. 1 Cor 1:1,4; Phil 1:1,3; Phlm 1,4). In addition, he reverts back to the plural when requesting prayers from the Colossians in 4:3 (see Lightfoot, *St. Paul's Epistle*, 231).

[4] This phrase goes beyond some of the more general references of giving "thanks to God" used in some of his other letters (cf. 1 Cor 1:4; 1 Thess 1:2; 2 Thess 1:3), which implies intentionality based on specific circumstances, particularly the Christological nature of the Colossian heresy he was confronting.

3:15,16,17; 4:2). The first portion of his prayer (vv. 3-5) is an expression of thanksgiving that reminded them, and informs us, of multiple reasons believers have to be grateful.

We Give Thanks for Our Saving Faith (1:3-4a)

The primary basis for Paul's gratitude was their testimony of "faith in Christ Jesus" (v. 4). This phrase certainly identifies Jesus as the sole object of their saving faith (Calvin, *Galatians–Philemon*, 138), but it primarily indicates that their faith abides and operates within the sphere or realm of Christ's lordship (v. 3; Moule, *Colossians and Philemon*, 49; see also O'Brien, *Colossians, Philemon*, 11). This corresponds with his later encouragement for them to "remain grounded and steadfast in the faith" (1:23; cf. 2:5,7). Paul was thankful for their saving faith in Christ and that it was continuing to operate as a living and active faith under the reign of King Jesus. The vitality and vibrancy of their faith resulted in a testimony that had made its way to Paul, and he was grateful.

The Colossians had received "the word of truth, the gospel" (v. 5) and were trusting exclusively in the person and work of Christ for salvation. As a result, their lives had been transformed. But Paul's prayer of gratitude did not congratulate and celebrate the Colossians; it directed praise and thanksgiving to God. In the same way, we should rejoice over the gift of our salvation through faith, giving thanks to the Lord for "his indescribable gift" in Christ (2 Cor 9:15). In addition, this prayer also encourages us to maintain a vibrant faith that continues to live for Christ in submission to his lordship.

We Give Thanks for Our Sincere Love (1:4b)

The saving faith of the Colossians had become evident through their "love . . . for all the saints." Paul uses the Greek term *agapē* to identify the sacrificial love of the Colossians that reflected the sacrificial love of Christ. As those who had been transformed by the Savior's love, they directed that love toward others (cf. 1 John 4:10-11). Specifically, Paul commended their love "for all the saints" (Col 1:4). This phrase does not limit their love by excluding others in a preferential or prejudicial manner. Rather, it highlights the indiscriminate nature of their love, "for all," and its particular expression toward God's people, "the saints" (cf. Gal 6:10).

Love for others is the evidence of a redeemed heart (cf. 1 John 3:14; 4:7-8) and the distinguishing mark of Christ's followers (John 13:34-35). Later in his letter Paul challenges the Colossians to, above all else, "put on love, which is the perfect bond of unity" (3:14). The sincere affection believers share for one another emanates from the undeserved love we have received in Christ. It unites us together and provides the strength and support we all need. Paul was grateful for their sacrificial devotion, and likewise, we should give thanks for the sincere love we share as members of God's family.

We Give Thanks for Our Secure Hope (1:5a)

For believers, the faith and love we exhibit spring from the hope we have in Christ. The construction of verses 3-5a explains the Colossians' "faith" and "love" as by-products of their "hope." Hope is the stimulating source for their abiding faith and active love. The hope Paul speaks of here is more than a presiding disposition of the heart or attitude of optimistic anticipation (cf. Rom 8:24). Here, "hope" is referring to the objective reality of that which is "reserved for [us] in heaven" by God (cf. 1 Pet 1:4-5) and has been revealed in "the gospel" (Col 1:5; cf. 1:23). Christ is the personification of this hope, "the hope of glory" (1:27), and abides in us, resides in heaven, and will one day reveal our hope when he appears (3:1-4; cf. Titus 2:13).

As with the previous two virtues of the Colossians, "faith" and "love," Paul is previewing a subject he will reintroduce later in his letter by way of further exhortation and practical implication (1:23,27). He also may be countering potential arguments from the false teachers and the doctrinal heresy plaguing the Colossians as it relates to heavenly encounters, "the worship of angels" (2:18; Pao, *Colossians and Philemon*, 53). But primarily, Paul is reminding them (and us!) of the infinite significance of our hope as the foundational anchor for our souls (Heb 6:19-20). Through this hope God supplies us with joy and peace as we trust in him (Rom 15:13). Because of its substance and its certainty (Rom 5:5), we can live with confidence and contentment as we give thanks for our secure hope in Christ.

The sum total of Paul's gratitude for the Colossians unites the three cords of Christian virtue—faith, love, and hope. These three abiding qualities are not temporal like our gifts and abilities (1 Cor 13:13). They are the motivation and the means for our work, labor, and perseverance in Christ (1 Thess 1:3). They unite us as we devote ourselves to drawing near to him and to encouraging one another (Heb 10:22-24; cf. 1 Pet 1:21-22). This familiar trinity of Christian virtues summarizes why we as members of God's family have countless reasons to be grateful.

As Members of God's Family, We Have Reasons to Be Going
COLOSSIANS 1:5B-8

While our reasons to be glad and grateful draw us together, Paul is quick to explain that they also send us out. Our identity in Christ is inextricably linked to his kingdom agenda, and as members of God's family, we have reasons to be going. In his prayer Paul acknowledges the life-changing experience of the Colossians that he ultimately intends to affirm with his letter to them. But imbedded within their conversion is the message, "the gospel," and the messenger, "Epaphras," that will serve as the impetus for them to continue to carry the mission forward. By recounting their experience, Paul provides two important reasons that compel all believers to be going.

The Truth of God Is the Gospel Message (1:5b-6)

As they consider the hope that transformed their lives, he reminds them of their initial encounter with Christ. The phrase, "You have already heard about this hope" (v. 5), most likely refers to their hearing and reception of the good news of Jesus from Epaphras (vv. 6-7).[5] Paul summarizes the message they received as "the word of truth, the gospel" (v. 5).[6] Paul uses "the word" multiple times in the letter with various modifiers that all emphasize the supreme and salvific nature of the gospel (1:25; 3:16). The "word of truth" positions the gospel in contrast to the false teaching of the Colossian heresy (O'Brien, *Colossians,*

---

[5] Some scholars see Paul's reference to their original reception of the message as a rank of precedent that stresses its validity over their subsequent encounters with the false teachers. See Moule, *The Epistles,* 50.

[6] In addressing the various possible renderings of the phrase in verse 5, Pao aptly states, "This reading ['the word of truth, the gospel'] best captures the sense of the verse in its context, as it both emphasizes truth as the content of the proclamation, and the apostolic gospel as one that is identified with truth. This paves the way for Paul's argument against the false teachers who have deviated from this gospel" (*Colossians and Philemon,* 53).

Philemon, 12).[7] But perhaps most importantly, these verses establish the content of the gospel as the truth of salvation (cf. Eph 1:13).

The construction of the corresponding phrases in verses 5 and 6 parallels "the gospel" with "God's grace." This synonymous use highlights the unmerited nature of our salvation. The gospel and the grace of God are inextricably intertwined (Gal 1:6). In contrast to the works-oriented Colossian heresy, God's gracious gift of salvation cannot be earned and is entirely undeserved. The Colossians had "heard" and understood the gospel of grace, they embraced it by faith, and as a result their lives had been transformed.

Paul reminded the Colossians of the gospel message they received in order to compel them to spread the good news. In the same way, the gracious and glorious nature of our salvation should humble us and motivate us to share the gospel. Our appreciation of God's grace is directly proportional to the understanding of our need for it. And when we are mindful of our own undeserving nature, we will be more aware of the desperate need of the lost world around us to hear the truth of God that is the gospel message.

The Truth of God Is a Global Message (1:6-8)

The universal need for salvation, combined with the universal availability of God's grace, means the gospel message is also a global message. Paul encouraged the Colossians that the truth of God was "bearing fruit and growing all over the world" in the same way that it was among them (v. 6). In contrast to the local delusion of the Colossian heresy, the power of the gospel was unlimited in its impact. The phrase "bearing fruit" emphasizes the reproductive nature of the gospel, and "growing" refers to its maturing capability (Melick, *Philippians, Colossians, Philemon*, 198). Paul uses the same terms in his intercession for the Colossians (1:10). In essence, he was praying for the effects of the gospel to be realized in their personal lives as well. The good news of Jesus was transforming lives everywhere, and Paul encouraged them that their testimonies had become part of a gospel wave that was sweeping around the world. They were a part of a global movement!

---

[7] Calvin also notes this aspect of Paul's phrase: "He calls the gospel, the *word of truth*, with the view of putting honour upon it, that they may more steadfastly and firmly adhere to the revelation which they have derived from that source" (*Galatians–Philemon*, 139–40).

In celebrating with the Colossians, Paul also reminded them of how they had received the gospel. Multiple phrases in these verses emphasize the means by which the good news had reached them. They had "heard" it (vv. 5,6), it had "come to" them (v. 6), and they had "learned" it from Epaphras (v. 7). More than likely Epaphras was a Pauline convert who was responsible for starting the Colossian church (ibid., 198–99). A native Colossian (4:12), he had been instrumental in evangelizing the Lycus Valley, including the flourishing churches of Hierapolis and Laodicea (4:13; O'Brien, *Colossians, Philemon*, 15). He was a close associate of Paul, a "fellow prisoner in Christ Jesus" (Phlm 23); and here in Colossians 1:7, he is described as Paul and Timothy's "dearly loved fellow servant." Like the co-senders of the letter, Epaphras was a surrendered bond servant operating under the lordship of Christ. Paul goes on to describe Epaphras as "a faithful minister of Christ." The term *minister* is often used to speak of Paul's associates, specifically in his missionary activity (ibid.). As a devoted follower of Christ, Epaphras was fulfilling his responsibility by sharing the good news and was therefore considered "faithful."

Epaphras was God's instrument that he used to reach the Colossians with the gospel. This reminds us of his designed plan for us to carry the gospel message to the nations. As Paul charged the Romans,

> *How, then, can they call on him they have not believed in? And how can they believe without hearing about him? And how can they hear without a preacher? And how can they preach unless they are sent? As it is written: How beautiful are the feet of those who bring good news.* (Rom 10:14-15)

As followers of Christ, we have the responsibility to share the good news that we received through the faithful testimony of others. As citizens of God's kingdom, it is our duty and our privilege. As members of God's family, our joint efforts in the mission of our Lord allow us to celebrate the "love" we have for one another (v. 8; cf. v. 4) as we share his love with others. This divine love is a manifestation of "the Spirit" (v. 8) that unites us and epitomizes the reasons we have to be going.

Conclusion

Paul begins his letter to the Colossians by welcoming the young church to the family of faith. He greets them with joy and enthusiastically reassures them of their irrevocable status as members of God's beloved people. In doing so, he also reminds them of the blessings, privileges, and responsibilities they have inherited. Paul's prayerful introduction assures us that we as modern Christ-followers are also recipients of these same glorious truths. As members of God's family, we have reasons to be glad, reasons to be grateful, and reasons to be going!

Perhaps the greatest truth for us as members of God's family is found in the rich theology of the passage. The presence of the triune God in these verses cannot be overlooked, and its significance cannot be overstated. The individual references imply the doctrine of the Trinity, and their collective presence implies an important familial truth as well. Through the mention of each divine member—"God the Father" (vv. 3,6), "our Lord Jesus Christ" (vv. 3,4,7), and "the Spirit" (v. 8)—we are reminded of the intimacy and fellowship God intends for us to share as members of his family. The interpersonal harmony of the Godhead, along with its functional unity, models the intimate bond and spiritual benefits we share as God's people.

Paul's companion letter to the Ephesians emphasizes these Trinitarian truths more explicitly (Eph 1:3-14), but their implicit reality in this passage reinforces the same practical implications we have seen throughout Paul's introduction to the Colossians. Our adoption by the Father should provoke us to praise him with gladness. Our redemption by the Son should motivate us to follow him with gratitude. And our conversion by the Spirit should empower us to obey him by going.

There is no doubt about it: as members of God's family, we have everything we need and more. Indeed, membership does have its privileges!

Reflect and Discuss

1. What does Paul identify in this passage as the reasons we have to be glad?
2. What does Paul identify in this passage as the reasons we have to be grateful?
3. What does Paul identify in this passage as the reasons we have to be going?
4. How does Paul highlight the work of each person of the Trinity in his prayer?
5. What is the significance of Paul's thanking God in his prayer for their faith, love, and hope?

6. What does Paul's prayer teach us about the gospel?
7. What does Paul's prayer teach us about community?
8. What does Paul's prayer teach us about how we should pray for others?
9. How does Paul show us the importance of being members of God's family in this passage?
10. What does this passage teach us about our relationships with fellow believers in the church?

A Maze or Amazing? Discovering God's Will for Your Life

COLOSSIANS 1:9-14

Main Idea: God has a plan for his people and graciously reveals it to us so that we can accomplish his will in order to advance his kingdom.

I. **We Must Recognize the Possibility of Finding God's Will (1:9).**
   A. God's will has been disclosed (1:9).
   B. God's will must be discerned (1:9).
II. **We Must Embrace the Purpose of Following God's Will (1:10).**
   A. We must long to please Christ (1:10).
   B. We must live to please Christ (1:10).
III. **We Must Adopt the Process of Fulfilling God's Will (1:10-12).**
   A. We are called to good works (1:10).
   B. We are called to go deep (1:10).
   C. We are called to grow strong (1:11).
   D. We are called to give thanks (1:12).
IV. **We Must Relish the Privilege of Freedom in God's Will (1:13-14).**
   A. We have been rescued from darkness (1:13).
   B. We have been redeemed for a purpose (1:14).

On Christmas morning when I (Scott Pace) was eight years old, I found a notepad in my stocking along with my favorite gum, some candy, and a customary pair of socks. It had my favorite team on it, the Duke Blue Devils, and each page was covered with grid lines. It wasn't the most exciting gift I had ever received, but I did find a creative way to enjoy it. I began to use the lines to carefully trace out mazes similar to those you would find on a kid's menu at a restaurant. Eventually I graduated to full size sheets of graph paper and would design intricate labyrinths with the goal of creating the most confusing mazes with as many dead ends as possible. Drawing them was a lot of work, but it was so entertaining to watch my parents and friends attempt to navigate their way through them and repeatedly have to backtrack and start over.

When it comes to finding God's will for our lives, many Christians approach it with a similar perspective. We are each easily convinced that

God has designed a plan for us with lots of dead ends, as though we are mice making our way through some experimental maze. Whenever we come to a point where we don't know which way to go, we are forced to reverse course and pursue a different path. This results in our wandering through life with uncertainty, second-guessing our decisions, feeling frustrated at every wrong turn, and hoping that somehow we will reach our destination and finally find God's will.

But discerning God's will for our lives was never intended to be like working through *a maze*. He designed it to be *amazing*! So, how can we know with certainty what his will is for us? And what is involved in accomplishing his plan? Paul answers these questions through the second portion of his prayer for the Colossians. This passage teaches us how we can determine God's will for our lives, both individually and corporately, and the necessary steps to fulfill it.

We Must Recognize the Possibility of Finding God's Will

COLOSSIANS 1:9

Verses 9-14 make up the second stanza of Paul's prayer for the Colossians. The intercessory couplets share several parallel components, including thanksgiving (vv. 3,12), prayer (vv. 3,9), hearing (vv. 4,9), bearing fruit, growing (vv. 6,10), and saints (vv. 4,12). These commonalities provide emphasis and highlight underlying themes, but the shared similarities do not eclipse the individual significance and progression within the second portion of Paul's prayer report (Pao, *Colossians and Philemon*, 64).

Paul's gratitude for their faith in the first section (vv. 3-8) spawns prayers of intercession on the Colossians' behalf—"For this reason" (v. 9)—in the second section. Because of their adoption into God's family and their simultaneous appointment into his service, Paul petitioned the Lord to reveal his will for them while praying that they would have the spiritual eyes necessary to discern it (cf. Eph 1:17-19). The apostle's concern did not stem from the rise of the false teaching; it had been consistent all along. He had not "stopped praying" for them "since the day" he had become aware of their faith.

Paul uses two verbs somewhat synonymously, "praying" and "asking," to describe his appeals on their behalf. The first term is the most common word Paul uses for prayers in his letters and is general in nature, describing the entirety of prayer life (Melick, *Philippians, Colossians, Philemon*, 200). The second term is more specific and focuses on a particular aspect of his prayers for the Colossians, namely, his intercession for their faithfulness and fulfillment of God's will.

Paul's example teaches us that we are all in constant need of intercessory prayer that is not occasional or based on impending circumstances. His immediate and ongoing prayers for the Colossians confirm for us that God's will for our lives is a present reality more than a distant fairy tale. And ultimately, his petition demonstrates that our ability to know and follow God's will for our lives begins with and depends on prayer!

God's Will Has Been Disclosed (1:9)

One of the most significant aspects of Paul's prayer for the Colossians is found in the request itself. He prays that God's people "may be filled with the knowledge of his will" (v. 9). The implied truth underlying his petition is that it is actually possible for believers to know and understand God's will for their lives. If it were not a possibility, Paul would not have prayed this for the Colossian Christians.

When determining God's will for their lives, most people take a *discovery* approach. Like a tourist on a beach looking for lost treasures, they approach it with a spiritual metal detector, sweeping the detector around as they wander through life hoping they stumble onto it. Yet when they uncover what they have found, they are often disappointed to see the equivalent of empty cans, tarnished objects, or worthless trinkets. This is like encountering a dead end in my maze, so they start the discovery cycle over again and hope the next beep will be it.

But God did not design his will to be found that way. He would not design a plan for our lives to hide it from us. Therefore, we must adopt more of a *discernment* approach. His will for us is outlined with clear instructions, so finding it is more like working with a treasure map than a metal detector. Instead of letting us aimlessly wander around, he gives us the specific steps that will lead us right to the place in life where we can enjoy the satisfying pleasures of knowing him and fully experiencing his will for our lives.

These steps are clearly prescribed in Scripture. In fact, at least five times in the New Testament God's will for people is explicitly stated. In 1 Timothy 2:3-4, the Bible teaches us that *it is God's will for us to be saved.* His desire for our salvation affirms his love for all people and his desire for their repentance and redemption (cf. 2 Pet 3:9). Spiritual conversion is the necessary first step in experiencing God's will for our lives. Paul's prayer acknowledges this in that our "knowledge of his will" is discerned with "wisdom and spiritual understanding" (v. 9). But it also demonstrates the reality that just like in the matter of salvation, God's further will and desire for our lives can be rejected.

Scripture also affirms that *it is God's will for us to be sanctified*. First Thessalonians 4:3 clearly asserts, "This is God's will, your sanctification." To be *sanctified* literally means to be "set apart" or to be "made holy." This is often understood as the process of our lives being increasingly conformed to the likeness of Jesus (Rom 8:29). God saves us so that we will become "holy and blameless . . . before him" (Eph 1:4). Therefore, his will for our lives includes our spiritual growth as we are transformed by his grace (2 Cor 3:18).

But the process of sanctification is only possible through another aspect of his will for our lives. The Bible makes clear that *it is God's will for us to be Spirit-filled*. Paul counseled the Ephesians to "understand what the Lord's will is," continuing: "Be filled by the Spirit" (Eph 5:17-18). While believers receive the Holy Spirit at salvation (Eph 1:13), yielding to his control and allowing him to permeate every area of our lives is an ongoing and deliberate process. Our moment-by-moment surrender to his abiding presence in our lives is an essential part of God's will for every believer.

As we faithfully live for Christ through the power of the Spirit, we also begin to recognize that *it is God's will for us to stand*. First Peter 2:15 teaches us, "It is God's will that you silence the ignorance of foolish people by doing good." Living in opposition to a world that is hostile to Christ and his ways requires believers to stand firm in our faith and devotion to him (1 Cor 15:58). This involves taking a stand against the enemy (Eph 6:11-14), standing up for the truth (Jude 1:3), and standing up for those who cannot stand for themselves (Jas 1:27).

Finally, his Word teaches us that *it is God's will for us to suffer*. This doesn't typically come to mind at graduation celebrations when we are being lavished with well-meaning assurances of the great lives God has for us. It certainly isn't what we visualize as we dream of God's best. But 1 Peter 4:19 tells us that believers "who suffer according to God's will" should continue to trust the Lord and live by obedient faith. This type of suffering is the natural result of God's people going against the grain—living counterculturally and experiencing resistance and opposition for their faith. Jesus prepared his followers with a warning about this hostility (John 15:18-21). Likewise, Paul instructed Timothy, "All who want to live a godly life in Christ Jesus will be persecuted" (2 Tim 3:12). As followers of Christ, we are not guaranteed to be spared from suffering. In fact, we are assured of the opposite. When we live according to God's will, we have to endure hardship for his name's sake.

Because these five aspects of God's will are clearly stated in the Scriptures, none of us have to blindly wonder, *What is God's will for my life?* He has told us. Granted, these elements of God's will do not answer specific questions about particular decisions. But these are even better! They are *clear*. We know with certainty that it is what God wants. They are *consistent*. They won't change tomorrow even if our circumstances do. And they are *customized*. Even though they are universally true, they are personal instructions and are applicable for each one of us.

These spiritual realities of God's will are also practical. When we devote ourselves to pursuing these things that God has clearly revealed, we will realize his more specific will for our lives. When we obey his clearly expressed desires and specific instructions, they ultimately translate into a knowledge and understanding of his intentions for our lives. By devoting ourselves entirely to those aspects of his will that he has plainly revealed, we will be able to discern the more personalized and specific plans he has for us. As a result, we can move forward with confidence, being convinced that it is possible to know and understand God's will for our lives.

God's Will Must Be Discerned (1:9)

While certain aspects of God's will have been clearly revealed, more personal and particular elements must be discerned. Paul's prayer for them to be "filled with the knowledge" of God's will could point to a true knowledge and fullness in contrast to the Colossian heresy's presumed distortion of knowledge (cf. 2:2-3; 3:10) and diminishing of Christ's fullness (cf. 1:19,25; 2:9-10).[1] But the primary significance of this phrase and its complementary term is that believers can have a clear and certain understanding of God's revealed will.

---

[1] Many scholars argue that the heresy was some form of Gnosticism, which derives its name from the Greek term for knowledge, *gnosis*. However, the evidence is inconclusive, and the precise form of the heresy (as covered in the introduction) cannot ultimately be determined. Here, as with other aspects of the letter, the heresy does not dictate Paul's understanding of the issues; and, therefore, we should not interpret the content through the lens of the heresy.

There are other significant aspects of Paul's prayer regarding God's will and our discernment that are important to note as well. First, it is a passive knowledge, "that you may be filled," indicating that we must rely on the Lord to grant us understanding that we cannot obtain on our own. Second, God's will is "spiritual" in nature and can only be discerned accordingly. Only believers have the capacity to recognize and discern spiritual truths that are disclosed and confirmed by the indwelling Spirit of God (1 Cor 2:10-14). And finally, the knowledge of his will goes beyond a casual or cognitive recognition and leads to a practical appropriation in "wisdom and . . . understanding." The wisdom from above is distinct from worldly understanding, and both are distinguished by their corresponding works (Jas 3:13-18).

Therefore, we must carefully discern God's will through prayer and the guidance of his Spirit. We must confirm his will in accordance with his Word. And we can evaluate its validity for our lives by the fruit it produces. Because God has graciously disclosed his will and provided everything we need to discern his will, through Paul's prayer in this passage, we can affirm the possibility of finding God's will for our lives.

We Must Embrace the Purpose of Following God's Will
COLOSSIANS 1:10

Paul's prayer for the Colossians not only reveals the possibility of knowing God's will; it also challenged them to embrace the purpose of following God's will. Too many times, especially in our culture, we can have a desire to know and follow the Lord's plan, but not for the right reason. If we are not careful, our motivations can subtly, and tragically, become selfish. Paul clearly explained to the Colossians that his desire for them to discern God's will was not for their own personal benefit; he had a far greater purpose in mind. In the same way, we must evaluate our own motives and align them with the ultimate ambition.

We Must Long to Please Christ (1:10)

The desired outcome of Paul's petition is clearly marked by the phrase "so that," which interprets the infinitive form of the verb *to walk* as denoting purpose. In addition, Paul's prayer uses two parallel phrases that identify the ultimate goal of fulfilling God's will: "worthy of the Lord" and "fully pleasing to him." This designates the honor of Christ and the glory of God as the intended outcome of obedience. In other words, Paul's desire for them to know God's will is not for their own personal pleasure but so that their lives may be pleasing to God! We must adopt this same purposefulness in our own lives. Most believers desire to discern God's will for their own personal benefit— what makes them happy, fits in their plans, achieves their dreams, answers their prayers, and satisfies their desires. But satisfying him must become our deepest passion and our highest goal. We must be willing to lay down our dreams and desires in order to pursue his will for our lives. God does not always ask us to relinquish these things, but he knows our hearts and whether we are willing to put his will over our own. It is easy to say that we will, but when it comes down to it, are we willing to lay anything and everything on the altar for him?

Many people expect the Lord to give them what they desire, and some may even quote Psalm 37:4 to justify their expectations: "Take delight in the LORD, and he will give you your heart's desires." But this misunderstanding portrays God as some cosmic genie who is obligated to grant us our wishes as long as we ask "in Jesus's name." What this verse actually means is that God will infuse our hearts with his desires when we learn to delight ourselves in what pleases him.

We Must Live to Please Christ (1:10)

Our desire to please Christ cannot simply be a sentiment or feeling; it must translate into action. We must not only *long* to please Christ; we must *live* to please Christ. Paul's emphasis on knowledge, wisdom, and understanding in verse 9 cannot be divorced from the action in verse 10. His prayer for the Colossians was intended to influence their behavior as noted by his use of the familiar metaphor "to walk."[2] This term, drawing on its Hebrew roots (cf. "live" in Gen 17:1), summarizes one's lifestyle and characterizes it as one of obedience and godliness (Melick, *Philippians, Colossians, Philemon*, 203). The accompanying phrase in this verse, "walk worthy of the Lord," depicts a manner of life that is consistent with their identity as saints (v. 2; cf. Rom 16:2), their "calling" (Eph 4:1), the "gospel of Christ" (Phil 1:27), and "God" himself (1 Thess 2:12; Pao, *Colossians and Philemon*, 70). This pattern of

---

[2] As O'Brien notes, "Paul often characterizes the life and behavior of the Christian by this verb *walk* (Gal 5:16; cf. v. 25; Rom 6:4; 8:4; 14:15; 2 Cor 4:2; Eph 2:10; 4:1; 5:2,15; Phil 3:17; etc.)" (*Colossians, Philemon*, 22).

behavior corresponding with their redeemed nature and abiding faith is ultimately what pleases the Lord and fulfills his will (cf. 1 Thess 4:1).

This means that pursuing God's will for our lives must be defined as comprehensively living in submission and surrender rather than living in comfort and convenience. It means our lives must be entirely and exclusively devoted to honoring him. We can't live the selfish way we want to and hide behind sanctified excuses like, "Well, God knows my heart." Our true desires will be revealed through our actual behavior as we embrace the ultimate purpose of following God's will: pleasing Christ!

We Must Adopt the Process of Fulfilling God's Will
COLOSSIANS 1:10-12

Paul's heart and desire for the Colossians are not limited to abstract spiritual thought. His prayer for believers also provides concrete instruction. The structure of these verses reveals a fourfold pattern that specifies practical aspects of the life that pleases the Lord. Paul uses four parallel participles, not always captured by contemporary translations, to describe the process of fulfilling God's will: "bearing fruit" (v. 10), "growing" (v. 10), "being strengthened" (v. 11), and "giving thanks" (v. 12). The verbs of ongoing action provide us with practical steps in the process of fulfilling God's will for our lives.

We Are Called to Good Works (1:10)

The first aspect of the process Paul identifies is "bearing fruit in every good work" (v. 10). This phrase "bearing fruit" speaks to the work of the gospel throughout the world (v. 6) but now references the specific work it performs in the life of the believer. Genuine faith inevitably produces good works (Jas 2:14-26), and God has redeemed us to be a people who are zealous for good works (Titus 2:14). These works are "fruit" produced by the Spirit (Gal 5:22-23)—fruit that glorifies God and distinguishes us as Jesus's disciples (John 15:8). As part of God's will for our lives, he has prepared good works for us to do (Eph 2:10), and he enables us to perform them (Phil 2:13).

We Are Called to Go Deep (1:10)

The process of fulfilling God's will also includes "growing in the knowledge of God" (v. 10). The ever-increasing nature of the gospel, "growing" (v. 6), is now personally experienced in the life of the believer through a deepening knowledge of God. Our relationships with the Lord are intended to increase in spiritual depth and personal intimacy (2 Pet 3:18). Just as Paul elevated knowing Christ above everything else (Phil 3:8), we must also set this as our ultimate goal and highest priority (Jer 9:23-24). We grow in our knowledge of him through spending time in prayer, personal Bible study, and faithful obedience. These disciplines not only enable us to discern his will; they also equip us to fulfill it (Rom 12:2).

We Are Called to Grow Strong (1:11)

Paul also points out that the process involves "being strengthened with all power, according to his glorious might" (v. 11). This is not merely encouragement for us to rely on the Lord. It means that fulfilling God's plan will be impossible apart from his divine strength. God's will for our lives will extend us beyond our own capabilities. It will require emotional and physical stamina that can be sustained only with his spiritual strength (cf. Eph 3:16). The use of the passive form of this participle, "being strengthened," accentuates the Lord as the active provider of divine enablement. The parallel phrases "all power" and "his glorious might" reinforce the supreme nature of his strength that enables us to fulfill his will. By his might, the Lord will empower us to have "great endurance and patience" (v. 11). These terms speak to the afflictions we will endure in this world as believers (John 16:33; 2 Tim 3:12) and the patience that must characterize our lives as we trust and follow him (Jas 5:7-8). Ultimately, if we pursue paths that can be accomplished in our own strength and ability, then we have achieved something less than God's will.

We Are Called to Give Thanks (1:12)

Finally, the process of fulfilling God's will concludes with our "giving thanks to the Father" (v. 12). This and the parallel thanks directed to the Father (vv. 3,12) serve as bookends for Paul's introductory section of prayer for the Colossians. He now clearly begins to shift his focus to the primary concern and content of the letter (Moo, *The Letters*, 99). He concludes this section with this fourth and final participle, "giving thanks," to describe the joyful and grateful hearts that should epitomize those who are devoted to God's plan.

The privilege of participating in the Lord's kingdom enterprise is only possible because he "has enabled [us] to share in the saints' inheritance in the light" (v. 12). The passive verb "has enabled" describes a divine qualification to participate in his will that is not based on our effort or merit. According to the subsequent verses, God's work of rescue and redemption positions us for participation in his kingdom (vv. 13-14). In order to make his point, Paul intentionally uses exodus terminology—"share" and "inheritance" (v. 12; cf. Exod 6:6-8), along with the deliverance language in verse 13—to evoke thoughts of Israel's divine rescue from Egypt and the allotted portions of the promised land among the tribes (Melick, *Philippians, Colossians, Philemon*, 205–6). As God's new covenant people, we share in the "saints' inheritance" and have been apportioned the spiritual privileges available in Christ to members of his kingdom of "light" (Moo, *The Letters*, 101–2).

In other words, God graciously includes us and willingly uses us to accomplish his divine purposes here on earth. This should prompt us to "give thanks in everything; for this is God's will for [us] in Christ Jesus" (1 Thess 5:18). When we are mindful of the Lord's undeserved kindness toward us, it should influence everything we do, saturating our hearts and lives with gratitude (Col 3:17). Therefore, thanksgiving is not simply a sentimental attitude of reflection but an intentional action of obedience. Being thankful is an integral part of fulfilling God's will.

We Must Relish the Freedom of God's Will
COLOSSIANS 1:13-14

The final two verses of this section elaborate on the Father's work of salvation to qualify his people for his service. These verses serve multiple literary purposes as they specify the nature of the work, identify the means by which it is accomplished, accentuate the work of the Son, and segue into the body of the letter. The transitional purpose of this section includes the shift from second person, "you" (v. 12), to first person, "us" (v. 13). This change in voice provides rhetorical force to Paul's argument (Pao, *Colossians and Philemon*, 75) while also referencing his own testimony with his metaphorical light/darkness terminology (see Acts 26:12-18; Moo, *The Letters*, 104). In the broader scope of the section, the rescuing work of the Father through the redemptive work of the Son assures the Colossians of the freedom they possess to enjoy and experience God's will.

We Have Been Rescued from Darkness (1:13)

In verse 13, Paul describes the positional status of the believer in before-and-after terms. This is foundational to his arguments throughout the letter and is first established here.[3] The two complementary verbs establish a stark contrast that reinforces the present reality of their sacred standing as God's people. The Greek term Paul uses for "rescued" speaks to the peril of our lost condition prior to Christ. The parallel term, "transferred," describes the sequential or simultaneous[4] act of the Father in salvation and reinforces the vast, insurmountable distance between the two conditions.

The contrast is deepened even further by the disparity between the positional realms, "the domain of darkness" and "the kingdom of the Son." These phrases not only describe positional standing, but the terms *domain* and *kingdom* imply the controlling influence over their respective residents. Furthermore, the two are polar opposite in their nature, as "light" (v. 12) and "darkness" (v. 13) cannot coexist (2 Cor 6:14). In Scripture, darkness commonly refers to the condition of the depraved world and is depicted by the physical and metaphorical blindness used to characterize the lost. Jesus described himself as "the light of the world" (John 8:12), and he invaded the darkness of sinful humanity and could not be overcome by it (John 1:4-5). Christ reigns over his kingdom of "light" (v. 12) as the One the Father "loves" (v. 13), and we are now citizens with the other saints and members of his household (Eph 2:19; cf. Phil 1:27; 3:20).

Being rescued from the darkness also includes the applied benefits of redemption. Through his death on the cross, Christ atoned for our sin and "in him" we have "forgiveness of sins" (cf. 2:13; Eph 1:7). Paul shifts the verb tense from the completed, threefold work of the Father in verses 12-13 to the present tense, "we have," in verse 14 to indicate the ongoing and permanent effects of our salvation (Harris, *Colossians and Philemon*, 37). As a result, we are released from the guilt, shame, and bondage of sin and are free to pursue God's will for our lives.

---

[3] This contrast is reflected in 1:21-23, is the basis for his argument in 2:11-15, serves as the fundamental contrast with the false teachers in 2:20-23 and 3:1-4, and is the premise for his practical instruction in 3:5-11 and 3:12-17.

[4] Moo acknowledges that the verbs could be interpreted either way, but that it may be best to understand them as concurrent, that we are rescued by being transferred (*The Letters*, 102–3).

We Have Been Redeemed for a Purpose (1:14)

Our freedom from sin is also a freedom to serve. The emphasis throughout this section focuses on the Colossians' purpose as a result of their new position. Paul's prayer desired a practical outcome: that they would "walk worthy of the Lord" and "fully pleasing to him" (v. 10). Each of the four participles in the passage were steps in the broader process of serving the Lord (vv. 10-12). The Colossians' position as recipients of God's gracious redemption highlighted their undeserving status and God's desire to rescue lost humanity through the work of his Son.

As God's people, we have a new position, a new purpose, and a new perspective. Our eyes have been opened and we can recognize the hopeless state from which we were rescued. We are free from our slavery to sin and free to serve Christ and fulfill his will. These truths also convict our hearts of the desperate condition of the world around us and heighten our awareness of our responsibility to live as light (Matt 5:14-16). We must live holy and blameless lives to shine as stars in the midst of a dark and perverse world (Phil 2:15). Above all, we must be faithful to proclaim the "light of the gospel" of our glorious King Jesus to penetrate the blindness of darkened hearts around us so that they too may be rescued (2 Cor 4:4-6). We have been redeemed for this purpose!

Conclusion

Paul's twofold prayer for the Colossians perfectly demonstrates how our identity as believers in Christ translates into our responsibility as disciples of Christ. As we reflect on and relish our membership in God's family, we are commissioned as his followers to fulfill his will for our lives.

God's will for our lives was never intended to be a mystery for us to solve. Instead, he has graciously provided everything we need to faithfully accomplish his plan (2 Pet 1:3). He has rescued us from blindly wandering in the darkness of our sin and has given us the redeemed ability to accurately discern and actively pursue his divine will. This means each of us has been appointed to serve in a particular role to collectively achieve God's kingdom agenda of sharing the good news of salvation through Jesus Christ. Therefore, we can live with purpose, with confidence, and with hope as we devote our lives to pleasing our Savior and participating in his plan.

Reflect and Discuss

1. What are some of the ways God has clearly and specifically revealed his will for our lives in Scripture?
2. What are some steps this passage gives us to help us discern God's will for our lives in an area that hasn't been as clearly revealed in Scripture?
3. How should knowing the purpose of finding God's will impact our motivation for seeking it?
4. How does knowing God's general will help us live in a way that pleases Christ?
5. What are the four ways we engage in the process of fulfilling God's will as discussed in this passage?
6. What are some of the reasons we are called to give thanks to God in this passage?
7. What is the significance of Paul's describing our salvation through Christ in terms from the book of Exodus? How does this help us better understand our salvation?
8. What does this passage tell us about both the past and the present benefits of our salvation?
9. How does God's redemption of us lead to service?
10. How does knowing God's will help us carry out our responsibilities?

The Preeminence of Christ

COLOSSIANS 1:15-23

Main Idea: The glory of Christ deserves our highest praise and deepest devotion because the gospel of Christ has rescued us from our rebellious hearts and hopeless condition.

I. **Jesus Is the Lord of Creation (1:15-17).**[1]
   A. He is the authority over creation (1:15).
   B. He is the agent of creation (1:16).
   C. He is the aim of creation (1:16-17).
   Application: Christ must be first in our worship.
II. **Jesus Is the Head of the Church (1:18).**
   A. He is the source of the church (1:18).
   B. He is sovereign over the church (1:18).
   Application: Christ must be first in our work.
III. **Jesus Is the Savior of the Cross (1:19-23).**
   A. He reveals the Father to us (1:19).
   B. He reconciles us to the Father (1:20-23).
   Application: Christ must be first in our witness.

Perhaps there is not a more magisterial depiction of King Jesus in all of Scripture than the Colossians Christ hymn. His cosmic reign over all creation, his divine authority over the church, and his sacrificial death on the cross are all clearly articulated and beautifully expressed in poetic fashion. Although there is much debate as to its classification as a hymn,[2] its original composition,[3] and its contents in relation to the

---

[1] Portions of this chapter, particularly the outline and some explanatory material, have been adapted from our previous work, *Pastoral Theology*, 69–73.

[2] David Pao provides a helpful summary of what constitutes a hymn and why this passage is commonly referred to as such. He also makes a critical observation based on its classification and the related importance of its contents for interpreting the rest of the letter: "To label this section a hymn is, therefore, not simply a conclusion concerning its style; it also highlights the significance of the subject" (*Colossians and Philemon*, 89–90).

[3] Douglas Moo aptly summarizes the extent of the debate on this issue and much of its hypothetical nature: "Further speculation about the original hymn's content, structure, and life-setting in the church has generated a veritable academic cottage industry. And

Colossian heresy,[4] there is zero debate as to the theological heights and doctrinal depths it spans. The Christology of this passage is unparalleled in that it not only articulates the most critical elements of Christian orthodoxy, but it also conveys these truths in grand fashion and with practical relevance.

Up to this point in the letter, Paul's prayer for the Colossians has focused on God's redemptive plan and their participation in it. In these next verses the apostle shifts his attention from the will of the Father to the work of the Son. The Colossians' identity as God's children and their ability to accomplish his plan are only possible through what the Son has already accomplished on their behalf. In other words, Paul establishes the gospel as the foundational truth for believers that serves as the basis for his practical instruction throughout the letter.

The structure of this passage is intentionally designed to highlight Christ's preeminence. The dual stanzas of the hymn (vv. 15-16 and vv. 18b-20) are connected by its central truth: the supremacy of Christ and his sustaining reign over creation (vv. 17-18a). The use of parallel terms and concepts in mirroring fashion serves as a literary chiasm that draws the reader's focus to this glorious and ultimate truth.

> A   He is the image of the invisible God,
>   the firstborn over all creation. . . . (vv. 15-16)
>
>   B   He is before all things (v. 17a)
>
>   C   and by him all things hold together. (v. 17b)
>
>   B'   He is also the head of the body, the church; (v. 18a)
>
> A'   he is the beginning,
>   the firstborn from the dead. . . . (vv. 18b-20)

'speculation' is, all too often, the appropriate word, for many of the theories rest on pretty weak or greatly debated foundations" (*The Letters*, 109). Richard Melick's summarizing thoughts as to whether Paul composed the hymn or adopted /adapted an existing hymn provide a balanced perspective: "Whether the hymn was original with Paul, he put his approval on it as though it were his own by including it in the letter. It is, therefore, in a general sense 'Pauline'" (*Philippians, Colossians, Philemon*, 213).

[4] Pao provides a helpful conclusion to this often times overcomplicated issue: "It is unclear exactly how Paul intends to use this hymn to respond directly to the false teachers. . . . What is clear is that believers should be mindful of what God has accomplished through his Son, as stated in this hymn" (*Colossians and Philemon*, 85).

In addition, a literary progression within the hymn transitions from Christ's ultimate and powerful reign over creation (vv. 15-17) to his intimate and personal redemption of his people (v. 20). This movement culminates in the practical reality and significance of the person and work of Christ for the Colossians (vv. 21-23).

This pivotal passage also signifies a transition into the body of the letter. By expounding on the person and work of Christ, Paul confronts the heretical doctrine that was infecting the church while simultaneously directing their attention upward to their glorious Savior who desires and deserves their highest praise and deepest devotion. The majestic portrait of Christ in these verses exalts him as the ultimate authority and supreme priority for our lives. Paul understood that when Jesus consumes our focus, everything else is put into its proper perspective. With Jesus as its centerpiece, this passage identifies three Christological truths, each with a corresponding application, that help us position our lives under the lordship of Christ.

Jesus Is the Lord of Creation
COLOSSIANS 1:15-17

In the preceding verses Paul affirmed the positional transfer of believers from the "domain of darkness" into the "kingdom of the Son" (v. 13). He now proceeds to exalt Jesus as the King and establishes his sovereign domain over all of creation. As the expressed revelation of God, and because of his instrumental role in the created order, Christ possesses the ultimate authority as the Lord of creation.

He Is the Authority over Creation (1:15)

Paul identifies Christ with two parallel assertions, declaring him to be "the image of the invisible God" and "the firstborn over all creation." These two phrases distinguish Christ as the unique revelation and representation of God. Since both of these idioms have been misunderstood or misused by interpreters, they require our careful consideration.

Here the term *image*—a translation of the Greek word from which we get the English word *icon*—is not to be understood in the sense that Jesus is a mere replica of God or similar to him. This misguided understanding of "image" violates God's command as that which was explicitly forbidden (Exod 20:4-6). More appropriately, "image" refers to the living manifestation of God with a precise and exact correspondence. Jesus is *the* revelation of God, exclusively and entirely. He is the embodiment of God's nature and makes what is otherwise "invisible" visible.

Based on Paul's reinforcement of this truth (Col 1:19; 2:9), it appears to be particularly relevant for the Colossians, perhaps in contrast to the competing heresy. But the reality of Christ's deity is not a truth that was just constructed to combat false teaching. Jesus repeatedly asserted his divine nature throughout his earthly ministry (cf. John 5:17-18; 8:58), and we see it repeated throughout the New Testament as well. For example, the author of Hebrews used similar terms by describing Jesus as "the exact expression of [God's] nature" (Heb 1:3). Paul uses the same terminology in 2 Corinthians 4:4 that he does here, referring to Christ as "the image of God." Additionally, John's prologue expresses the concept with further clarification, asserting, "No one has ever seen God. The one and only Son, who is himself God and is at the Father's side—he has revealed him" (John 1:18).

Paul's use of the term *image* ultimately underscores the deity of Christ while also emphasizing his authority. The term, especially considering the immediate context, evokes reference to the creation account where God created mankind "in his own image" (Gen 1:27). As Pao observes,

> In the Genesis context, to be created in God's image is not to resemble God in all aspects and attributes, but to represent him as the authority over his created realm (Gen 1:28).
> (*Colossians and Philemon*, 94)

Therefore, the *image* concept in this verse includes both Jesus as God's ultimate revelation (deity) and Jesus as God's personal representation (humanity). In other words, he is the divine authority over all creation as the epitome of the earthly image and embodiment of the heavenly image of God.

The second phrase in Colossians 1:15, "the firstborn over all creation," is also meant to emphasize Christ's authority. This statement has been abused by historical and contemporary cults and other religions. In the third and fourth centuries, Arianism used it as a proof text. Today several other religions have interpreted this phrase to assert that Jesus is a created being. But considering the context, "firstborn" clearly does not describe the order in which Jesus was created in relation to the rest of creation. Rather it conveys his position of primacy, prominence, and prestige over creation.

The term *firstborn* is used elsewhere in Scripture to speak of rank or supremacy rather than temporal sequence. For example, David (and the foreshadowed messianic ruler) is granted the title of "firstborn," despite his being the youngest of his brothers (1 Sam 16:11), and as such he was regarded as "greatest of the kings of the earth" (Ps 89:27). Similarly, Israel is referred to as God's "firstborn" (Exod 4:22) with clear allusion to its status. Furthermore, in a legal sense, this title is used to speak of the primary heir that is entitled to the inheritance, including the father's power and authority over the household (Pao, *Colossians and Philemon*, 95). Based on this textual evidence, the CSB properly translates the phrase, "firstborn *over* all creation" (emphasis added).

Furthermore, the universal aspect of Jesus's rule and reign is clearly the point of this entire passage. As Moo notes, the term variously translated "all," "each," or "every" is used eight times in verses 15-20 and is the "thread that binds the verses together" (*The Letters*, 111). This opening verse initiates this understanding through the parallel phrases in which Christ is uniquely identified, and therefore uniquely qualified, as the Lord, the supreme authority over creation.

He Is the Agent of Creation (1:16)

Christ's authority over creation also derives from his role as the agent of creation. The contents of 1:16, introduced by the explanatory preposition "for," provides additional basis for Christ's authority and further endorses our understanding of the two phrases in the previous verse. Jesus cannot be seen as part of creation when "everything" was created "by him . . . through him and for him."

Paul's emphasis here is on Christ's primary role as the agent by which all of creation exists. The initial phrase, "by him," denotes his divine ingenuity and omnipotence. John specifies Christ as "the Word" through whom creation was spoken into existence (John 1:1,3). If God the Father is the divine architect who conceived of creation, God the Son is the causal agent by which it was accomplished (cf. Heb 1:2-3). This first of three prepositional phrases, more literally "in him," also identifies Christ as the domain that encompasses the entirety of the cosmos, the sphere in which it was created and continues to exist.

His unique agency and universal authority are also reinforced by the supporting expressions that follow. Paul uses polar extremes, "in heaven and on earth" and "the visible and the invisible," to demonstrate the all-inclusive totality of his reign. He also specifies "thrones or dominions or rulers or authorities" to emphasize Christ's unrivaled supremacy over all spiritual and physical beings (cf. 2:15,18; Eph 6:12). Paul repeats the phrase "all things have been created" and uses a second prepositional phrase, "through him," to further expound on Christ as the agent of creation and, as such, the inherent and exclusive authority he possesses over it.

He Is the Aim of Creation (1:16-17)

The final prepositional phrase, "for him," is a significant point that identifies Jesus as the aim of creation. Paul asserts that Christ's preexistence and active agency in creation are bookended in eternity by his glory as its ultimate goal. Jesus is "the Alpha and the Omega, the first and the last, the beginning and the end" (Rev 22:13; cf. Rev 1:8; 21:6). In the Philippians Christ hymn this is also the crescendo of the created order:

> *so that at the name of Jesus every knee will bow—in heaven and on earth and under the earth—and every tongue will confess that Jesus Christ is Lord, to the glory of God the Father.* (Phil 2:10-11)

In other words, all things, in heaven and on earth, were created to find their fulfillment and consummation in Christ (Eph 1:10).

As the aim of its existence, Christ is worthy to be exalted and glorified as the Lord of his creation. Paul reinforces this understanding in Colossians 1:17, describing him as being "before all things." This phrase has a dual meaning that affirms both his primacy and his preexistence. Similar to the case of the "firstborn" in verse 15, "before" reinforces Christ's ultimate greatness and is therefore translated in some versions as "above all things." In addition, the temporal sense of "before" speaks of the real preexistence of the person of Jesus Christ prior to creation and further justifies his supremacy over it.

Paul goes on to state, "By him all things hold together," explaining that Jesus not only existed prior to creation and actively participated in creation, but he continues to sustain creation (cf. Heb 1:3). Christ is actively involved in his creation as the sovereign King of the universe. "By him" the existence and coherence of the universe was established and is maintained. He rules over all things and his authoritative reign and universal supremacy cannot be denied. As Dutch theologian Abraham Kuyper famously proclaimed, "There is not a square inch in the whole domain of our human existence over which Christ, who is sovereign over *all*, does not cry, 'Mine!'" (Bratt, *Abraham Kuyper*, 488; emphasis in original).

Application: Christ Must Be First in Our Worship

These verses all combine to convey the central idea that Jesus Christ is Lord. As the Lord of creation, he is the ruler and authority over everything else. All of creation was made to bring glory to its Creator. Therefore, Jesus must be exalted and should have first place in our worship. As the Lord of creation, he is worthy of our adoration, our allegiance, and our awe! The psalmist captures this response best in Psalm 95:3-7:

> For the LORD is a great God,
> a great King above all gods.
> The depths of the earth are in his hand,
> and the mountain peaks are his.
> The sea is his; he made it.
> His hands formed the dry land.
> Come, let's worship and bow down;
> let's kneel before the LORD our Maker.
> For he is our God,
> and we are the people of his pasture,
> the sheep under his care.

Paul wanted the Colossians to understand that our worship of Christ should correspond with the comprehensive nature of his reign. It should consume every area of our lives. This includes both our personal worship that submits every aspect of our lives to his lordship (Rom 12:1) and our corporate worship that celebrates Jesus as the eternal King and glories in his exaltation (Rev 4:11). Jesus is the Lord of creation!

Jesus Is the Head of the Church
COLOSSIANS 1:18

In addition to presenting Jesus as the Lord of creation, Paul describes another aspect of Christ's supremacy in this passage. Verse 18 asserts that Jesus is the head of the church. Having established Jesus's supremacy over physical creation, Paul now seeks to proclaim Jesus's dominion over his spiritual creation, the church.

He Is the Source of the Church (1:18)

Paul identifies Christ as "the head of the body, the church." The metaphor Paul uses here, and in multiple other New Testament letters, communicates several aspects of Christ's relationship with the church. These characteristics include the unity and mutual dependence of the various parts of the body (1 Cor 12:12-26), the growth of the body toward maturity (Eph 4:15-16), and the governing superiority of the head over the body (Col 1:18; Melick, *Philippians, Colossians, Philemon*, 221).[5] Paul also uses the metaphor to describe the instrumental role of the head in the redemption of the body (Eph 5:23).

As the hymn transitions from the creative work of Christ to the redemptive work of Christ, Paul affirms that Jesus is the source from which the church derives its life, sustenance, and growth (cf. Col 2:19). Paul elaborates on his preeminence in the church and clarifies this understanding with the next phrase that parallels the "head of the body" in the chiastic structure of the hymn, "he is the beginning." While this phrase reiterates his supremacy in rank and affirms his precedence in time, Paul is also highlighting Christ's creative initiative as the source or "founder" of the church (Moo, *The Letters*, 129). This understanding is especially pronounced considering the context of Christ's role in creation (vv. 15-17) and this phrase's clear allusion to the creation narrative, "In the beginning" (Gen 1:1). By comparison, the church is his spiritual creation, his body, which is his holy people that he obtained with his blood (Acts 20:28; cf. 1 Pet 1:18-19) and ordained with his blessing (Matt 16:18; 28:18-20).

He Is Sovereign over the Church (1:18)

In addition to being the source of the church, Christ is also sovereign over the church. As the head, Jesus is its governing faculty. He alone

---

[5] Melick also summarizes the significance of the various uses of the metaphor by Paul and their related nature rather than their isolated understanding. He says, "These diverse applications of the illustration point out the adaptability of the concept. Perhaps the emphases overlap on occasion since the metaphor is pregnant with possibilities. The common element in all is that of organic interrelationship" (ibid.).

is the leader of the church, the living organism that is his body. This metaphor and its context also denote a key difference between Christ's relationship with the church and his relationship to the rest of creation. The relationship between Christ and his body is organic. It is far more personal and intimate, yet his leadership is just as sovereign.

The spiritual nature of the body is further clarified by the phrase, "the firstborn from the dead" (v. 18; cf. Rev 1:5). This phrase expounds on the preceding concept of Christ as "the beginning," clarifying his personal inauguration of the church when he was the first to rise from the dead (Acts 26:23). It also clearly parallels the earlier use of the identical term "firstborn," signifying Christ's primacy and authority over creation (Col 1:15) and now, through his death and resurrection, as head over the new creation (v. 18). Establishing this truth is essential for the Colossians (and all believers!) who positionally have been buried and raised with Christ (2:12) and now live in anticipation of the eschatological reality of his reign (3:1-4).

Therefore, Paul summarizes not just this immediate section but everything that has been stated thus far, culminating in Christ's obtaining and occupying "first place in everything" (v. 18). The phrase of confirmation, "so that he might come to have," does not diminish his eternal dominion over creation, but it reflects the definitive declaration of his sovereignty and lordship through his bodily resurrection (cf. Rom 1:4; Phil 2:9-11). Therefore, in the church, in creation, in salvation, and even in death, Christ holds the titles and privileges of the firstborn. He is preeminent over all. All hail King Jesus!

Application: Christ Must Be First in Our Work

What should our response be to Jesus as the head of the church? Submission. Obedience. Service. As the Lord's people we must relinquish control and submit to his authority and his agenda. No personal desires, programs, or controlling group of people should determine our direction and ministries. Jesus, as the head of the church, must be given ultimate authority and leadership in the local church. It is important to note that these aspects of Christ's leadership over the church assume a corporate nature in the spiritual life of every believer. Active involvement in the local body is essential to our existence and function as individual members of the spiritual body of Christ (Rom 12:4-5; cf. Eph 4:15-16). Every believer is an active member that he has gifted and works through to accomplish his purposes (1 Cor 12:12-27).

But this understanding is much deeper and much more personal than the local church body. As the head of the church, Christ does not just have dominion over the corporate body; he desires and deserves the thrones of our individual hearts and lives as well. This involves our daily service as members of God's global church beyond the ministries of the local church. In every capacity of our lives, as employees or neighbors, as students or ball players, as parents or children, we must work as though we are working for the Lord (Col 3:23). Paul will later summarize this with the practical and comprehensive admonition, "And whatever you do, in word or in deed, do everything in the name of the Lord Jesus, giving thanks to God the Father through him" (Col 3:17). In our labor and with his love, Jesus, as head of the church, must have first place in our work.

Jesus Is the Savior of the Cross
COLOSSIANS 1:19-23

The final aspect of Christ's supremacy that Paul identifies in this passage shifts from Jesus's person and position to his work of redemption. In verses 19-20, Paul pronounces that Jesus is the Savior of the cross. The identity of Jesus as Lord over creation and head of the church are sufficient for Paul to dispel any rival doctrines, philosophies, or religious figures. But the greatest and most glorious aspect of Christ's identity lies in Paul's next statements. He describes the incarnation of Jesus, his coming to inhabit his own creation, and his purpose for doing so. He then appropriates the redemptive work of Christ to the Colossian believers (vv. 21-23) so that they may recognize their positional standing in him, live according to their redeemed status, and participate in the mission of the gospel.

He Reveals the Father to Us (1:19)

As part of the redemptive work of Jesus, Paul explains that Christ reveals the Father to us (v. 19). Paul describes Christ's incarnation with the phrase, "For God was pleased to have all his fullness dwell in him." The "dwell" language speaks to the reality of God's inhabiting presence as when he chose to abide in the tabernacle and the temple in the Old Testament (Exod 29:44-46; Ps 68:16). Christ's eternal nature as God was present in his physical existence on earth (cf. John 1:14), as he truly was "Immanuel," God with us (Matt 1:23). This parallels Paul's statement in Colossians 2:9, which elaborates further: "For the entire fullness of God's nature dwells bodily in Christ."

The phrasing in 1:19 distinguishes God the Father from Christ the Son, while affirming the full deity of the Son and maintaining the passage's focus on him. "God was pleased" implicitly refers to the Father as the architect of redemptive history (vv. 12-13). It also echoes the multiple affirmations of the Father during Christ's earthly ministry (Matt 3:17; 17:5) without dividing their oneness (John 8:19; 10:30; 14:9). Paul is ultimately reiterating the truth of the deity of Christ we saw in verse 15 as the "image" or physical manifestation of God. This is significant because it was only *as God* that Christ was able to provide the suitable sacrifice Paul goes on to describe in verse 20.

He Reconciles Us to the Father (1:20-23)

Not only does he reveal the Father to us, but Christ also reconciles us to the Father. The deity of Jesus highlights Christ alone as the exclusive Mediator who is able to "reconcile everything" (v. 20; cf. 2 Tim 2:5). Jesus accomplishes this reconciliation "by making peace through his blood, shed on the cross." What is implied here in the text must be stated explicitly for us. Reconciliation and the need for "peace" clearly mean that all of creation, "whether things on earth or things in heaven," have become estranged and brought into conflict with the Creator. The universal reality of sin's devastating effects is described in parallel language with the comprehensive scope of Christ's work in creation (v. 16; cf. Rom 8:19-22). Just as all things were created "through him," all things must also be reconciled "through him."[6] Paul summarized this same truth for the Corinthians: "In Christ, God was reconciling the world to himself" (2 Cor 5:19).

Paul also specifies the means by which the reconciliation with God is made possible. It is only "through his blood" that the price of redemption can be paid (cf. Heb 9:13-14; 1 Pet 1:18-19). Christ's atonement for our sin, "his blood," was "shed on the cross" (v. 20) to satisfy God's wrath toward our sin (cf. Rom 3:25), to purchase our forgiveness (cf. Heb 9:22), and to secure our "peace" so that he might "reconcile" us,

---

[6] This final section of the hymn contains the same prepositions used in parallel fashion with the first stanza of the hymn: "by/in him" (vv. 16,19), "through him" (vv. 16,20), and "for him/to himself" (vv. 16,20).

along with all of creation, "to himself." But his sacrificial death and resurrection, while universal in availability and scope, are only applied by grace to those who receive them by faith (cf. Rom 5:1; Eph 2:8-9).

As the hymn concludes, Paul transitions with words of application for the Colossians as noted by the shift in voice and the recurring direct address, "you." The verses in this paragraph (vv. 21-23), one sentence in the original, not only summarize and apply the truths of the Christ hymn, but they establish a thesis for the rest of the letter. The unrivaled beauty and supremacy of Christ (vv. 15-20) and the Colossians' redeemed identity in him (vv. 21-22) serve as the impetus for their devotion and obedience to the gospel mission (v. 23). In familiar Pauline fashion, he uses a before-and-after approach, "once . . . now," to describe their salvation. He traces their personal time line with a past, present, and future sequence to provide them with a gospel-oriented trajectory moving forward.

First, Paul reminds them of the vast gulf of separation that had to be overcome through Christ's death by describing the nature of their relationship with God prior to Christ. The expanse of their separation and the corresponding extent of God's mercy magnify the extreme nature of their previous condition and the remarkable nature of their reconciliation. They were estranged from God, "alienated," enemies of God, "hostile in [their] minds," and evil before God: "expressed in [their] evil actions" (v. 21).

"But now," because of God's grace through the atoning work of Christ, "by his physical body through his death," they have been "reconciled" (v. 22). The means of the reconciliation, "through" (vv. 20,22), is clearly emphasized as Paul describes the incomparable Christ (vv. 15-20) as the incarnate Christ ("by his physical body") who was the substitute for sinful humanity. Through "his death" (cf. vv. 18,20), believers are positionally presented, both now and in eternity, as "holy, faultless, and blameless before him" (v. 22).

These terms carry a sacrificial connotation and reflect the nature of the sacrifice itself and the resulting status of the one on whose behalf it was offered. In this sense believers are instructed to offer their lives as living sacrifices, "holy and pleasing to God," as those who have been changed by the mercy of Christ's sacrifice (Rom 12:1). The terms also have a judicial overtone that affirms believers' new status as those who will stand justified, "holy and blameless" in Christ, before God in the final judgment (Eph 1:4; 5:27).

The transforming nature of our salvation (vv. 21-22) mirrors the transferring nature of our salvation described earlier (vv. 13-14). These positional realities—including the death/life, buried/raised, old/new—are the basis for many of the letter's practical instructions (cf. 2:12-13,20; 3:1,5,10). Their immediate application in this section focuses on the Colossians' continued faithfulness to "the hope of the gospel that [they] heard" (1:23; cf. 1:5-6). Paul's use of the conditional clause, "if indeed," does not cast doubt on the genuine nature of the Colossians' faith, and he certainly does not make the eternal security of their salvation conditional on their future obedience. However, he is able to assume, based on the theological realities he has asserted (vv. 21-22) and practical realities he has affirmed (1:4-6), that they will continue "grounded and steadfast in the faith" (v. 23).

Paul's confidence is ultimately in the life-changing power of "the gospel" (v. 23) that had transformed them, produced fruit throughout the world (1:6), and was being "proclaimed in all creation under heaven" (v. 23). This phrase summarizes the universal nature of Christ's lordship over creation (vv. 15-17) in conjunction with the universal availability of reconciliation through him (vv. 18-20). It is the message of good news to which Paul had devoted his life as a "servant" (v. 23). Just as Epaphras had done on their behalf (1:7), and now by way of his own example, Paul is challenging the Colossians to dedicate themselves as servants of Christ to his mission.

Application: Christ Must Be First in Our Witness

As the Savior of the cross, Jesus died and rose again to make redemption and reconciliation possible for all who will trust in him (Rom 10:13). This final aspect of Christ's supremacy means that Christ must be first in our witness. Because of Christ's reconciling work in our lives, we are called to carry this message of reconciliation to the lost world around us. As a result of our salvation and corresponding new identity in Christ (Col 1:21-22; cf. 2 Cor 5:17), God's Word commissions us: "We are ambassadors for Christ, since God is making his appeal through us. We plead on Christ's behalf, 'Be reconciled to God'" (2 Cor 5:20).

The urgency of our mission is determined by the authority of Christ (Col 1:15-17; cf. Matt 28:18), due to humanity's need for Christ (Col 1:19-20), and, ultimately, for the glory of Christ (v. 18). Therefore, Paul would go on to challenge the Colossians: "Act wisely toward outsiders, making the most of the time" (Col 4:5). We must embrace this same challenge by praying for open avenues for the gospel and by seizing every opportunity to share the good news with those whom God brings into our lives and across our paths.

Conclusion

The late Bible expositor Haddon Robinson astutely pointed out the importance of priorities in sermon preparation by citing a simple anecdote: "An old recipe for a rabbit stew starts out, 'First catch the rabbit.' That puts first things first. Without the rabbit there is no dish" (*Biblical Preaching*, 53). In essence, Paul's message to the Colossians highlighted a similar fundamental principle. Without Christ, nothing else matters. Christ must be first in every area of our lives.

For all of the recognition this passage receives for its Christological beauty and theological depth, its practical implications are rarely considered. But Paul recognized the correspondence between the reality and the relevance of Christ's preeminence. As the Lord of creation, Jesus wants and is worthy to occupy first place in our worship. As the head of the church, Jesus desires and deserves first place in our work. And as the Savior of the cross, Jesus compels and commissions us to honor him with first place in our witness.

Reflect and Discuss

1. What does Paul tell us about Jesus in this passage that makes him worthy of our worship?
2. What are the ways this passage teaches us that Jesus is God the Son?
3. What is so significant about Jesus being "the image of the invisible God"?
4. What is the significance of Jesus's being Lord over not only the first creation but the new creation as well?
5. Why should Jesus be first in our work?
6. Why is it so important that Jesus is God in human flesh? Why is it necessary for him to be the God-man (v. 19)?
7. What does it mean for Jesus to reconcile all things to himself through the blood of his cross?
8. How does Jesus's reconciling work on the cross change our identity?
9. Why should Jesus be first in our witness?
10. In what areas of your life are you failing to put Jesus first?

Faithful Servants of Christ

COLOSSIANS 1:24–2:5

Main Idea: God has entrusted each of us with the privilege and responsibility to serve the cause of Christ by sharing the gospel of Christ to build up the body of Christ.

As Faithful Servants of Christ, We Must Be Devoted to . . .
I. Suffering as Ministers of the Church (1:24-25).
   A. We must embrace suffering for Christ (1:24).
   B. We must endure suffering for Christ (1:25a).
II. Striving for the Mission of the Church (1:25-29).
   A. Labor for them to know the mystery of Christ (1:25b-27).
   B. Labor for them to grow to maturity in Christ (1:28-29).
III. Strengthening the Members of the Church (2:1-5).
   A. We must affirm God's people with our love (2:1-2a).
   B. We must anchor God's people in the truth (2:2b-3).
   C. We must alert God's people to the risk (2:4).
   D. We must assure God's people in the faith (2:5).

The measure of our success in life, and certainly in ministry, is ultimately summarized by one standard in God's kingdom—faithfulness. Jesus illustrated and emphasized this truth in multiple ways and in various contexts. For example, in admonishing his disciples to be prepared for his return, he was looking for the "faithful" servants (Matt 24:45-47). He told the parable of the shrewd manager to illustrate their responsibility to be "faithful" in every way (Luke 16:10-12). And describing their role in the kingdom of God, Jesus told the parable of the talents to evaluate his disciples' stewardship and commended them with, "Well done, good and faithful servant!" (Matt 25:14-30).

Likewise, as servants of Christ and stewards of the gospel, we must "be found faithful" (1 Cor 4:1-2). This is not a standard reserved for those who occupy posts in vocational ministry; it is true for every Christian. Throughout his letter to the Colossians, Paul uses the term "faithful" to characterize any and all believers who are fulfilling their roles and responsibilities for the Lord (1:2,7; 4:7,9). And by way of his own example in this passage, Paul demonstrates what faithful service for Christ and his church looks like.

As Paul transitions into the body of the letter, he offers a brief description, and in essence a defense, of his ministry. His identity as a "servant" of the gospel at the end of the previous section (v. 23) provides the launching pad into his personal testimony. Having referenced his apostolic and authoritative role (1:1), he makes his broader platform and common role as a "servant" of the church (v. 25) the focus in this passage. He uses the pronoun "I" repeatedly in these verses (1:24-25,29; 2:1,4-5), with the one exception of the plural "we" in verse 28 to signify that he is not alone in his mission. Paul understood that the mission of the church is a collective effort to which all believers are called to devote themselves.

From a literary perspective, a notable progression in the first chapter transitions in focus from God the Father (1:3-14), to Christ the Son (1:15-23), to Paul as his servant (1:23-25; Pao, *Colossians and Philemon*, 119). This traceable succession elevates Paul and his doctrine above the false teachers who were propagating the Colossian heresy. Paul's spiritual heritage validates his apostolic authority and his doctrinal orthodoxy to a community of Christians that he had never met personally. Spiritually speaking, his ministerial resumé also provides the theological warrant for his subsequent instructions while simultaneously inviting the church to join him in serving Christ.

Perhaps most significantly, Paul's personal testimony in this passage exhibits a tangible expression of his genuine love for the Colossian church through his willing sacrifice for them and for other congregations. His sacrificial love for Christ and his church fueled Paul's obedience and provided a compelling motivation for the Colossians to participate in the gospel mission.

This passage breaks down into two sections that are connected by common terms and themes. Paul's ministry to the churches (1:24-29) and Paul's ministry to the Colossians (2:1-5) are wedded together with repeated concepts that mirror each other and form a literary chiasm.

A　"Rejoice" and "my flesh"/"his body" (1:24)
　　B　"make known," "wealth," "mystery" (1:27)
　　　　C　"striving" (1:29)
　　　　C'　"struggling" (2:1)
　　B'　"knowledge," "riches," "mystery" (2:2)
A'　"rejoicing," "body" (2:5) (Moo, *The Letters*, 148)

The parallel terms in 1:24 and 2:5 provide textual bookends that distinguish the passage as a complete thought. The purpose of Paul's mission—making known the mystery of the gospel—provides the movement within the passage that ultimately centers on his unwavering devotion to the cause of Christ.

Through Paul's testimony we see the nature of God's mission, what it requires from each of us, and ultimately what he desires to accomplish through us. In this passage God calls us as his servants to be fully devoted to the mission of the gospel by sharing the good news of Christ and participating in the sufferings of Christ, in order to grow the body of Christ. In short, these verses teach us how to be the faithful servants God desires.

Suffering as Ministers of the Church
COLOSSIANS 1:24-25

Paul saw himself as a "servant" in the global mission of Christ (vv. 23,25). This term, sometimes translated as "minister," was not one of positional status but one of personal demeanor. Despite his lofty accomplishments, Paul never rose above his posture of humility. He saw himself as an undeserving servant of the Lord. As a result, in selfless deference to others and in tireless devotion to Christ, he willingly sacrificed himself for the sake of the church in gratitude for the cross. As faithful servants of Christ, we must adopt this same perspective by embracing and enduring suffering for Christ.

We Must Embrace Suffering for Christ (1:24)

The concept of suffering is woven throughout this passage (1:24,29; 2:1). The original terms carry the connotation of struggles and afflictions. Elsewhere Paul uses the term appearing in verse 24 to describe the sufferings that are common for all believers who follow Christ (Rom 8:18; 2 Cor 1:5-7; O'Brien, *Colossians, Philemon,* 76). Paul himself had endured extreme forms of suffering (cf. 2 Cor 11:23-33) and had been called for this purpose (Acts 9:16). Although the specific forms of his afflictions may have been unique, their nature and occurrence are typical for all of Christ's disciples and should be an expected part of faithfully serving him (cf. 2 Tim 1:11-12; 3:11-12).

Paul's ability to "rejoice" in his sufferings resulted from an eternal perspective on his earthly circumstances. His afflictions were not only on behalf of the Colossians, "for [them]," but were for the universal cause of Christ, "for his body, that is, the church" (v. 24). Paul recognized that his personal role was part of a larger whole. His sacrifices for the sake of the gospel, along with those of other devoted believers, would result in the expansion of Christ's church. As a result, he could embrace suffering with joy.

Similarly, the various afflictions we suffer for Christ should be embraced with an eternal perspective that considers the temporal nature of our earthly lives in contrast to the everlasting glory of God's kingdom (Rom 8:17-18; 2 Cor 4:16-18). Giving our lives for the cause of Christ will require personal sacrifice and suffering that this world will not comprehend, but it is a cause we can deliberately embrace with joy as we follow Jesus's own example (Heb 12:2-3) and claim his victory (John 16:33).

We Must Endure Suffering for Christ (1:25a)

As Paul describes his own "sufferings" in his "flesh," he affirms their function in "completing," or filling up, "what is lacking in Christ's afflictions" (v. 24). While interpreters have historically wrestled over the precise meaning of this phrase, the apostle's adamant defense of the sufficiency of Christ's death (1:19-20; 2:15) clearly eliminates any understanding that attempts to interpret it as Paul's contributing anything of redemptive value to the substitutionary atonement of Christ.[1] While this may eliminate heretical misinterpretations, the immediate context and clear teachings of Scripture can help us determine the affirmative meaning of this phrase.

Contextually, the spiritual reality of the body of Christ was established in the preceding hymn and exalted Christ as the "head" of the church (v. 18; cf. 2:19). Paul also explained the material reality that was necessary for our personal redemption and was accomplished by Christ's "physical body through his death" (v. 22; cf. 1 Pet 2:24). He now combines the spiritual and physical concepts by expounding on his physical "sufferings" in his "flesh" in conjunction with Christ's "afflictions" for the sake of his spiritual "body, that is, the church" (Col 1:24).

---

[1] The term used for Christ's "afflictions" or tribulations is never used in Scripture to refer to his redemptive work. Instead, Paul refers to Christ's suffering in the act of redemption with the concepts of blood, cross, and death (O'Brien, *Colossians, Philemon*, 77).

There is some theological and textual precedent for understanding this passage to refer to believers' participation in Christ's suffering as part of his body (2 Cor 1:5-6; 4:10-11; Phil 3:10).[2] And certainly, the parallels between Paul's suffering and Christ's are real. "Both suffered in the flesh; both suffered vicariously; both suffered for the gospel; and both suffered for the church" (Melick, *Philippians, Colossians, Philemon*, 240).[3] But an exclusive interpretation of the verse as a spiritual participation fails to address the pressing question of "what is lacking" in Christ's afflictions and how Paul's "sufferings" are "completing" them.

Christ suffered and satisfied the divine wrath for the sin of humanity on the cross (1 John 2:2). But Jesus also affirmed that there were earthly afflictions still yet to come that his followers would endure (Mark 13:19-24; cf. Rev 6:9-11). The delimited extent of these tribulations helps address the issue of what is "lacking" and what Paul is "completing." In addition, these sufferings are directly related to the expansion of the messianic kingdom, which also seems to be Paul's concern here based on the terminology of the surrounding verses.[4] Furthermore, Paul's specific reference to his missional calling to the Gentiles (Col 1:27), its corresponding suffering (Acts 9:15-16), its vicarious nature on the church's behalf, and the unfolding revelation of God's salvation (Col 1:26) all seem to support an eschatological *fulfillment* of his participation in Christ's afflictions.

Paul's suffering in order to fulfill his personal calling was in service to the Colossian congregation and the church as a whole. "According to God's commission" Paul was called as an apostle to the Gentiles (Col 1:25,27; cf. Gal 1:15-16); and the Colossians, a predominantly Gentile congregation, were the fruit of Paul's labor and the benefactors of his "sufferings." As such, they were also the object of his devotion, a source of his motivation, and recipients of his ongoing ministry.

While Paul's individual role was distinct, it mirrored Christ's ultimate example of sacrifice and provides a model for us to follow. Too many times we are quick to avoid situations or alleviate struggles that

---

[2] Jesus's confrontation at Paul's conversion certainly would have contributed to the apostle's understanding of this concept (Acts 9:4).

[3] Melick makes this observation but also notes differences between Paul and Christ, primarily that Paul did not suffer redemptively.

[4] For example, he uses "mystery" (1:26-27; 2:2), "kingdom" (1:13), and "afflictions" or, more literally, "tribulations" (1:24).

may be part of God's providential plan for our growth and for his church. But Jesus uses the suffering of his servants to advance his kingdom to places and people it has never reached. Believing that God's plan includes our participation and will inevitably involve "sufferings," we can embrace them with joy as we anticipate the consummation of Christ's kingdom and usher it in through our devoted service to him and to his church (Acts 14:22; cf. 1 Thess 3:2-4,7).

Striving for the Mission of the Church
COLOSSIANS 1:25-29

In addition to suffering as ministers of the church, our role as Christ's servants also involves our tireless devotion to the mission of the church. Paul's striving for the mission is recounted through his personal calling and experience within the broader context of redemptive history (vv. 25-27). His compelling testimony motivates all believers and culminates in a collective goal for the mission, to "present everyone mature in Christ" (v. 28). It is to this end that Paul strives and labors (v. 29). Through his inspirational example and by the power of the gospel, the Lord invites us to join together in striving for the mission of the church. Simply put, God's mission for Paul is the same mission he has for each of us, and it requires the same tireless devotion.

Labor for Them to Know the Mystery of Christ (1:25b-27)

The purpose of Paul's calling and service to the church was to "make the word of God fully known" (v. 25). He devoted his life to this singular mission while recognizing dual aspects of what this mission involved. Paul's stewardship of God's message, to make it "fully known," included both the explanation of the gospel's fulfillment in Christ and the expansion of the gospel's impact throughout the world.

Paul describes the gospel of Christ as "the mystery hidden for ages and generations" (v. 26; cf. Rom 16:25). The "mystery" in relation to the past "generations" certainly speaks of the fulfillment of God's messianic promises to his covenant people. The "mystery" that was previously "hidden," or not in plain sight, has been "revealed" in Christ, who is the substance of the shadows throughout the Old Testament (cf. Col 2:17).

But the term "mystery" also refers to the specific aspect of God's inclusion of the Gentiles in his redemptive plan. Paul uses the term elsewhere to describe this particular facet of the gospel (Rom 11:25), and he expounds on its significance as part of God's eternal purpose in his covenant promises (Eph 3:1-7). Through Paul's ministry as an apostle to the Gentiles, the "word of God," the "mystery" of the gospel— Christ as the Redeemer of all nations—was made "fully known" (cf. Eph 3:8-11).

While God used Paul as his agent, the mystery was not reserved for him, it was "revealed to his saints" (Col 1:26). This term refers to all believers (cf. vv. 2,4,12) as recipients of the truth of the gospel, and it reminds us that we now possess the "mystery" within us, "Christ in [us]," who is "the hope of glory" (v. 27). Our status in Christ and his presence in us secures our hope and provides us with a confident assurance of the "glorious wealth," the future inheritance (v. 12) that God has extended in Christ to all people (v. 27).

As recipients of the eternal inheritance, we have been entrusted by God with this "mystery" that we might be his messengers, laboring on behalf of the nations, so that he may reveal the glory of Christ to them through the gospel message he has commissioned us to share. Indeed, we must labor for them to know the mystery of Christ.

Labor for Them to Grow to Maturity in Christ (1:28-29)

Despite current distinctions Paul never differentiated between evangelism and discipleship in God's mission. He understood his commission as part of the Great Commission—not to win converts but to "make disciples" (Matt 28:19-20). This divine mandate for all believers, based on the cosmic reign of Christ (Col 1:15-20; cf. Matt 28:18), begins and ends with Jesus, leading Paul to declare, "We proclaim him" (Col 1:28; cf. 2 Cor 4:5). The plural pronoun, "we," includes his partners in the gospel mission, Timothy (1:1) and Epaphras (1:7), and distinguishes their ministry from that of the false teachers. But the sudden shift within this otherwise personal testimony also incorporates all believers into the mission of proclaiming Christ (Pao, *Colossians and Philemon*, 131).

The good news of the gospel is made known through the faithful witness of Christ's followers. Paul explains how we are to accomplish our mission and identifies its strategy, its audience, and its goal. The strategy for making disciples is to "proclaim him," declaring Jesus as the sole means of salvation, by "warning and teaching" others (v. 28). These two terms are complementary functions that extend beyond simply sharing the facts of the gospel. "Warning" includes cautioning and counseling others in light of the truth, while "teaching" involves informing and instructing them how to live according to the gospel.

In addition, as we strategically engage others with the gospel, we must do so "with all wisdom" (v. 28; cf. 1:9). This phrase describes a contextualized approach with an uncompromised message. It includes the content of our message since Christ is the source and personification of all "wisdom" (2:3). But it also describes our approach, reminding us that we must act with wisdom toward outsiders (4:5) as we courageously and compassionately share the gospel of Christ. Jesus commissioned his disciples with a similar caution (Matt 10:16), and we must exercise the same wisdom as we share the good news.

Along with the strategy, Paul also identifies our universal audience for the mission through his repeated use of the term "everyone" (v. 28). Our God does not discriminate. He desires all people to be saved through repentance and personal faith in Christ (1 Tim 2:3-6; 2 Pet 3:9). The inclusive terminology broadens the scope of our gospel mission beyond the superficial barriers and roadblocks we typically construct based on our personal prejudices or preferences. "Everyone" extends the range of the mission to the borderless domain of our Savior and King. Therefore, we cannot restrict the breadth of the mission by focusing on a select few or reduce the depth of the mission by simply winning converts.

The strategy and audience of the mission culminate in its ultimate goal, to "present everyone mature in Christ" (v. 28). While this phrase includes the individual growth and sanctification of the believer during earthly life, its ultimate focus is on Christ himself and our perfected union with him in eternity. Our lives here, while being conformed to his likeness (3:10), will ultimately be presented "holy" and "blameless" (1:22) as we become mature and complete in the stature measured by the fullness of Christ (Eph 4:13; cf. Rom 8:29).

With this eternal perspective in mind, Paul devotes his entire life to the mission of Christ. He is convinced that his struggles and his suffering are not in vain (cf. 1 Cor 15:58). Therefore, he continues to "labor" for this purpose (Col 1:29). Yet he also recognizes that it requires strength beyond his own, and he is careful to make sure that his effort and ability are not the point of focus. Paul's "striving" is not just *for the sake of* Christ; his tireless devotion is *enabled by* the "strength" of Christ that "works powerfully" in him (v. 29). By God's grace Paul is empowered to labor and persevere in order to see the Lord's mission accomplished.

In the same way, we must devote ourselves to striving for the mission of the church. As we are strengthened by his glorious might, we must tirelessly serve to help others come to know the mystery of Christ and to grow to maturity in Christ.

Strengthening the Members of the Church
COLOSSIANS 2:1-5

Having described his ministry to the church at large, Paul now focuses his specific attention on the local congregations, particularly the church at Colossae and his service on their behalf. These verses are more personal and convey the apostle's affection for the Colossians with an endearing passion that should reflect our hearts for God's people. Paul's efforts to encourage and build up the church provide a paradigm for our ministry as we devote ourselves to strengthening the members of the church.

We Must Affirm God's People with Our Love (2:1-2a)

Paul's encouragement for the church begins with a personal address that affirms God's people. In the previous verses his use of the pronoun "you" was much more broad and inclusive, addressing the Colossians as part of "the church" (1:24-25), the "saints" (v. 26), and including "everyone" (v. 28). In this section "you" is far more personal and accentuates their individual value and communal identity. The transitional phrase, "For I want *you* to know," and the explanatory clause, "I am struggling for *you*," signal a more direct address that is naturally affirming (2:1; emphasis added).

In addition to his tone, the extent of Paul's personal sacrifice, "how greatly I am struggling for you," conveys their value (2:1). His "struggling" corresponds with the term "striving" in the previous verse (1:29) and describes the physical hardships associated with his ministry, including his current imprisonment (4:3,18), as well as his emotional and spiritual burden for them (cf. 2 Cor 11:28). Paul assumed personal responsibility for the Colossians' spiritual well-being, and he was laboring for their sake, along with "those in Laodicea" and other neighboring congregations that had "not seen [him] in person" (2:1).[5]

---

[5] The church of Laodicea, along with Heirapolis (4:13-17; cf. Rev 2–3), was also located in the Lycus Valley and was roughly twelve miles from Colossae. While Paul's

The personal affirmation implicit in his language and tone is made explicit in his stated purpose. Paul desires for "their hearts to be encouraged and joined together in love" (2:2). This affectionate expression reflects his hope for them, that they would be spiritually uplifted and united by the mutual love they share for one another in Christ (cf. 3:14). Similarly, we should look for ways to affirm God's people in order to encourage their hearts, stimulate their affection for one another, and knit them together in love.

We Must Anchor God's People in the Truth (2:2b-3)

In addition to affirming God's people in love, we must also anchor God's people in the truth. Paul's encouragement for the Colossians was not limited to their emotional comfort. Their personal edification also included a verbal exhortation "so that" they would be propelled forward in their spiritual walks. Paul desired that, through their united effort and loving encouragement, they would grow deeper in their faith and stronger in their conviction regarding the truth of the gospel.

Paul wanted them to experience and enjoy "all the riches of complete understanding" that come from "the knowledge of God's mystery— Christ" (2:2). These phrases complement each other and speak to the Colossians' level of comprehension of God's unfolding plan of redemption (1:26). But an individual's depth of understanding is intended to be more than intellectual. It is developed through a personal encounter and spiritual relationship with Jesus Christ in whom "are hidden all the treasures of wisdom and knowledge" (2:3).

In other words, the immeasurable value of the gospel can only be realized through the inexhaustible glory that is expressed and experienced in Christ. While contextually Paul is refuting false teachings that would have prioritized religious and mystical practices (2:18,21-23), he is primarily establishing the ultimate reality that all true "wisdom and knowledge" are personified in Christ. As a result, only through a deeper, more intimate knowledge of him can we experience the fullness of the "riches" and "treasures" of our faith. Therefore, as believers, our faith must be anchored in him.

---

strategic efforts and partnerships had most likely led to the formation of these churches, he was not directly responsible, as evidenced by this phrase. Despite his lack of personal interaction, he possessed a genuine affection for these churches and likely had all of them in mind here.

We Must Alert God's People to the Risk (2:4)

Strengthening the members of the church also includes alerting God's people to the dangerous influence of the world and the risk of deception. Being affirmed in our faith and anchored in Christ prepare us to discern and resist the deceptive teachings that attempt to mislead us. Paul recognized the prevalent dangers, and out of genuine concern for the Colossians, he cautioned them. But much like his approach in the rest of the letter, rather than directly refuting the specifics of the false teachings, he encourages believers to be grounded in the truth. Paul believed the best defense against deception is discipleship.

Therefore, he admonishes believers to grow in their faith "so that no one will deceive [them] with arguments that sound reasonable" (2:4). His caution alerts us to the real threat of false teachers, the risk and possibility of being deceived, and the convincing nature of their message. Most people relegate false teachings to blatant heresies and obvious violations of orthodoxy. But more often than not, we are deceived by counterfeits that closely resemble the truth, cultural lies that are camouflaged to the undiscerning heart, and convincing personalities that are persuasive and seem sincere. Therefore, it is crucial for us to alert God's people to the risk and equip them to discern the truth and stand firm in it.

We Must Assure God's People in the Faith (2:5)

Paul concludes this section on strengthening the members of the church with one final pillar of support—assurance. On the heels of his admonition, Paul needed to reassure the Colossians, especially since he was "absent in body" (2:5). The tenuous situation in the church warranted his involvement, but he was unable to intervene with his physical presence, so his letter served as an authorized representation of his authoritative voice (4:18). But his letter, and his imprisonment that necessitated it, also reflected his care and concern for the church. Paul's absence demonstrated his willingness to suffer for them and validated his faithfulness since it was the result of him being in prison or "chains" for the gospel (4:3,18). Therefore, his instruction and encouragement assured the Colossians of his personal support and genuine affection by reminding them, "I am with you in spirit" (2:5; cf. 1 Cor 5:3-5).

In addition to his support, Paul also expresses his confidence and hope for them. His joyful anticipation of their continued faithfulness, "rejoicing to see" (Col 2:5), parallels the joyful endurance of his faithfulness on their behalf at the beginning of the passage (1:24). Despite the impending threats they are facing, he is certain that their unity will be proven through their being "well ordered" resulting from, and evidenced by, "the strength of [their] faith" (2:5). Ultimately, the object of their faith and their positional status "in Christ" give him confidence and serve as the basis of their assurance.

As with the Colossians, our faith can also be challenged by the weight of our circumstances or the intimidation from our adversaries. But in Christ we have the full assurance of our security through his victory; and, therefore, we can encourage one another to stand firm in our faith. As a result, by affirming, anchoring, alerting, and assuring God's people, we can strengthen one another as members of the church.

Conclusion

Paul's faithfulness as a servant of Christ did not qualify him for a lofty status and a life free of troubles and trials. In fact, he encountered exactly the opposite. It was precisely because of his devotion to Christ that he was subjected to the suffering and struggles he endured. In gratitude for what Jesus had suffered on his behalf and for the eternal glory he secured, Paul willingly and joyfully subjected himself to hardships for the sake of Christ's church.

Many Christians today take the opposite approach to finding joy in the church. Sadly, members and guests often adopt a consumer mindset, looking for the highest rate of return with the least amount of required investment. They want to benefit from the ministries of the church and escape from the misery of the world without recognizing that the church was founded on and functions on servants' hearts, not selfish ones (Matt 20:28).

Ultimately, the greatest joy in the Christian life is not found in the comfort and conveniences offered in the local church; it is found in offering ourselves in sacrifice and service to its Savior and Lord. By suffering as a minister of the church, striving for the mission of the church, and strengthening the members of the church, we can participate in the cause of Christ, be commended as his faithful servants, and share in our Master's joy (Matt 25:21).

Reflect and Discuss

1. What is the motivation for suffering Paul talks about in this passage?
2. What are some implications of this passage for global missions?
3. What are some of the reasons Paul gives in this passage for laboring passionately for Christ?
4. How does Jesus use our suffering to further spread the gospel?
5. What does Paul teach us about how we are to labor to grow people to maturity in Christ?
6. What are some things we learn about Jesus in this passage? Why should he be the center and content of our preaching and proclamation (1:28)?
7. What are some of the ways Paul gives us in this passage to help strengthen other members of the church?
8. What does this passage teach us about ministry in the church, both vocational and nonvocational?
9. What is the significance of all the treasures of wisdom and knowledge being hidden in Christ? How should that truth influence our lives?
10. What does this passage teach us about the relationship between evangelism and discipleship?

Learning to Walk

COLOSSIANS 2:6-15

Main Idea: God calls us to grow in our walks with Christ in order to strengthen our faith and find our fulfillment in him.

I. **We Must Deepen Our Intimacy with Christ (2:6-7).**
    A. We are called to be grounded (2:6-7).
    B. We are called to be growing (2:7).
    C. We are called to be grateful (2:7).
II. **We Must Denounce the Insufficiency of Christ (2:8-10).**
    A. False teaching deceives us and denies Christ (2:8).
    B. Faithful teaching edifies us and exalts Christ (2:9-10).
III. **We Must Define Our Identity in Christ (2:11-15).**
    A. He circumcised our hearts (2:11).
    B. He conquered over death (2:12-13).
    C. He canceled our debt (2:13-14).
    D. He condemned the enemy (2:15).
    E. He confirmed our victory (2:15).

The first steps of any child who is learning to walk are a major accomplishment. The excitement on a child's face in that experience of forward progress in an upright position is a sight to cherish and celebrate. But the jubilation of a proud parent is immediately tempered with the realization that the child's walking introduces a whole new set of challenges and cautions. Falling is inevitable, the ability to wander into harm's way requires safeguarding, and opening new doors (literally and figuratively!) exposes the child to possibilities and pitfalls that most little ones are not prepared to handle. Taking steps is one thing, but taking on a flight of steps is another!

Scripture describes the Christian life in similar terms. Walking with God is a metaphor for the believer's life that appears on the earliest pages of Scripture (Gen 5:22; 6:9; 48:15). It is used throughout the Old Testament to describe God's people as they journey through life and live according to his ways (i.e., Deut 30:16; Pss 1:1; 119:1). In the New Testament "walking" describes a life of faith (2 Cor 5:7) and the nature of our spiritual growth and progress that parallels the physical development of a child (3 John 4). It is important for us to recognize what this familiar metaphor of walking is meant to communicate. Like life, walking spiritually requires strength and stamina, it involves direction and a destination; one must avoid pitfalls and overcome obstacles to stay on course.

Like a spiritual parent, Paul recognized these aspects of walking with God and the Colossians' need to be encouraged, supported, and protected as they learned to take steps on their individual spiritual journeys. He used the phrase previously in the letter to describe the Christian life God desires for his children that ultimately honors him (1:10). He uses it here, to "walk in him" (2:6), as he begins to offer his guidance for their growing faith.

These verses are essentially a synopsis of the entire letter and reflect the heart of the book. Paul transitions from his prayerful and personal introduction and bases his practical instruction through the remainder of the letter on the foundational truths he established in his extended opening. The use of "so then" (v. 6) clearly identifies the preliminary material (1:3–2:5) as the theological and circumstantial impetus for the Colossians to "continue to walk in him" (v. 6).[1]

The rest of the letter describes what a life devoted to Christ looks like, and this passage prescribes the initial steps of the lifelong journey. Paul teaches the Colossians what God wants all believers to know—that a faithful walk with Christ requires us to pursue intimacy with Jesus, find fulfillment in the sufficiency of Jesus, and claim our victorious identity in Jesus.

We Must Deepen Our Intimacy with Christ
COLOSSIANS 2:6-7

In order to learn to walk with the Lord, the first step we must take is to deepen our intimacy with Christ. Paul describes this process in the initial verses of this passage that could also be characterized as the thesis of the letter. The initial phrase reminds the Colossians of their positional

---

[1] Moo notes that this phrase at the end of 2:6 is the first imperative in the letter and introduces a string of twenty-nine commands that extend to 4:6. This not only signifies a transition from the introductory material into the body of the epistle, but it also serves as the "overarching point of the whole letter body" (*The Letters*, 175–76).

status as those who had trusted "Christ Jesus as Lord,"[2] with the goal of provoking their further spiritual progression (v. 6). This phrase/title Paul uses in reference to their salvation draws from the description of Christ's identity as the supreme and sovereign Lord in the Christ hymn of 1:15-20 and reinforces his deity and distinction over and above any rival teachings of the Colossian heresy. Therefore, "just as" the Colossians had "received" him as the "Lord," they should "continue to walk in him" in complete submission and obedience.

This ongoing "walk" with Christ is the subject of Paul's intercession for them (1:10), and the same term is used here as the focus of his instruction for them (2:6). Paul prescribes a life that honors the Lord by using four participles in 2:7 that mirror the four in his earlier prayer on their behalf—"being rooted" / "bearing fruit" (1:10), "built up" / "growing" (1:10), "established" / "being strengthened" (1:11), "overflowing with gratitude" / "giving thanks" (1:12; Pao, *Colossians and Philemon*, 156). His petitions, now directives, inform us how to deepen our intimacy with Christ.

We Are Called to Be Grounded (2:6-7)

Paul uses this horticultural metaphor, "rooted" (v. 7), to describe our positional status in the Lord and our need to remain firmly planted in him. His terminology evokes thoughts of the psalmist's description of the "happy" man who is "like a tree planted beside flowing streams that bears its fruit in its season, and its leaf does not wither" (Ps 1:1,3). In order to mature in our walk with Christ, we must be nourished by the source of life, Jesus himself, and be planted in the soil of God's truth that allows us to abide in him.

The term also echoes Jesus's use of agricultural imagery as he instructed his disciples to "remain" in him (John 15:4-7). Not only do the roots provide access to the source of life, but they also provide stability and keep us from shifting or ultimately falling away. Similar to the way one may use the concept of *roots* to refer to one's heritage, being "rooted" in Christ includes remaining grounded in the faith by which we "received" him (Col 2:6). Like the Colossians, our faith must

---

[2] This unique phrase in the original language literally reads, "Christ Jesus the Lord," and its syntactical construction is not used anywhere else in the New Testament (Melick, *Philippians, Colossians, Philemon*, 247).

continue in its original soil and not be uprooted. By continuing to draw from the streams of living water that never run dry, we will deepen our intimacy with Christ and produce fruit that remains.

We Are Called to Be Growing (2:7)

Our personal fellowship with Christ also fuels our continued growth in him. Paul shifts to a construction metaphor, "built up," to describe our personal and corporate spiritual progress "in him" (v. 7). The combination of agricultural and architectural metaphors weds the shared concept of a necessary foundation to produce and sustain growth (O'Brien, *Colossians, Philemon,* 107). This reflects the same blended use of metaphors Paul combined to describe the growth God produces through the sowing and watering ministries of his servants as well as their construction efforts to build on the foundation of Jesus Christ (see 1 Cor 3:5-11).

As a construction term, "built up" is almost certainly an allusion to the people of God as his dwelling place (Pao, *Colossians and Philemon,* 157); we are being formed together and growing together "into a holy temple" (Eph 2:19-22; cf. 1 Cor 3:16). As we are rooted in Christ, we grow in intimacy with him and in community with his people, as "living stones" who are "being built" into a "spiritual house" (1 Pet 2:5). Therefore, God desires for us to grow deeper in our personal walk with Christ and in our corporate devotion so that we might be "built up" and draw closer to him.

Being "rooted and built up" will ultimately fortify the Colossians so that they may be "established in the faith" (Col 2:7). While some commentators interpret this as a legal metaphor, Paul is more likely using it to describe the collective effect of being grounded and growing (Moo, *The Letters,* 181). As believers, they will be strengthened and will persevere in their faith as it is reinforced through a continual commitment to the truth, "just as [they] were taught" (v. 7) In other words, Paul is challenging them and cautioning them to grow deeper in what they know (and *whom* they know!) in order to prevent their being seduced by false teachers with competing and conflicting doctrines that do not exalt Christ. Being "rooted . . . built up . . . and established" (v. 7) will allow us to "remain grounded and steadfast in the faith" and not be "shifted away from the hope of the gospel" (1:23).

We Are Called to Be Grateful (2:7)

The first three participles are all in passive form and emphasize God's role in accomplishing our grounding and growth. The final one, "overflowing with gratitude" (v. 7), is an active participle that highlights our response to God's redemptive and renewing work on our behalf. As we grow in Christ and stay focused on the gospel, the undeserved nature of God's grace toward us should humble us and produce gratitude in our hearts.

Thanksgiving is a consistent theme throughout the letter and is meant to characterize the life of the believer (cf. 1:3,12; 2:7; 3:15,17; 4:2). It certainly includes a prevailing *attitude* of gratitude, but it also should be apparent through intentional *expressions* of thanksgiving. This seems to be the goal of Paul's exhortation in this verse as he characterizes it as "overflowing" from our lives. Our gratitude to the Lord will be evident through acts of kindness and benevolence to others, offerings of praise and worship to the Lord, and lives spent in humble submission to him. As a result, our intimacy with Christ will perpetually deepen by producing further gratitude as we are grounded and growing in him.

We Must Denounce the Insufficiency of Christ
COLOSSIANS 2:8-10

In addition to deepening our intimacy with Christ, learning to walk with him also requires us to find our fulfillment in his total and utter sufficiency. The Colossians were being besieged with false teachings about the person and work of Jesus, and these deceptive and destructive heresies were threatening to undermine the foundation of truth on which their faith had been established. Pursuing the prescribed religious practices and adopting false ideologies that ultimately distort and diminish the nature and redemptive work of Christ would eventually leave them empty and derail their faith.

In similar fashion, our culture attempts to entice us with persuasive philosophies and worldly values that denigrate the person and work of our Savior and subtly seek to render our faith ineffective. In order to combat these dangerous influences, we must recognize the infinite worth of Christ as the only source of true fulfillment and denounce any teaching to the contrary. Paul goes on to explain how we can distinguish between faithful teaching and the contemporary versions of false teaching.

False Teaching Deceives Us and Denies Christ (2:8)

The nature of Paul's warning is stronger than a cautionary awareness. "Be careful" alerts his readers to the threat of an imminent danger that has serious consequences (v. 8). Likewise, his vivid metaphorical admonition to avoid being taken "captive" by false teachers speaks to the influential and delusional nature of their doctrine and its ability to enslave those who become convinced. His warning is further strengthened by the irony of the perceived freedom offered by those who take spiritual hostages contrasted with Paul's genuine freedom in the gospel despite his physical imprisonment.

His description of the false teaching also underscores its convincing and devious nature. The deceptive teaching of this world distorts its victim's entire perspective: "philosophy"; it is misleading and worthless: "empty deceit"; and it is not according to God's eternal truth but is "based on human tradition" and "the elements of the world" (v. 8).[3] Paul describes the shallow and hollow foundation that these captivating doctrines are "based on" to intentionally contrast his previous instruction to the Colossians to be "rooted" and "established" in Christ (v. 7).

The fundamental flaw of all false doctrine is the distortion and denial of the foundational truth of the gospel, the person and work of Jesus. Paul accentuates this distinguishing factor, "rather than Christ" (v. 8), and thereby denounces any alternative teaching as that which is diametrically opposed to the gospel of Jesus. In other words, faith in Christ must be exclusive and cannot be enhanced, either by addition (through religious practices and good works) or by subtraction (by abstaining from sin or depriving yourself of privileges). While the

---

[3] The precise meaning of this phrase has been thoroughly debated, and Melick provides a concise summary of the various interpretations (*Philippians, Colossians, Philemon*, 253). For a more expanded summary of the issues and arguments, see Moo, *The Letters*, 187–93. The majority of the discussion stems from possible connections between Paul's use of this phrase and the implied understanding it offers regarding the Colossian heresy. However, his ultimate point in this verse, regardless of the specific reference of this phrase (whether cosmic forces, religious principles, or physical elements) is that the competing teachings and corresponding worship practices were inferior to the supremacy of Christ, his sovereignty over all of creation, and the exclusive worship he is worthy to receive.

deceptive philosophy and values of this world may not explicitly reject Christ, their failure to affirm his sole sufficiency ultimately denies him.]

Faithful Teaching Edifies Us and Exalts Christ (2:9-10)

In contrast with the false teaching that deceives us and denies Christ, Paul characterizes faithful teaching as that which edifies us and exalts Christ. Having established the ultimate distinguishing factor as the person and work of Christ (v. 8), Paul now elaborates on the crucial distinctions of the gospel that set their faith apart.

His description of the essence and effect of faithful teaching is in direct contradiction to that of the false teaching. The barren emptiness of the deceptive doctrine is exceeded by the divine fullness of Christ, "the entire fullness of God's nature dwells bodily in Christ" (v. 9). The concept of "fullness" excludes room for any competing doctrines or practices. But Paul's ultimate point was to affirm the comprehensive nature of Christ's essence as the "entire" embodiment of divine nature. It reiterates Paul's earlier declaration, "God was pleased to have all his fullness dwell in him" (1:19), with emphatic force as he explicitly and exclusively affirms that Christ is the real and actual presence of God himself in bodily form.

This would not only have rejected any aspects of the Colossian heresy that denied the reality of the incarnation; it also definitively asserts with unassailable clarity that Jesus is God. It further conclusively affirms the substitutionary nature of Christ's atonement through his bodily sacrifice on our behalf (1:22; cf. 1 Pet 2:24). It is through his physical death and bodily resurrection (Col 2:13) that he offers salvation and the possibility of a reconciled and resurrected life. This is the basis for our edification in him that is impossible through any other means and, therefore, cannot be compromised with doctrinal error.

The Colossians' attempt to find fulfillment in any other source would ultimately prove futile. But "in Christ" (v. 9) they possessed everything they needed or could ever desire. Paul's overlapping use of words is intentional, and the fulfillment we experience, "filled by him" (v. 10), is directly connected to the "fullness" of Christ himself (v. 9). This is in contrast to the "empty" nature (v. 8) of the false teaching. [In other words, Jesus, as "the head over every ruler and authority" (v. 10; cf. 1:6-18), supersedes every perceived benefit that any competing philosophies, rival spiritual beings, or religious practices could offer.]

The implications of these crucial theological truths are significant and multifaceted. First, Christ is preeminent and worthy of all worship. Any teaching or practice that attempts to diminish his worthiness by elevating other beings or beliefs must be denounced. Likewise, any form of worship that dishonors or dilutes his infinite worth should be avoided. Second, Christ's universal supremacy translates into his ultimate sufficiency. He is not lacking in any way; therefore, in him neither are we. In Christ we possess everything from true wisdom to eternal wealth to personal worth. Jesus is our everything!

Finally, as God's people, we "have been filled by him" (v. 10) and can experience our true fulfillment in him. Apart from Christ there is no genuine satisfaction, but through his fullness we are made complete. "In him," and through him in us, we can fulfill our created purpose and experience life in its fullest expression (cf. John 10:10). Therefore, as we continue to walk in him, we must affirm his sufficiency in both our theological beliefs and our everyday behaviors, while denouncing every principle or practice that attempts to undermine his fullness.

We Must Define Our Identity in Christ
COLOSSIANS 2:11-15

Progressing in our walk with him also requires us to define our identity in Christ. The letter to the Colossians follows the common being-doing pattern of New Testament epistles. This is sometimes referred to as the indicative/imperative approach, and Colossians provides a prime example of this design (Moo, *The Letters*, 176). This model is a synopsis of the Christian life: it is based on timeless theological truths and the reality of who we are in Christ (indicative), and the corresponding behavior and practical implications are prescribed and commanded (imperative).

As the hinge passage in Paul's letter to the Colossians, these verses not only encourage us to progress in our walk (vv. 6-7) based on the timeless truths of Christ's identity (vv. 8-10); they also propel us forward based on the fullness and reality of our identity in him (vv. 11-15). Paul repeatedly uses the phrase "in him" or "with him" in succession throughout these verses to signify the union we share with Jesus and the corresponding status we have as believers. The person and work of Christ are clearly the focal point, but, as Paul explains, our identity is defined by his redemptive work that is applied to us through every aspect of the salvation he secured on our behalf.

He Circumcised Our Hearts (2:11)

In conjunction with the fullness of Christ and our fullness in him, Paul now expounds on our status as his people by referencing the Jewish custom of circumcision (v. 11). As the covenant sign of God's people in the Old Testament, circumcision was the defining physical distinctive that set his people apart from the pagan nations (Gen 17:9-14). It not only signified the covenant relationship; it also indicated the means by which the covenant would be ratified and fulfilled in the promised Messiah through Abraham's seed (Gen 12:1-7) and the seed of woman (Gen 3:15). Moses recognized the spiritual nature of circumcision and the circumcision of the heart that it ultimately represented (Deut 30:6).

Similarly, Paul affirmed the spiritual nature of circumcision (Rom 2:25-29) as well as the spiritual nature of the "seed" promise and its covenant fulfillment in Christ (Gal 3:16,29). Therefore, he describes it here as a personal reality we possess in Christ, as those who "were also circumcised in him," and the spiritual covenant that has been performed by God, "a circumcision not done with hands" (Col 2:11).

The last half of this verse has two distinct interpretations that are both viable as they clarify our identity in Christ. The various ways this verse is translated reflects the different interpretive possibilities and warrants our consideration. On one hand, Paul could be elaborating on the nature of our circumcision and its implications, "putting off the body of flesh," as our new status before God based on the spiritual operation, "the circumcision of Christ," performed by him on our hearts. In addressing his readers, "you," he explains that believers have put off "the body of flesh" (v. 11; cf. 3:9; Rom 6:6) and in Christ have the power to overcome the sinful desires of our previous nature.

The second option interprets the verse as using the covenantal metaphor to refer to the substitutionary death of Christ, "putting off the body of flesh," and his crucifixion as "the circumcision of Christ." Paul's use of the phrase "body of flesh" in this verse is identical to the previous one that clearly refers to Christ's "physical body" (Col 1:22). This also agrees with the incarnational understanding of Christ's embodiment of God's nature in the immediate context (2:9). Other parallels are found in Paul's summaries of the gospel—the death, burial, and resurrection of Christ (1 Cor 15:3-4; Rom 6:3-4)—with a similar pattern in this passage—the circumcision, burial, and resurrection of Christ (Col 2:11-13). Likewise, the corresponding passage in Ephesians explicitly refers to "the blood of Christ" as that which accomplishes our spiritual circumcision (Eph 2:11-13). In this sense Christ's death is understood as his "circumcision" that permanently ratifies God's covenant with his people, whose hearts are spiritually circumcised in him.

While both interpretations have merit and are theologically valid, contextually Paul seems to be addressing the positional status of believers by emphasizing the work Christ performed in order to secure it. It is through his substitutionary atonement that our hearts have been circumcised in order that we as believers may receive covenantal status as members of God's people. This emphasis would eliminate the need for any further "severe treatment of the body" that the false teachers may have been promoting, which ultimately provided no value in overcoming the indulgence of the flesh (Col 2:23). But through the sacrifice of Christ's entire body, not simply the removal of a piece of flesh, our hearts are spiritually circumcised and converted.

He Conquered over Death (2:12-13)

The spiritual circumcision we receive in Christ is accomplished through his sacrifice and our participation in it by faith. In addition to this redemptive truth, Paul goes on to explain that through Christ's substitutionary atonement and his bodily resurrection he also conquered death, defeating the ultimate penalty of sin (Gen 2:15-17; Rom 6:23), and offers us new life. Both aspects of Christ's work and our corresponding status in him are spoken of as that which have already occurred and are established, "*were* also circumcised" (Col 2:11), "*were* buried," and "*were* also raised with him" (v. 12; emphasis added). In addition, they also are both received and applied "through faith in the working of God" (v. 12).

Our communion with Christ in his death as those who "were buried with him in baptism" (v. 12) reinforces our "circumcised" status as his covenant people.[4] But Paul's continued explanation, "You were

---

[4] Paul's reference to baptism here mirrors his use of circumcision, and both are used metaphorically to point to the spiritual reality. While Paul's description of baptism as that which reflects the death, burial, and resurrection of Christ endorses immersion as the proper mode of the ordinance, he is not advocating that baptism has replaced circumcision as a sign of the covenant that should be administered ceremonially to infants or as a religious rite. The "baptism" here is performed by the "working of God" (v. 12) and therefore is understood as a reference to the spiritual baptism believers experience on conversion (c.f. Rom 6:4; 1 Cor 12:13; Gal 3:27).

also raised with him" (v. 12) and "He made you alive with him" (v. 13), highlights an additional aspect of our identity in Christ that has several implications. First, it offers us assurance of the eternal hope that is secured for all believers through Christ's resurrection (cf. 1:5,12). Additionally, this crucial aspect of understanding is also the foundational truth and motivation for Paul's practical instructions through the remainder of the letter as that which corresponds to our new identity in him (3:1). And finally, not only should our godly lifestyle be consistent with our resurrected status, the power of God, "who raised him from the dead" (2:12), now dwells within us through the Holy Spirit and enables us to live according to our identity in Christ (cf. Rom 8:11). Because he has conquered death, "we are more than conquerors through him" (Rom 8:37), and we have the ability to say no to sin and yes to righteousness (cf. Rom 6:3-13).

He Canceled Our Debt (2:13-14)

The third aspect of Christ's work that defines our identity in him is the redemptive forgiveness that his work secures: he canceled our debt. Paul helps the Colossians understand the correlation between Christ's death, burial, and resurrection and the atonement it provides for our sin. The description of their previous status as those who "were dead in trespasses and in the uncircumcision of [their] flesh" (v. 13; cf. Eph 2:1-3) unites the two spiritual concepts from the preceding verses, Christ's "baptism" and "circumcision," and underscores the dramatic nature of spiritual conversion. It also establishes his atoning sacrifice as the source from which this third facet of our identity in Christ derives.

The sacrificial system of the Mosaic covenant was established to foreshadow Christ's sacrifice that would ultimately atone for sin (cf. Heb 9:11–10:18). Jesus died as "the Lamb of God, who takes away the sin of the world" (John 1:29) and will be worshiped with eternal praise as the "Lamb who was slaughtered" on our behalf (Rev 5:11-12). Through his blood, Christ atones for our sin, thereby securing our forgiveness through God's mercy and grace (Col 2:13; cf. Heb 9:22; 1 Pet 1:18-19). This forgiveness is comprehensive, "all our trespasses" (Col 2:13), and is complete (cf. John 19:30; Heb 9:26-28;).

While forgiveness has a forensic component that cleanses our sin (1 John 1:7,9), it also has a financial connotation that cancels our debt. Paul emphasizes the second aspect in this passage, which corresponds to his previous description of salvation in payment terms: "redemption, the forgiveness of sins" (Col 1:14; cf. Eph 1:7). Christ's sacrifice satisfied and "erased" our "certificate of debt," the payment of death that our sin deserved and was owed to God (Col 2:14; c.f. Rom 6:23). This record of our sin, the violation of God's decrees and our required obedience, "its obligations," was "against us and opposed to us." In other words, we were indicted and stood condemned before God. But Christ, through his sacrifice, removed it "by nailing it to the cross" and canceled our debt. Therefore, we believers now stand before God forgiven, without guilt or shame, because the Lamb of God suffered the punishment for our sin!

He Condemned the Enemy (2:15)

Our spiritual conversion, "circumcision," resurrection, and "baptism" have not only provided us with new life and forgiveness of sin, but the work of Christ has also condemned the enemy. Paul previously declared Jesus's supremacy "over every ruler and authority" (2:10; cf. 1:16) by virtue of his sovereign nature. He now asserts Christ's supremacy based on his redemptive work on the cross and his resurrection that "disarmed the rulers and authorities" (v. 15). While Jesus voluntarily stripped off his body of flesh (v. 11), by his sacrifice he victoriously stripped the opposing spiritual forces of their power as he "disarmed" and defeated them.

These cosmic powers of darkness are the agents of the ultimate enemy, Satan, who wage war against our souls with fear, guilt, shame, and the threat of punishment (cf. Eph 6:11-12). But through Christ these enemies and their weapons are rendered powerless, and we have the ability to overcome their relentless, though impotent, attacks. Ultimately, Christ's death on the cross and his resurrection from the grave secured our eternal redemption, but it sealed his enemies' fate of eternal condemnation (Rev 20:10-15).

He Confirmed Our Victory (2:15)

The final aspect of our identity in Christ is our triumphant status through the confirmation of his victory. Paul explains that Jesus not only disarmed and defeated the enemy, but he also "disgraced them publicly" (v. 15). This phrase includes a dual understanding, a temporal and an eternal sense, that characterizes Christ's triumph as both a humiliating defeat for his enemies and a glorious celebration for his people.

While the cross of Christ satisfied God's wrath toward sin and disarmed the enemy, Jesus's conquering the grave ultimately secures our victory as believers (1 Cor 15:54-57) and declares him to be the "powerful Son of God . . . by the resurrection of the dead" (Rom 1:3-4). In addition, his ascension exalts him to his rightful throne (Heb 1:3), restores his preexistent and preeminent glory (John 17:5), and proclaims his victory from "heaven . . . at the right hand of God" (1 Pet 3:18-22; Moo, *The Letters*, 215–16). In other words, through Christ's physical and visible resurrection and ascension, Jesus put on public display his victory and his enemies' defeat.

The phrases in this verse also carry a familiar cultural connotation for Paul's original audience and provide a vivid picture of Christ's victorious celebration when he "triumphed over them" (Col 2:15). In ancient literature the victorious term Paul uses typically described a triumphant procession that Roman generals would lead through the streets of Rome to celebrate a military victory (Pao, *Colossians and Philemon*, 173). As the powerless captives were paraded behind the conquering victor, their defeat and public humiliation were declared through their forced submission to his rule and authority (O'Brien, *Colossians, Philemon*, 128–29).

In the same way, Christ has defeated his foes, and their public disgrace has confirmed and certified our victory. Therefore, we have the confidence that whatever hardships and heartaches must be endured in this world through trial or temptation, Christ has defeated the enemy (John 16:33), and we who are "in him" (Col 2:15) by faith are able to overcome the world (1 John 5:4). This final aspect of our identity in Christ allows us to walk in victory with the assurance of our secure status in him.

Conclusion

Paul's challenge for the Colossians to continue to "walk" in Christ is the same call of God for believers today (Eph 4:1). But as in the case of the original recipients of his letter, this requires us to pursue intimacy with Jesus, to find fulfillment in the sufficiency of Jesus, and to claim our victorious identity in Jesus. Each of these steps in our walk faces specific challenges that attempt to trip us up and detour us in our journey.

For instance, as believers we will face the temptation to drift away from the foundational truth of the gospel and personal intimacy with Christ as we grow comfortable and complacent in our salvation. We can become distracted by the busyness of our lives and ministries or even begin to explore other sources of spiritual nourishment and fulfillment. Instead, we must deepen our intimacy with Christ through the renewing grace and mercy of the gospel so that we may continually be grounded, growing, and grateful.

Likewise, our world will continue to entice us with its indulgent values, its empty promises, and even its spiritual counterfeits in an effort to convince us that they can satisfy and stabilize our lives. Rather than abandoning Jesus entirely, we may be persuaded to compromise our faith by attempting to synthesize worldly beliefs and behaviors with our commitment to Christ. But the sufficiency of Christ requires us to denounce any competing means of fulfillment as that which is ultimately empty and can never truly satisfy. His fullness is the only source of true satisfaction that can never be diluted or depleted.

Ultimately, our walk with Christ must also overcome the temptations to find our identity in what we know, what we can do, or what we have. Our identity as believers is determined by *who* we know, what *he* has done, and all that *he* offers. Through his death, burial, and resurrection, Christ has adopted us into his family, he has purchased our salvation, and he has given us new life with the power to walk in the victory that he has secured on our behalf!

Reflect and Discuss

1. What does it mean to walk in Christ in the same way we received him?
2. How do worldly philosophies take us away from Christ? What is Paul's antidote to such false teaching?
3. What is the significance of the "entire fullness of God's nature" (v. 9) dwelling in Christ's body? What are the implications of this truth for our lives?
4. What does this passage teach us about how our union with Christ transforms our identity?
5. How does Paul describe the different aspects of our identity that we have received in the gospel? For example, what is the significance of being "raised with him" (v. 12)?
6. What is the significance of Paul's stacking different metaphors to show the comprehensiveness of Christ's forgiveness of our sins?

7. What is the significance of Christ's disarming "the rulers and authorities" (v. 15) when it comes to our dealing with guilt, shame, and the accusations of the enemy?
8. What are some of the implications of Christ's triumph and victorious resurrection?
9. How does this passage teach us to stay centered on Jesus?
10. How does this passage highlight the sufficiency of Christ in his person and work?

Learning to Live in Freedom

COLOSSIANS 2:16–3:4

Main Idea: Through the power of the gospel and according to our identity in Christ, we have been delivered from the demands of religious performance and are free to live for his glory through loving obedience.

I. **Our Death in Christ Releases Us from the Law (2:16-23).**
   A. We are free from the shackles of reputation (2:16,18).
   B. We are free from the bondage of religion (2:16-19).
   C. We are free from the chains of regulations (2:20-23).

II. **Our Faith in Christ Raises Us to New Life (3:1-4).**
   A. Jesus redirects life's pursuits (3:1).
   B. Jesus reshapes life's perspective (3:2).
   C. Jesus redefines life's purpose (3:3-4).

Paul wrote the letter to the Colossians with heavy chains on his wrists. This certainly was not the first time he had been in prison (2 Cor 11:23), and it would not be the last (2 Tim 1:8). But Paul knew better than anyone that the bars and shackles of an earthly jail did not determine his ultimate freedom. He also recognized that civic freedom did not always equate to authentic liberty.

Perhaps his understanding of true freedom was most influenced by his experience in Macedonia with Silas (Acts 16:16-38). As they were spreading the gospel, they were harassed by a young girl who was enslaved in every way. Physically, she was a slave to her masters who were exploiting her for financial gain. Spiritually, she was possessed by a demonic spirit who had seized control of her life. By the power of Christ, Paul instantly freed her from both.

As a result, Paul and Silas were flogged and imprisoned. The Scriptures vividly describe how they were heavily guarded, thrown into the most secure area of the jail, and their feet were shackled with chains. Yet none of these could restrain their hearts from worshiping. As they expressed their praise to God, an earthquake shook the prison, the doors opened, and their bonds were broken. While others may have fled and sought what they supposed was freedom, Paul and Silas continued to operate in the spiritual liberty they had never lost. Paul reassured the jailer that they had not escaped, and the guard responded with a request for true freedom, salvation in Christ!

Perhaps this is why Paul was so emphatic as he cautioned the church at Colossae. He knew the dangers of spiritual shackles were far more severe than those of physical chains, and the Colossians found themselves being drawn into a yoke of religious bondage. Their church had been infiltrated by false teachers who were captivating God's people with embellished spiritual experiences and saddling them with ritualistic expressions of piety. But the Colossians already possessed the keys to unlock these fetters of futility. Paul pointed them out in the early portion of his letter when he confirmed the Colossians' salvation in Christ and celebrated their Savior's supremacy. This section of his writing expounds on the implications of these theological keys that Paul began to explain in the preceding passage.

The instructional portion of the letter opened with his challenge to "continue to walk" according to the finished work of Christ and the Colossians' corresponding identity in him (Col 2:6-15). He now shifts to the resulting mindset and practical implications of this established reality. The transition is signified by the change in verb tense from the previous section. He moves from describing our spiritual status secured through faith in the atoning work of Christ—you "*were* . . . circumcised . . . buried . . . raised*" (2:11-12; emphasis added)—to the redemptive significance of these spiritual realities—"Therefore, don't let anyone judge [or] . . . condemn you" (2:16-19), "If you died with Christ" (2:20-23), and "if you have been raised with Christ" (3:1-4).[1]

Paul's instructions for the Colossians are based on the doctrinal truths that have secured their freedom in Christ. Because of their identity in him, they have been liberated from the oppressive demands of

---

[1] In following Paul's train of thought, the positional status of 2:11-12, "buried" and "raised," is the basis for the liberating perspective of the believer in 2:20 ("If you died with Christ . . .") and in 3:1 ("If you have been raised with Christ"). These same dual aspects of Christian identity then provide the impetus for Paul's practical instruction in 3:5 ("Therefore, put to death . . .") and 3:12 ("Therefore, as God's chosen ones, holy and dearly loved, put on . . ."). Textually, Paul seems to trace these characteristics of our status in Christ (buried/raised) from the believer's position (2:9-15), to the believer's perspective (2:16–3:4), to the believer's practice (3:5-17). This combination also serves as the basis for the textual divisions and corresponding sermon passages.

the false teachers (2:16-23) and are free to live according to the eternal hope of the gospel (3:1-4). In the same way, we must learn to embrace our freedom in Christ and avoid the deceptive snare of pious performance. Even though we may not directly encounter the blatant heresy of such false teachers in our church contexts, we can certainly observe the influence of contemporary leaders who distort the Scriptures. They mislead and entangle undiscerning Christians in a hopeless web of guilt and failure by promoting religious moralism. As a result, many believers unintentionally subject themselves to a works-based righteousness and live enslaved to self-imposed rules and regulations according to assumed expectations. At the same time, other believers elevate themselves in self-righteousness, parading their legalistic lifestyle cloaked in false humility that presumes God's favor. However, as this passage teaches, through the power of the gospel and according to our identity in Christ, we have been delivered from the demands of religious performance and are free to live for his glory through loving obedience.

Our Death in Christ Releases Us from the Law
COLOSSIANS 2:16-23

The concept of freedom and the joy of deliverance are the underlying truths in this section. In the previous passage Paul's exhortation for the Colossians to grow in their faith (2:6-7) was combined with a caution not to be taken "captive" by the false teaching that had permeated their culture and invaded their church (v. 8). In these verses he describes specific aspects of the heresy that would potentially hold the Colossians hostage, and he confronts them with three related exhortations: "Don't let anyone judge you" (v. 16), "Let no one condemn you" (v. 18), and "Why do you submit to [the world's] regulations?" (v. 20).

Each of these admonitions hinges on the conditional clause in verse 20: "If you died with Christ. . . ." This phrase is central to the passage and provides the interpretational lens by which to understand the premise for each exhortation and their relationship to one another (Pao, *Colossians and Philemon*, 184). Paul explained how the finished work of Christ, and their corresponding participation in his death, frees them from the related obligations of the false teaching.

This theological truth not only provides the basis to refute the doctrinal error and religious rituals that were being propagated in Colossae;

it also eliminates the need to precisely define the Colossian heresy[2] and establishes the timeless doctrinal truth that has contemporary relevance for all believers. In this passage God reminds us of the freedom we possess in Christ that liberates us from the enticing deception and exhausting demands of a works-based righteousness.

We Are Free from the Shackles of Reputation (2:16,18)

Paul recognized that much of the adherence to a strict code of behavior stemmed from the pressure of other people's expectations. His two liberating admonitions regarding the judging (v. 16) and condemning (v. 18) by others reveals the posture of the false teachers and the pressure to perform that they were exerting. Evidently, these teachers were boasting about their adherence to religious dietary laws and festivals, ascetic practices, worship of angels, and reported visions (vv. 16,18,21-23). Their hubris reflects the underlying, self-righteous pride that led Paul to characterize them as those who "are inflated by empty notions of their unspiritual mind" (v. 18).

The false teachers' condescending demeanor was oppressive and had coerced the Colossians into lives of shame, guilt, and obligation. As a result, Paul commands the believers not to "let anyone judge" (v. 16) or "condemn" them (v. 18). While the Colossians could not prevent the critical and condemning judgment of others, they could control how they responded, and this is Paul's primary concern (Melick, *Philippians, Colossians, Philemon*, 266). In both of these instances, Paul demonstrates how the basis for the unfounded reproach conflicts with a proper understanding of "Christ" (v. 17) and their relationship to him as "the head" (v. 19). For Paul, Christ is the delineating factor by which all doctrines and

---

[2] Scholars have explored a variety of possibilities as to the exact nature of the Colossian heresy in an attempt to better understand the historical context of the letter and assist in its interpretation. Moo provides a helpful summary of the research and various related arguments (*The Letters*, 46–60). Ultimately, the precise nature of the Colossian heresy does not influence or inform the timeless theological and Christological truths that Paul asserts to refute the false teachings. In other words, doctrine is not defined by a conflicting error; it is declared for the purpose of correcting error. Therefore, while an in-depth investigation of the issues may be helpful in interpreting the specifics that Paul alludes to in this passage, a conclusive and comprehensive understanding of the Colossian heresy is not plausible or ultimately necessary to faithfully interpret and apply these verses or the letter as a whole.

duties must be measured and why his initial caution warned them against being taken "captive" by anything that is not based on Christ (v. 8).

Therefore, he challenges them to view themselves based on their true positional standing in Christ. "If you died with Christ" (v. 20) refers to his previous explanation of their salvation and their current status as believers (vv. 11-12) and clearly draws the implications from its conditional wording, "if" or "since." In other words, as a result of their acceptance in Christ, they are not controlled by, and do not need to be consumed with, man's approval.

Today the shackles of other people's expectations, real or perceived, continue to enslave many of God's people. We struggle to manufacture or maintain our reputations in a culture that is captivated with façades and personas. What is even more concerning is that in the church we have created a culture and a climate that expects people to submit to our self-imposed standards or unrealistic expectations of perfection. As a result, God's people oftentimes feign a superficial obedience to conceal their struggles, cover up their pasts, or conform to the prevailing customs. But our death in Christ has freed us from the shackles of reputation.

We Are Free from the Bondage of Religion (2:16-19)

In addition to the presumptuous and suffocating disposition of the false teachers, the Colossians were being burdened with the weight of their religious bondage as well. In general, the false teachers were promoting a view of God that was a merit-based theology entrenched in human performance. This was primarily demonstrated in their misunderstanding and misuse of the law. While there is no direct reference to the Mosaic law, the questions of a restricted diet, "food and drink," and religious days, "a festival or a new moon or a Sabbath day" (v. 16)[3] were being held over their heads. These are most certainly aspects of the law with ethnic implications and are categories that were points of contention throughout the early church (Acts 15; Rom 14:1–15:6; 1 Cor 8–10).

As Paul notes, these customs and regulations were given as a "shadow of what was to come" (Col 2:17; cf. Heb 8:5; 10:1). Not only does this

---

[3] Pao (*Colossians and Philemon*, 185) notes that the reference to these religious days is clearly Jewish based on the use of these three terms together in multiple Old Testament passages (i.e., 1 Chr 23:31; 2 Chr 2:4; 31:3; Ezek 45:17; cf. 2 Kgs 4:23; Neh 10:33; Isa 66:23; Ezek 46:1; Amos 8:5).

term *shadow* imply the temporary and preparatory purpose of the law, but Paul's contrasting and definitive phrase, "the substance is Christ," demonstrates Christ's supremacy over the law and his fulfillment of it. The law revealed God's character through principle, but Christ was the full expression of his character in person (Col 1:15,19; 2:9; cf. Heb 1:3).

The transitional term "therefore" at the beginning of the passage (Col 2:16) draws on the preceding truths as the basis for his explanation. The fullness of Christ (v. 9), his ultimate authority (v. 10), his sacrificial and substitutionary death (vv. 11-14), and his corresponding victory (v. 15) collectively serve as the unassailable fortress of our freedom. Because of who Christ is and what he has done, the legal demands of the law have been satisfied, and we are free from the obligations of religious obedience as an effort to secure or maintain our forgiveness and acceptance by God. As a result, Paul admonishes them, "Don't let anyone judge you" according to the law (v. 16).

The additional elements of the false teaching he describes fall into a somewhat different category and are distinguished by the second declaration of emancipation: "Let no one condemn you" (v. 18). The two terms Paul uses in his exhortations, "judge" and "condemn," describe more than just criticism from the false teachers. While this particular term *condemn* could include an athletic connotation of an umpire who could disqualify you, it primarily seems to build on the concept of Paul's initial term *judge* in verse 16 (Pao, *Colossians and Philemon*, 188). Combined together, the two terms describe an authoritative pronouncement of God's judgment that the false teachers were presuming and portraying themselves to have (Moo, *The Letters*, 218).

In addition to attempting to usurp God's authority, the false teachers were using idolatrous criteria as the basis for their judgment and seeking to impose their practices on the Colossians. Paul lists several aspects of their heresy that are difficult to specifically define for contemporary readers, but each of them clearly reveals a prideful spirit that elevates the individual. In false humility they deprive and denigrate themselves, "delighting in ascetic practices"; they deify and venerate angelic beings ("the worship of angels"); and they fabricate and exaggerate spiritual experiences, "claiming access to a visionary realm" (v. 18). In exalting these practices, the false teachers were ultimately inflating their own egos with "empty notions" to satisfy their fleshly desires, their "unspiritual mind" (v. 18).

Ironically, as Paul points out, the indulgence of their own "mind" actually disconnects them from the true "head," who is Christ (vv. 18-19;

cf. 1:18; 2:10). As the "head of the body, the church" (1:18), Christ alone is the source and authority by which the body is "nourished and held together" (2:19; cf. 3:15). The false teaching was essentially decapitating the body of Christ, severing it from its life-giving and unifying "head" that supplies each member and the collective whole with the spiritual sustenance to promote "growth from God" (v. 19).

Burdening God's people with religious principles and practices that spiritually starve them is a serious issue in the contemporary church as well. While the types of cultic customs the Colossians faced may not be common, we can be guilty of creating a similar culture of performance that distorts a healthy view of God's mercy and grace, cultivates a judgmental climate, and imprisons God's people in religious bondage. We must be careful not to create contemporary versions of these practices; rather, we must continue to point people to Christ and their freedom from the bondage of religion that is found in him.

We Are Free from the Chains of Regulations (2:20-23)

In addition to the shackles of reputation and the bondage of religion, the Colossians were being hindered by proverbial chains of regulations. Paul has described the intimidating demeanor of the false teachers, their distorted view of God, and the toxic religious culture they had established (vv. 16-19). In 2:20-23, he provides the theological and practical warrants for rejecting their teaching and prepares to shift the Colossians' perspective to its proper focus (3:1-4).

The conditional clause, "if you died with Christ" (2:20), serves as the culmination of his indictment against the false teachers and invites the readers to consider the implications of the theological and spiritual reality of their salvation. The direct tone of these verses is felt through the shift in verb forms, from third-person commands—"Don't let anyone judge" (v. 16) and "Let no one condemn" (v. 18)—to second-person discourse and repeated pleas—"Why do you . . . ?" (v. 20).

Paul wants the Colossians to understand that their shared death with Christ, the "head over every ruler and authority" (v. 10), who "triumphed over" rulers and authority (v. 15) and emptied "the elements of this world" of any power in their lives (v. 20; cf. v. 8). Therefore, he challenges them: "Why do you live as if you still belonged to the world?" (v. 20). Their willing subjugation to the world, as they "submit to [its] regulations," is inconsistent with their freedom in Christ.

The false teaching enslaving the Colossians is incompatible with their salvation in Christ for several reasons. First, Paul summarizes the rules of the false teachers: "Don't handle, don't taste, don't touch" (v. 21); and he explains that they are commands of abstinence that focus on things that are temporal in substance and value: "All these regulations refer to what is destined to perish by being used up" (v. 22). Second, he contends these regulations derive from a source that is inferior and impotent: "They are human commands and doctrines" (v. 22). Finally, Paul points out that the rules and regulations are worthless and ineffective. Since they correspond to the false teachings—"self-made religion, false humility, and severe treatment of the body" (v. 23; cf. v. 18)—they have "a reputation for wisdom," but ultimately, "they are not of any value in curbing self-indulgence" (v. 23). In other words, rules and regulations do not have the power or ability to change the heart's affections and overcome sinful desires.

The words of Paul in these verses seem to echo Jesus's indictment of the Pharisees for "teaching as doctrines human commands" and "abandoning the command of God" in order to "hold on to human tradition" (Mark 7:7-9). Jesus was ultimately focused on the heart, and Paul shared the same concern for the Colossians. It is possible to outwardly appear close and clean, while inwardly the heart remains distant and dirty (Matt 15:8; 23:27-28). But a focus on the heart does not disregard righteousness and obedience; it actually ensures it. It is by cleaning the inside of the "cup" that the outside will become truly clean (Matt 23:25).

Therefore, living according to our death in Christ will enable us to walk faithfully and resist the indulgence of the flesh. Forced compliance, especially to traditions, preferences, or legalistic practices, will only subject us to a religious version of the same slavery from which Christ died to liberate us. But our death in Christ releases us from the law. And through his death we have been freed from the shackles of reputation, the bondage of religion, and chains of regulations.

Our Faith in Christ Raises Us to New Life
COLOSSIANS 3:1-4

Our freedom in Christ is claimed through our identity in him and our spiritual participation in his redemptive work. As Paul indicted the false teachers for their religious rules and practices, he simultaneously reminded the Colossian believers of their liberty from these enslaving teachings. The conditional statement in the previous verses, "If you died with Christ," explained that through Christ's death they possess a corresponding freedom that releases them from legalistic obligations (2:20). This section begins with a parallel conditional statement, "So if you have been raised with Christ" (3:1), which establishes the continuity of thought, transitioning from the negative cautions to the positive exhortations of Paul's argument.

While death in Christ frees us from the law, our faith in Christ raises us to new life. This redeemed life certainly includes a behavioral component Paul will describe in the next passage, but it begins with a spiritual change that occurs in the heart. As he explains, new life in Christ transforms us at a more fundamental level by redirecting our pursuits, reshaping our perspective, and redefining our purpose.

Jesus Redirects Life's Pursuits (3:1)

While the false teachers were preoccupied with personal performance and experience, Paul describes our identity in a passive voice: "You *have been raised* with Christ" (v. 1; emphasis added), emphasizing God's work rather than our efforts. This fundamental difference is significant because it establishes the positional starting point for our spiritual growth. The opening phrase in these verses is a declaration of certainty that is grounded in the spiritual reality of believers' identity in Christ rather than in our vain attempts to earn his favor. As a result, he challenges them to consider how their life-direction should be determined accordingly.

As a result of our new life in Christ, Paul directs the Colossians to "seek the things above, where Christ is" (v. 1). This phrase intentionally describes a shift upward, away from the false teaching that was grounded in worldly things and human traditions (2:8,20). Directing their affections toward the resurrected Lord also supersedes the false teachers' elevated claims of visions and the worship of heavenly beings (2:18) while reiterating Christ's ultimate supremacy and honor as the one who is "seated at the right hand of God" (3:1).

It is important to note that Paul is not prescribing a mystical experience with Christ that would parallel or compete with the claims of the false teachers. He is challenging the Colossians to reorient their lives toward the heavenly reality that is already theirs through their authentic union with Christ (cf. Eph 2:6). To "seek the things above" carries the connotations of directing our hearts' passions and pursuits toward our eternal dwelling in Christ's presence and his glory. This phrase contrasts our potential captivity by false ideologies and the things of this world, and it redirects our hearts' affections toward those things that possess eternal value and substance.

Practically speaking, redirecting our pursuits begins with recalibrating our hearts' desires. As we become captivated by Christ through our union with him, we should seek to filter our passions through his throne of majesty to ultimately align our will with his. Our pursuits, what we devote ourselves to, should be measured by their value in Christ's kingdom, their purpose in accomplishing his mission, and their contribution to building his church. This may require us to reevaluate our careers or to reallocate our resources. It may involve reconsidering how we spend our time or invest in our relationships. Ultimately, our union with Christ should stir our affections for him and redirect our pursuits.

Jesus Reshapes Life's Perspective (3:2)

Paul continues to describe the transforming impact of our union with Christ by expanding on the concept of our *seeking* with a specific admonition for our *thinking*. These two verses offer parallel and complementary thoughts, but they are not synonymous concepts. To "seek the things above" (3:1) describes the reorientation of our hearts' affections. To "set your minds on things above" (v. 2) involves the reorientation of our volitional will (Moo, *The Letters*, 248).

The terminology in 3:2, "Set your minds," describes a reshaping of the thought process and overall perspective of believers based on the eternal realities of their salvation. The apostle clearly recognized the holistic change that our redemption involves, especially the crucial importance of renewing our minds. If the false teachers were advocating an emotional and mystical experience, this rational and objective perspective certainly countered their doctrine. In contrast to their approach, Christians should not determine eternal truths according to "earthly things"; we must interpret the world around us according to the heavenly reality "above" us (v. 2). This means that the significance of reshaping the mind in the process of sanctification is not situational or optional; it is foundational.

Allowing Christ's redemptive work to reshape our perspective is necessary for several reasons. Its primary significance is that it enables us to fulfill the great commandment by loving God with our entire selves, including our "mind[s]" (Matt 22:37-38). It is also essential because it protects us from the world's influence as the culture attempts to conform our thinking to its pattern. Through the constant renewing of our minds, we can experience God's transformation in our lives (Rom 12:2).

This renewed perspective also guards our hearts and minds with God's supernatural peace as we dwell on the things that are above (Phil 4:6-8). In addition, by focusing on that which is eternal, we can renew our hope in the midst of temporary afflictions (2 Cor 4:16-18). And ultimately, through new life in Christ, setting our minds on things above reshapes our perspective by allowing us to be led by the Spirit (Rom 8:6-7) and to "have the mind of Christ" (1 Cor 2:16 NIV).

Jesus Redefines Our Purpose (3:3-4)

Our identity in Christ not only redirects our pursuits and reshapes our perspective. Paul concludes this section by explaining how our union with Christ redefines our purpose. He summarizes both of the premises in the passage by establishing them as the collective baseline for his final admonition. The two conditional clauses (2:20; 3:1) are now asserted as a single statement: "For you died, and your life is hidden with Christ in God" (3:3). This assertion points backward and forward in the text. "For" establishes this maxim as the basis for why the Colossians are to "seek" and "set [their] minds on" the "things above" (vv. 1-2). But the declaration also serves as the warrant for Paul's continued exhortation. The flow is sequential from the established past, "you *died*," to the present, "your life *is* hidden," to the future, "you also *will* appear" (vv. 3-4; emphasis added). He now proceeds to explain how the present reality of these truths is intended to reset the trajectory of our lives toward eternity.

The description of the believer's "hidden" life in Christ signifies our personal relationship with him, affirms the security of our salvation in him, and certifies our glorious inheritance in him that is yet to be revealed. For our lives to be "hidden" in him not only positions us in Christ but also positions Christ in us (1:27). We have "died" with Christ, yet by faith we continue to live through Christ's abiding presence in hope of his promised return (cf. Gal 2:20). Paul clarifies that Christ "is

[our] life," and that which is "hidden" will appear. And when Christ "appears," we "also will appear with him" (Col 3:4). In other words, both our "hidden" life in Christ and his indwelling "life" in us will be fully revealed when he returns "in glory" (cf. 1 John 3:2). In the same way that the mystery of Christ was "hidden" in previous generations (Col 1:26), our identity in Christ and his pending return is "hidden" until he comes again "in glory" (3:3-4).

This future fulfillment of our current identity in Christ should redefine our purpose in multiple ways. For example, the glory of Christ's return reminds us of the temporal nature of this world and the fleeting value of its possessions and pleasures. Therefore, we should not be deceived by the vain pursuit of earthly wealth, achievement, status, or gratification (1 John 2:15-17). In Christ we are citizens of heaven and should not be deterred or distracted by the enticing desires of the flesh or ways of this world (Phil 3:20-21). Rather, since we have an eternal inheritance that awaits us (Col 1:5,12), we should "seek the things above" (3:1) by pursuing his kingdom and his righteousness (Matt 6:33).

In addition, the certainty of Christ's return gives us assurance that allows us to live with confidence in a world filled with uncertainty. As a result, we can endure hardships and persevere by fixing our hope on the grace and glory that will be revealed at the coming of Christ (Col 1:27; cf. 1 Pet 1:13). This hope is sure and steadfast, "firm and secure," as an "anchor for the soul" because Christ entered the holy place on our behalf (Heb 6:19-20) and is "seated at the right hand of God" (Col 3:1).

Finally, the imminence of Christ's return should motivate us to live with urgency. The coming of our Savior delivers hope, but it also ushers in his impending judgment. While the promise of justice may comfort us as believers, it should also burden us as it seals the destiny of the unbeliever who will be separated from God for eternity (2 Thess 1:5-10). Therefore, we must live as Christ's ambassadors, appealing to the lost to be reconciled to God through the power of the gospel (2 Cor 5:20).

As we anticipate the second coming of Christ, we can celebrate our life in him and rejoice at the glory we will share in his presence. But his imminent return is not intended to simply foster dreams of a heavenly eutopia that disregards the eternal significance of our earthly lives. Instead, we must allow our identity in Christ and his promised return to redefine our purpose. These truths should inspire us to live as citizens of heaven, strengthen us with hope, and motivate us to live with a gospel urgency.

Conclusion

Paul challenged the Colossians to grow in their faith and cautioned them not to be captivated by false teachings (Col 2:6-8). While addressing the specific issues of their church and community, he also established timeless principles for all believers to embrace that are grounded in our identity in Christ. As believers, our death in Christ liberates us from a life of insecurity, performance, and bondage under the law. Our life in Christ frees us to serve him with loving obedience and allows us to seek him with renewed passion.

Our personal union with Christ is comprehensive, and it associates us with every aspect of his work. We died with Christ (2:20; 3:3), we were buried with Christ (2:12), we have been raised with Christ (2:13; 3:1), and, therefore, we will appear with Christ in glory (3:4; Moo, *The Letters*, 251). As those who have been united with Christ through faith, we should let our entire lives be transformed and devoted to his mission and will. Through our new life in him, Jesus intends to redirect our pursuits, reshape our perspective, and redefine our purpose.

While these truths define our personal identity in Christ, they also have corporate implications. Within the body of Christ, we should cultivate a spiritual community that does not shackle God's people with unnecessary guilt or pressure to perform. Christ's death has liberated us from the rules and regulations of this religious mindset that breeds a culture of shame. At the same time, this does not lead to a culture that accepts or endorses sinful behavior. Instead, as we dwell within the community of faith, we should collectively seek and set our minds on things above that we share in common with other believers. We should live with holy anticipation of Christ's return as we celebrate our new life in him and devote ourselves to the mission of seeing others liberated from the bondage of sin to inherit the eternal promises of King Jesus!

Reflect and Discuss

1. How does our freedom in Christ free us from the shackles of reputation?
2. How does our freedom in Christ free us from the bondage of religion?
3. How does our freedom in Christ free us from the chains of regulations?

4. How should being raised with Christ redirect your life's pursuits?
5. How should being raised with Christ reshape your perspective?
6. How does being raised with Christ redefine your life's purpose?
7. How does this passage call us to renew our minds?
8. What does it mean for our lives to be hidden "with Christ in God" (v. 3)?
9. How should this passage motivate us to live with evangelistic urgency?
10. What does this passage teach us about our future hope?

How to Dress for Success

COLOSSIANS 3:5-17

Main Idea: God has called us to live according to our identity in Christ by putting off the sinful habits of our former nature and by putting on the godly virtues of our redeemed nature.

I. **We Must Cleanse Ourselves from Sinfulness (3:5-11).**
   A. We must put to death our sinful passions (3:5-7).
   B. We must put off our sinful practices (3:8-10).
   C. We must put down our sinful pride (3:11).
II. **We Must Clothe Ourselves in Godliness (3:12-17).**
   A. We must put on spiritual clothes in which we can accurately reflect our Savior (3:12-14).
   B. We must put on spiritual clothes in which we can comfortably rest in our Savior (3:15).
   C. We must put on spiritual clothes in which we can gratefully rejoice in our Savior (3:16).
   D. We must put on spiritual clothes in which we can actively run for our Savior (3:17).

Having grown up in eastern North Carolina, I (Scott) can remember countless days of yard work that would leave me covered in the fine black grit from the sandy soil of our coastal region. On hot summer afternoons a cloud of dust would chase me around the yard as I cut the thin, weedy grass. The thick humidity would blend with my dripping sweat to cover me with a sticky film that trapped the dirt against my skin as my clothes absorbed it. The only relief would come when the chores were complete and I could escape inside for a much-needed shower.

The sanitizing process began with my peeling off the sweat-saturated clothes that were clinging to my body. The damp and smelly garments would smack the bathroom floor as I stepped into the cool, clean flow of water in the shower. As I watched the dirt rinse off, it created a dirty creek circling into the drain. Even with the warm lather of shampoo and fragrant soap, I sometimes had to go through multiple washes to extract the grit from my scalp, ears, and nasal cavity; all had seemed to attract the filth like magnets. But once it was washed away, I felt great. It was invigorating. I felt like a completely different person.

After I stepped out of the shower and dried off, I would go through the typical hygiene routine, complete with deodorant and Q-tips, and smile with a refreshing sense of satisfaction. But imagine if after experiencing such a thorough cleansing, I made the unthinkable decision to dress myself in those cold, damp, grimy clothes that I had previously stripped off. The feel of that wet shirt as it pulled down over my face and chest, the smell of those damp socks as they stretched on my feet, and the touch of those drenched shorts as I stepped back into them would be enough to make anybody cringe!

Of course, we could not imagine why anyone would ever choose to defile his freshly washed body with soiled, smelly clothes. Yet many of us believers often clothe ourselves with sinful behavior that does not fit with our purified identity in Christ. By God's grace our sin has been cleansed through the atoning work of Christ, and we have been called to "dress" ourselves accordingly. But like many directives in Scripture, this is easier read than done! In fact, it is impossible apart from the redemptive power of the gospel. Therefore, Paul grounds his exhortation to the Colossians in the accomplished work of Christ.

The instructive nature of this section of the letter is built on the foundational truths Paul previously established. His train of thought has continued to progress from the believer's position (2:9-15), to the believer's perspective (2:16–3:4), and now to the believer's practice (3:5-17). Each of these passages follows the same dualistic pattern based on our parallel status in Christ—"buried"/ "raised" (2:12), "if you died with Christ" (2:20) / "if you have been raised with Christ" (3:1), and "put to death" (3:5) / "put on" (3:12). The structure of this passage emerges from these foundational pillars of death/life and old/new (Melick, *Philippians, Colossians, Philemon*, 286).

As Paul identifies the behaviors that correspond with their respective spiritual condition, death (vv. 5-11) and life (vv. 12-17), he describes the practical implications for believers. He challenges the Colossians to figuratively clothe themselves with a lifestyle that corresponds to the purifying work of Christ and their redeemed nature. The passage includes three lists of vices (vv. 5,8) and virtues (v. 12) that each occur in clusters of five. These lists provide additional structure to the passage and identify specific conduct that believers are called to "put off" or "put on" (vv. 9-10).

As God's people we are called to live in a way that reflects the character of our Savior. This requires us to progress in our sanctification as the vices of our previous spiritual condition are replaced with the virtues of our new life in Christ. In this passage God teaches us how to live according to our identity in Christ by putting off the sinful habits of our former nature and putting on the righteous conduct of our redeemed nature.

We Must Cleanse Ourselves from Sinfulness
COLOSSIANS 3:5-11

The process of sanctification always includes two components: the negative aspect of sins that are forsaken and the positive aspect of holiness that is pursued (2 Cor 7:1). In this passage Paul exhorts the Colossians in both areas through his use of the clothing metaphor and the process of taking off and putting on. As he explains, in order to clothe ourselves in righteousness, we must first cleanse our lives from sinfulness.

We Must Put to Death Our Sinful Passions (3:5-7)

These verses begin with a transitional "therefore," which clearly makes the Colossians' instruction dependent on the theological truths of the previous verses. This passage, on the premise of the preceding texts, explains the practical implications of their death in Christ (2:12,20; 3:3) that requires them to "put to death what belongs to [their] earthly nature" (3:5). That command emphasizes our active participation in the sanctification process, but it does not make it dependent on our ability or efforts. As Moo observes, "The imperative 'put to death' in this verse must be viewed as a call to respond to, and cooperate with, the transformative power that is already operative within us" (*The Letters*, 255).

The call to crucify "what belongs to [our] earthly nature" also distinguishes our true identity in Christ from the sinful behaviors that characterize our previous condition. While the residue of sin's desire remains, we as believers are able to subdue the members of our physical bodies and resist and strip away the passions of the flesh (cf. Rom 6:12-14). Therefore, Paul identifies five specific vices we should deal with accordingly.

Paul's initial list of sins in this passage deals primarily with those of a sexual nature. The first four sins are explicitly illicit, and the final one addresses the root of their depraved behavior. Certainly these vices were common struggles of the Colossians just as they are universal struggles to which all adult believers can relate. Beyond its widespread relevance, this list is also appropriate because of the intensity of sexual sin and the ability for believers to overcome other temptations if they can learn to deal with these.

The term "sexual immorality" is generic and refers to any kind of sexual sin. Our English word *pornography* derives from this term. "Impurity" speaks to moral corruption in general, but it is commonly used regarding sins of a sexual nature (cf. Rom 1:24; Gal 5:19). Likewise, "lust" describes the shameful passions associated with the sexual sins of those "who don't know God" (1 Thess 4:5; cf. Rom 1:26). The fourth vice, "desire," derives its sexual connotation from its immediate context and the modifying adjective that characterizes it as "evil."

While initially the final sin in the list appears unrelated, "greed" refers to the insatiable desire for more that often characterizes the enticing nature of sexual sin. In this sense it could describe the driving motivation for the previous four sins (Pao, *Colossians and Philemon*, 220). The sexual connotation and related connection between this final vice and the previous ones can also be determined textually. As Beale observes,

> That "covetousness" likely includes "sexual greed" is apparent from the exhortation against sexual immorality in 1 Thess 4:3-7, where the combination of the same Greek words for "immorality," "uncleanness," "passion," and "desire" all occur and are equated with sexual "greed." (*Colossians and Philemon*, 274)

In verse 5, this sin is distinguished from others in the list by the modifying phrase, "which is idolatry" (cf. Eph 5:5). While the clarifying phrase is true of the final sin, it also speaks to the nature of the entire list. By describing the collective whole in this way, Paul reveals the idolatrous root of the listed sinful behaviors, and he challenges believers to consider the more significant underlying issue. Failure to adopt and abide by a scriptural sexual ethic ultimately constitutes a refusal to submit to the lordship of Christ (Pao, *Colossians and Philemon*, 221). Categorizing these sins as idolatrous also introduces the cautionary aspect of Paul's instruction, warning believers to consider God's impending wrath that these sins invite (Col 3:6).

It is not uncommon for vice lists in the New Testament to conclude with a warning of God's judgment (1 Cor 6:10-11; Gal 5:19-21; Eph 5:3-6; Moo, *The Letters*, 258). The vices in this passage clearly violate the holiness of God and rightly deserve God's just anger and punishment. Yet many people in today's culture resist or deny the concept of God's wrath. But the reality of God's judgment is also a validation of God's righteous character and an invitation to repentance.

> A holy God does not stand idly by when men act unrighteously, transgress the law, show disdain to him as their creator or spurn his love and mercy. He acts in a righteous manner[,] punishing sin in the present and especially on the final day. Yet God also acquits the guilty, and only the person who understands something of the greatness of his wrath will be mastered by the greatness of his mercy. (O'Brien, *Colossians, Philemon*, 184–85)

In Christ, we are spared from the coming wrath (1 Thess 1:10) and can live in the freedom of our salvation in him.

Paul continues to draw an important line of distinction between the Colossians' identity in Christ and these incompatible behaviors. He reminds them of their previous condition when they "once walked in these things" when they "were living in them" (Col 3:7). Prior to our salvation in Christ, all of us were born as "sons of disobedience" (ESV) and "children under wrath" (Eph 2:1-3). This left us "alienated and hostile" in mind, which was manifested in our "evil actions" (Col 1:21). But now we are called to strip off these sinful behaviors that correspond to an unregenerate condition. As those who have died with Christ, we can "put to death" our sinful passions (3:5).

We Must Put Off Our Sinful Practices (3:8-10)

Paul begins these verses with a transitional phrase, "but now," that further contrasts the Colossians' previous spiritual status (v. 7) with their current standing in Christ. It reinforces the proper correspondence between their positional and practical righteousness and places an emphasis on their personal responsibility to "put away" (v. 8) that which does not align with their true identity. This command parallels the previous imperative, "put to death" (v. 5), and describes the act of denouncing, doing away with, or putting off the sinful behavior. The parallel understanding of the verbs is also supported by the subsequent fivefold list of sins that follow each command.

While the previous list of vices focused on sexual sins, this list is more directed to social sins. The first two, "anger" and "wrath," are closely related. While a slight distinction between a volatile attitude and vicious action is possible, the frequent combination of the two in Scripture and their inseparable nature in practice require them to be addressed together.[1] The two terms regularly describe God's righteous disposition toward sin; but when brandished by us, they usurp God's divine authority. When joined with "malice," a general term for evil intentions toward another person, these three sins are a toxic combination that poisons relationships and promotes conflict and division.

The final two sins in this list, "slander" and "filthy language," describe the verbal manifestations of malicious attitudes and actions toward others. When directed toward God, the term "slander" is translated as "blasphemy" (Matt 12:31; John 10:33). But it is also a word used to describe derogatory and defamatory speech against other people (Eph 4:31; 1 Tim 6:4). Ultimately, speaking against those who are made in God's image can be understood as blasphemous (Jas 3:9; Pao, *Colossians and Philemon*, 224), and as believers we are instructed to "slander no one" (Titus 3:2). Paul also calls for the Colossians to put away "filthy language," which in this context is best understood as harsh and abusive talk toward others.

The concluding phrase, "from your mouth," clearly relates to the final two verbal sins. But it also is a collective reference that includes all of the sins in this verse that were initially joined by the umbrella phrase "all the following" (Col 3:8). Not only is the final phrase parallel in summarizing function to the concluding phrase regarding idolatry in the first list (v. 5); it also corresponds in its rebellious nature against God. Evil speech derives from a sinful heart (Matt 12:34), reflects the whole of one's spiritual inability to refrain from sin (Jas 3:2), and is characteristic of those who are opposed to God (Rom 3:10-18). In addition, considering its direct contrast to proper worship filled with praise and thanksgiving (Col 3:15-17), these verbal vices are understood to constitute idolatrous sin.

These particular vices are not only sinful on a personal level, but they undermine unity in the body of Christ. This seems to be part of Paul's focus as he immediately follows the list with the collective

---

[1] Moo observes that the rough equivalence of the terms is reflected in their combined translation more than forty times in the Septuagint, typically as "fierce anger" (*The Letters*, 263).

prohibition, "Do not lie to one another" (v. 9). This command not only fits with the list of verbal vices, but it also seems to be a direct reference to the false teachers' attempts to deceive (2:4,8). The content of their doctrine and their abusive tone caused animosity and strife among the Colossians. But the message of the gospel, along with its corresponding tone of mercy and grace, promotes harmony and unity among God's people.

Once again Paul grounds his practical instruction for the Colossians in the proper understanding of their identity in Christ through his previous use of *stripping off* terminology. Since the spiritual circumcision of their conversion was "putting off" the body of flesh through Christ's crucifixion (2:11), and since Jesus stripped off the power of the rulers and authorities (2:15), they have spiritually already "put off the old self with its practices" (3:9; Moo, *The Letters*, 266). Concerning the positive aspect of their identity, they have also "put on the new self" (v. 10). The clothing metaphor is most clearly depicted in these verses as Paul includes the negative, "put off," and the positive, "put on," aspects of sanctification.

While their new identity is certain, the practical transformation is still a work in progress. They are "being renewed in knowledge according to the image of [their] Creator" (v. 10). The passive form of the verb emphasizes God's active role in the sanctifying process. It is through true "knowledge," as opposed to the false claims of the heretical teachers, that their spiritual growth will continue (cf. Rom 12:2). Ultimately, a believer's "new self" is being conformed to the likeness of Christ, "the image of [the] Creator," since Jesus is the "image of the invisible God" (Col 3:10; 1:15) and the agent of creation (1:16). The "new self" is our redeemed nature that practically speaking is being "created according to God's likeness in righteousness and purity of the truth" (Eph 4:24). Therefore, according to Paul's instructions to the Colossians, we must align our practical righteousness with our positional righteousness in Christ. We must put off the sinful practices of our previous nature and put on that which corresponds to our new life in him.

We Must Put Down Our Sinful Pride (3:11)

The final verse in this section highlights the collective significance of Paul's individual instruction for the church. Paul uses several combinations of artificial distinctions that are eliminated through the Colossians' identity in Christ. The categories he uses are culturally specific to their historical context, but the principles have contemporary implications for God's people today.

The communal tone of Paul's declaration in this verse is evident by the opening and concluding terms. The initial phrase translated "in Christ" simply denotes the corporate sphere of the "new self," and the closing phrase speaks to the supremacy of Christ and the equality among his people as "all and in all" (v. 11). Between these verbal parentheses of communal terminology, Paul identifies and eliminates potential obstacles that would hinder them from experiencing the genuine community they spiritually already possess.

The first two descriptive terms, "Greek and Jew," are common throughout the New Testament and typically represent two broad categories of people in order to symbolize the universal availability of the gospel (see Rom 1:16). Paul used these classifications to speak of the general need for salvation and the shared depravity of all people (Rom 3:9) while also identifying them both as beneficiaries of the salvation found in Christ (Rom 10:12). This ethnic distinction was the source of much division, and each group is often depicted in light of their religious and social opposition to each other. As Paul points out, this distinction is removed as all redeemed Greeks (Gentiles) and redeemed Jews are combined into one new humanity in Christ (Eph 2:15).

The next distinction their new identity removes is that of "circumcision and uncircumcision." God established circumcision as the sign of his covenant with Abram and his descendants, the nation of Israel (Gen 17:11). This symbol became a source of division in the early church concerning its necessity for Gentiles who came to faith in Christ. The issue was formally resolved at the Jerusalem Council (Acts 15:16-35) but remained a source of conflict in many congregations. Paul had previously clarified that the spiritual circumcision of the heart was accomplished through Christ's sacrificial death (Col 2:11). Therefore, in Christ this distinction is also nullified as all people become part of God's covenant community and are valued equally (Gal 6:15).

The exact meaning of the next couplet is debated among scholars. The terms "barbarian," those who do not speak Greek, and "Scythian," inhabitants of a region north of the Black Sea, do not seem to have the contrasting connotation that the previous distinctions possess. Since both of these categories of people were known for their cruel behavior and uncivilized actions, some scholars see this as a point of comparison (Melick, *Philippians, Colossians, Philemon*, 298). Others attempt to maintain a contrast by identifying Scythians as those who were slaves and barbarians who were free (Campbell, "Unraveling Colossians 3:11b").[2] Perhaps the simplest explanation is that these terms expand the previous category by referencing particular examples of those who were uncircumcised among the Colossians. Regardless of the relations of the terms, this superficial distinction is also invalidated in Christ.

The final terms, "slave and free," are frequently used in contrast throughout Paul's writings (cf. 1 Cor 12:13; Eph 6:8). This social distinction seems more substantial since he goes on to address the functional aspects of the relationship (Col 3:22–4:1). But its lingering cultural significance only underscores Paul's point further, that Christ redefines what it means to be a slave and free (1 Cor 7:22). His letter to Philemon, a member of the Colossian church, regarding his escaped slave, Onesimus, whom Paul led to Christ in prison, exemplifies the abolition of this distinction (Phlm 1,16). Paul concludes with a summarizing and emphatic declaration, "Christ is all and in all" (Col 3:11), that echoes the sovereign lordship of Jesus pronounced in the earlier Christ hymn (1:15-20) while also reinforcing their unified nature in him (cf. Gal 3:28).

Although the categories may be different, the church today continues to make superficial distinctions, which Christ eliminates in order to unite us as one body. Our culture and our churches draw invisible lines and build invisible walls based on ethnic, social, gender, and economic factors. But we must recognize that preferential treatment of any particular group should be considered prejudicial treatment against every other group (cf. Jas 2:1-13).

The root of these types of sinful behavior is pride. An elevated view of ourselves promotes a condescending view of others and devalues them. Most importantly, it devalues the work of Christ, whose death destroys every barrier and reconciles us to the Father and unifies us as his children (Col 1:18-20). The beauty of the body of Christ is found in its cohesive unity with its blended diversity. Divisive pride not only causes division among God's people; it ultimately hinders our individual and collective spiritual growth and impedes our universal mission (1:6). Therefore, as we strip off our sinful passions and practices, we must also

---

[2] Despite the efforts of modern scholarship, disagreement among evangelical scholars remains. For example, Pao is persuaded by Campbell's work (*Colossians and Philemon*, 228–29), while Moo remains unconvinced (*The Letters*, 270–71).

strip ourselves of the sinful pride that divides the body of Christ so that we can experience his fullness.

We Must Clothe Ourselves in Godliness
COLOSSIANS 3:12-17

We all know what it is like to be dressed for the occasion. There are times when we would prefer to dress in our house clothes rather than our work clothes, but our responsibilities require a certain uniform of sorts. At other times we would like summer seasonal attire, but colder weather may force us to bundle up. And sometimes certain occasions or situations may dictate more formal attire when we wish we could just relax or go for a run. Jogging in dress shoes and a suit just does not work!

However, putting on the practical righteousness of Christ is fitting for all occasions! There's no situation or season in life when clothing ourselves in him is inappropriate or inadequate. While in the previous verses Paul described what should be taken off, in these verses he prescribes what should be taken up.

We Must Put On Spiritual Clothes in Which We Can Accurately Reflect Our Savior (3:12-14)

In contrast to what corresponds with unredeemed nature and its lifestyle, Paul now uses the clothing metaphor that corresponds with our identity in Christ and challenges us to consider the practical implications. Based on our positional status, "as God's chosen ones, holy and dearly loved," we are to live accordingly (v. 12). The first description of our identity, "as God's chosen ones," reinforces the removal of the Greek/Jew distinction in the previous verse. All believers are members of his covenant family, and we are considered "saints" (1:2,12) who have been "circumcised" in Christ (2:11) and have become heirs of his eternal "inheritance" (1:12; Pao, *Colossians and Philemon*, 224). In Christ, we are also "holy and dearly loved," those who have been set apart by God's undeserved loving-kindness to be his ambassadors (cf. 1 Pet 2:9-10).

In parallel fashion to his previous two lists, Paul now identifies five virtues that should characterize our lives as Christ's followers. "Compassion" describes a heartfelt mercy toward others that reflects Jesus's concern for people who were hurting (see Matt 9:36). "Kindness" is a disposition that is thoughtful and considerate and is demonstrated through acts of benevolence, often to people who do not deserve it. As those who have been rescued by God's undeserved kindness toward us in Christ (Titus 3:4), we should adorn ourselves with this same caring posture.

We are also called to clothe ourselves with "humility," an honest assessment of ourselves (Rom 12:3), and a selfless perspective that values others as more important (Phil 2:3-4). "Gentleness," sometimes translated as "meekness," describes a peaceful and unassuming attitude that Paul used to characterize Christ (2 Cor 10:1) and that Jesus used to describe himself (Matt 11:29 NIV). The final attribute, "patience," speaks to a measured response to others, especially in the face of opposition, that exhibits a confident trust in the Lord who patiently extends grace to all people (2 Pet 3:9). Collectively, this list of virtues identifies characteristics that reflect our Savior and essentially equate to our putting on Christ (cf. Rom 13:14).

Paul's instruction to "put on" these attributes is immediately explained by corresponding actions. The two parallel participles in Colossians 3:13, "bearing with one another and forgiving one another," modify the command and provide practical examples of how we are to demonstrate the preceding virtues. In "bearing with one another" we lovingly and patiently cooperate with others for the sake of unity (cf. Eph 4:2-3). "Forgiving one another" involves a willingness to extend the mercy we have received in Christ to those who hurt or offend us (Eph 4:32). While the "grievance against another" may be valid, our forgiveness does not excuse their sin (Col 3:13). Instead, it allows us to cover the offenses with grace (1 Pet 4:8), preserves unity, and prevents bitterness from taking root in our hearts (Heb 12:15).

The capstone virtue, "above all," is that we are to "put on love" (Col 3:14). Loving others is always elevated as the supreme quality we are called to demonstrate (1 Cor 13:13). Love is evidence of our salvation, it is a testimony of the gospel, it expresses our love for God in response to his love for us, it epitomizes the character of God, and it ultimately fulfills the law (1 John 4:7-21; cf. Rom 13:10). God's love for us and our love for one another is the "perfect bond of unity" (Col 3:14) that weds us together and blends the virtues in complete harmony.

This list of virtues describes an outfit of loving sacrifice and service. Following Jesus requires us to "put on" the disposition and duties of a servant. Just as Jesus wrapped himself with the towel of humility to wash the disciples' feet (John 13:1-5) and clothed himself in humanity in willing submission to the Father (Phil 2:5-9), we are called to dress ourselves in humble acts of service to God on behalf of others. But too often we are more concerned with feeding our desires than ministering to those in need. Instead, we must take off our spiritual bibs and put on our spiritual aprons that reflect the compassionate heart of our Savior by loving others and willingly sacrificing on their behalf.

We Must Put On Spiritual Clothes in Which We Can Comfortably Rest in Our Savior (3:15)

In addition to being suitable for service, clothing ourselves in Christ also allows us to be ready to relax. Paul goes on to encourage us, "Let the peace of Christ . . . rule your hearts" (v. 15). In our culture it is easy for our hearts to become filled with tension, anxiety, and fear. Frustrations can fester and worries can weigh on us, causing our lives to be characterized as anything but peaceful.

But in Christ we can have peace with our Creator (1:20), peace with our consciences (Phil 4:7), and peace with our circumstances (John 14:27). His peace can "rule" or control our hearts as we trust the Lord and place our confidence in him. This peace is an inherent aspect of our salvation, "to which [we] were also called." It is cultivated individually through prayer and corporately through the comfort and assurance of God's people as part of "one body" (Col 3:15; cf. 1:18). When our hearts find peace in Christ, we will have a proper perspective that allows us to "be thankful" (v. 15). A heart filled with gratitude can be thankful for all things (Eph 5:20) and in all circumstances (1 Thess 5:18).

As we submit ourselves to him through prayer, we can allow his supernatural peace to guard our hearts and minds in Christ Jesus (Phil 4:6-7). By immersing our hearts in gratitude, we can fix our eyes on him and abide in his peace (Isa 26:3). In doing so, we put on clothes that allow us to comfortably rest in our Savior.

We Must Put On Spiritual Clothes in Which We Can Gratefully Rejoice in Our Savior (3:16)

Just as clothing ourselves in Christ makes us suitable for service and ready to relax, dressing according to our identity in him also helps us be prepared for praise. A proper understanding of our positional status in him not only saturates our hearts with love and peace but also primes our hearts to overflow in celebration of our Savior!

In order to worship in Spirit and truth (John 4:24), God's people must worship according to the "word of Christ" (Col 3:16). This phrase is best understood as a summary of the redemptive work of Jesus and parallels the previously used expression, "the word of truth, the gospel" (1:5). In other words, the same message of salvation that adopts us into God's family and unites us as his people must be the central truth that saturates our corporate worship and everything we do. As we allow the gospel to "dwell richly" among us, we uphold Christ as the source of "all wisdom" (cf. 2:3) and his truth serves as the substance for our "teaching and admonishing" one another (3:16). These same terms summarized Paul's personal ministry and spiritual ambition (1:28), and they must become our collective goal as well.

While many contemporary churches approach the musical portion of our corporate worship as a formality, according to Paul it is actually meant to be formative. He uses a variety of expressions, "psalms, hymns, and spiritual songs," as the means by which we teach and admonish one another (v. 16; cf. Eph 5:19). The variety of musical terms validates multiple styles of "singing to God," while the content of all forms must be carefully evaluated by its faithfulness to "the word of Christ." When Jesus and his redemptive work are exalted, the transforming grace of the gospel will promote "gratitude" in our "hearts" where true worship occurs (Col 3:16).

Just as reverent occasions require appropriate attire, our identity in Christ deserves and demands a life that is adorned with praise and thanksgiving. Therefore, we must put on spiritual clothes that gratefully rejoice in our Savior. Our worship must be infused with the truth of the gospel as we promote deeper intimacy with Christ, stronger unity as his people, and higher praise for our King!

We Must Put On Spiritual Clothes in Which We Can Actively Run for Our Savior (3:17)

The Christian's figurative wardrobe is not only appropriate attire that is suitable for service, ready to relax, and prepared for praise; it is also active gear that helps us run the race. Scripture often refers to our lives as a competitive marathon that requires strenuous effort and tremendous endurance (1 Cor 9:24-27; 2 Tim 4:7; Heb 12:1-2). This verse echoes similar coaching sentiments in the form of a challenging exhortation.

Its opening phrase, "whatever you do," speaks to the comprehensive nature of its instruction. This is reinforced by the all-inclusive behavioral phrase, "in word or in deed," that spans our entire lifestyle, from our words to their works. And this wholehearted devotion is further emphasized by the cumulative phrase, "Do everything in the name of the Lord Jesus." Paul wants believers to understand the magnitude of the cosmic reign of Christ and the gravity of its practical implications. This verse translates his universal sovereignty into personal supremacy as we submit ourselves to his lordship in complete obedience.

The conclusion of the verse continues to carry the theme of thanksgiving that flows through this entire section (Col 3:15,16,17). Paul reminds us that wholehearted devotion stems from our identity in Christ by directing our gratitude to our heavenly Father through Jesus (v. 17). This final phrase, "giving thanks to God the Father through him," reflects his previous prayer that explicitly based our continual thanksgiving on our redeemed status in Christ (1:12-14). By connecting it to such a comprehensive lifestyle, he clearly intends a spirit of gratitude to permeate every aspect of our lives.

The closing verse in this section serves a dual purpose as it summarizes the virtuous lifestyle described in the preceding verses (3:12-16) and previews the specific practical instructions for the Christian home that follow (3:18–4:1). It also reviews and renews the primary appeal of the letter: walk in humble submission to the lordship of Christ while growing and giving thanks (2:6). As we clothe ourselves in Christ, we are dressed and ready for action. We can run with maximum effort and with gratitude for the privilege to be on his team!

Conclusion

From the earliest pages of Scripture, we see the futility of mankind's best attempts to cover our sinfulness. As a result of original sin, Adam and Eve's view of themselves and each other became tainted and distorted. They now recognized their literal and figurative nakedness, and they were ashamed and afraid before God (Gen 3:10). In an attempt to cover up their sin and conceal their shame, they "sewed fig leaves together and made coverings for themselves" (Gen 3:7).

Of course, their efforts to clothe themselves were completely inadequate. It was only by God's grace and his provision of a blood sacrifice that their sin and shame were able to be covered as "he clothed them" (Gen 3:21). In the same way, our sinful adamic nature, the "old self," is clothed in our unrighteous works, and any attempt we make to strip them away apart from God's grace is futile. But in Christ the sacrifice was made to cover and cleanse our sin. And through him we are made righteous (2 Cor 5:21) and clothed in Christ and his righteousness (Gal 3:27). Through Jesus, the new and better Adam, we are re-created and being conformed into his image.

Therefore, as we live with an eternal perspective (Col 3:1-4), we must dress accordingly. We must strip off the sinful works associated with the flesh and put on a lifestyle of holiness that corresponds to our righteousness in him. And one day even our corruptible bodies will be clothed with incorruptible immortality (see 1 Cor 15:54; 2 Cor 5:4). We will don the white robes of righteousness that have been washed in the blood of the Lamb, and we will worship our glorious King for all of eternity (Rev 7:9)!

Reflect and Discuss

1. Why is our new identity in Christ foundational for obeying Paul's commands in this passage?
2. What sexual sins described in this passage do you need to put off?
3. What social sins described in this passage do you need to put off?
4. How does our union with Christ bring unity with others in the church?
5. What should we put off as hindrances to that unity?
6. How might this passage address racial tensions in our day?
7. How does Jesus embody the characteristics we are called to put on? How does knowing this help us to "put on" these characteristics?
8. How do we let the peace of Christ rule in our hearts?
9. What are some ways this passage encourages us to help one another grow in the Christian life?
10. How does this passage prepare us to run for our Savior?

God's Blueprint for Building a Home

COLOSSIANS 3:18–4:1

Main Idea: When Christ is the Lord of a family, they can build their home according to God's design and desire.

I. **We Must Dedicate Our Homes to the Lord (3:18–4:1).**
   A. We must submit to his leadership.
   B. We must serve with his love.
II. **We Can Dwell with Harmony in the Lord (3:18–4:1).**
   A. Wives should respectfully lift up their husbands (3:18).
   B. Husbands should sacrificially love their wives (3:19).
   C. Children should humbly listen to their parents (3:20).
   D. Parents should faithfully lead their children (3:21).
   E. Believers should diligently labor for their Master (3:22–4:1).
III. **We Should Display Our Hearts for the Lord (3:18–4:1).**
   A. We must carefully consider different situations.
   B. We must prayerfully consider difficult seasons.

Perhaps one of Jesus's most recognizable parables is the one he used to conclude the greatest sermon ever preached. In the Sermon on the Mount, Jesus provided a holistic description of the life he desired for his followers (Matt 5–7). He summarized his message and the importance of obeying his instructions by contrasting the wise and foolish builders (Matt 7:24-27). Yet one of the most important and often overlooked aspects of the parable is what the two builders were constructing—their houses.

While clearly Jesus was teaching the necessity of a strong foundation for life and the stability of his word as the only reliable basis, he did not simply reference an old generic building, an important government office, or even a structure for corporate worship. He chose the house for the parable because it is the most important dwelling one can envision. It is a home to the family, protects that which is most cherished, serves as a place of personal rest and private refuge, and is the base of operations for everything else. Each "house" is equated to its respective builder and serves as the physical domain that essentially represents all of life.

Just as it was for the builders in Jesus's parable, the most significant aspect of life remains the home—not just the dwelling but everything it represents. And to Jesus's point, an attempt to build a house on anything other than his Word is foolish and futile, because everyone, including believers, will experience the proverbial storms of life that come from every direction—rain, wind, and floods. Our ability to persevere will be determined by the foundation we build on and the instructions we follow. Paul understood this and made sure to address this fundamental aspect of our lives in the practical portion of his letter.

As he continues to provide the implications of the believers' identity, Paul directs his attention to the crucial aspect of their homes. His concentrated focus on this area stems from a variety of factors, including: (1) the redemptive significance of the family in God's plan, (2) the reflective significance of the family for the covenant relationship between God and his people, and (3) the relational significance for the personal and social implications of the family.

Several literary features distinguish this passage from its surrounding context. Textually, the absence of a transitional phrase into the household instructions sets them apart from the broader corporate imperatives in the preceding paragraph. The lack of a conjunction or connecting participle also creates an authoritative tone based on the imperatival force of the instructions and the pointed brevity of the household commands.

In addition, this passage is set apart as a distinct literary unit based on the features shared by the surrounding passages. The verses that immediately precede it are corporate instructions for mutual submission to the lordship of Christ. The final three exhortations are coupled with thanksgiving (3:15-17). Likewise, the verses that immediately follow this passage are additional corporate instructions that are also commended with thanksgiving (4:2-5). These collective appeals bookend the household passage and set it apart as more of a self-contained unit.

But these literary distinctions do not isolate the passage from its surrounding context; they accentuate the significance of its contents. The domestic guidelines of these verses flow directly from the comprehensive instruction to "do everything in the name of the Lord Jesus" (3:17). The household instructions also fit within the broader conversation of Colossians by demonstrating the practical implications of the redemptive work of Christ for believers. Paul's dialogue that has established the redeemed identity for believers now finds its practical outworking in the most important personal, relational, and social context—the home.

In terms of the historical context, Paul addresses the members of the household according to the domestic code of his day. However, in contrast to its cultural standards, Paul demonstrates how the redemptive work of Christ redefines our familial and social relationships. This is vitally important for us to consider as we preach this passage in our contemporary and cultural context. As we address domestic roles, gender differences, and his instructions to slaves and masters, we must be abundantly clear on the truth of the biblical equality of all people, both in essence and in value. In Christ, all social and superficial factors that are used to discriminate against others have been eradicated (3:11; cf. Gal 3:28). Therefore, as we address the various roles and responsibilities in the home, we should affirm the timeless biblical distinctions while also affirming the worth of every individual member.

The structural symmetry of the passage is also important to observe. There are three pairs of relationships that are each described in relation to the male leader in the home—wives/husbands, children/fathers, slaves/masters. The collective sequence of these three relationships progresses in a prioritized manner while their individual pattern consistently describes the supportive roles and responsibilities in relation to the leadership of the husband/father/master. Most importantly, the Christian household is clearly intended to operate in submission to the ultimate leadership of "the Lord Christ" (3:24) who is the sovereign "Master in heaven" (4:1).

This passage not only reoriented the domestic structure of their culture with the supreme leadership of Christ; it also demonstrates Paul's point of the entire letter: Jesus is the exalted Lord over everything! When Christ is the Lord of my family, my wife and I can build our home according to God's design and desire. In this passage God provides the blueprint and gives us the necessary steps to build a home according to his plan.

We Must Dedicate Our Homes to the Lord
COLOSSIANS 3:18–4:1

God established the family as part of the created order (Gen 2:18-25). His design for the husband and wife reflects the covenant relationship between God and his people through its relational unity and intimacy. It also provides the context for procreation and the continued expansion of his people through the godly heritage of faith that is intended to be cultivated in the context of the home. But when sin entered the world, the family unit was devastated. The relationship between husband and wife became strained (Gen 3:16), the covenant concept that marriage was intended to display grew distorted, and the spiritual habitat of the home was contaminated.

But through the redemptive power of Christ, God has provided a way for our homes to be redeemed and their original design to be restored. Paul has already referenced the familial nature of the covenant community of faith that is established through our salvation in Christ (1:1-8). He now explains how our immediate families can be redeemed through him.

We Must Submit to His Leadership

Scripture is clear: any attempt to build our homes apart from the Lord's leadership is futile. "Unless the LORD builds a house, its builders labor over it in vain" (Ps 127:1). For the Lord to build our homes, our families must be established under his authority, according to his instructions, and with his ongoing involvement. In many ways this supremacy and comprehensive leadership reflect his sovereign lordship over all of creation (1:15-20). But now, on a more personal and practical level, it means that every aspect of our homes must be offered in submission to his authority. And as "builders" who diligently "labor," we must participate in his work according to his design and desire.

Christ's authority over every aspect of our households is reflected in his personal leadership for the individual roles and responsibilities Paul describes. The term "Lord" occurs six times through this passage (3:18,20,22,23,24; 4:1 ["Master"]), and each of the relationships includes at least one reference to him. This clearly identifies Christ as the ultimate leader of our families. But while most believers would acknowledge his authority, we often struggle with the practical implications of this for each of our roles.

First, submitting to his leadership in the home means that *our roles are specifically assigned by him*. While Paul addresses the domestic structure of his culture, the roles of husbands, wives, and children were all established as part of God's original design for the family and should be honored as such. Although these roles are distinct from one another, the individual members that occupy the roles have equal value before God, and their particular functions are vital within God's design.

While the specific aspects of these roles and their related responsibilities will be considered individually, the specific instructions for each member of the home must all begin with an initial submission to the leadership of Christ. In other words, in order to be the Lord of our homes, he must first be the Lord of our hearts. The irreplaceable foundation of a home that is built according to God's design must be a personal relationship with him. Otherwise, his instructions are reduced to practical advice that will collapse under the weight of personal responsibility that cannot be fulfilled apart from him. Just as Christ is the cornerstone of God's house and spiritual family (1 Pet 2:5-7), he must be the cornerstone of our homes as well.

In addition, submitting to his leadership in the home means that *our roles are ultimately accountable to him.* Many times we are guilty of determining our personal obedience and the fulfillment of our particular roles based on the faithfulness of the other members of our households. But our responsibility is not contingent on their obedience. In other words, a wife's unwilling spirit does not negate a husband's responsibility to love her and not be harsh. Likewise, a wife's devotion to her husband cannot be determined based on his level of commitment to love her well. Similarly, children's submission to their parents is not optional.

God does not expect family members to subject themselves to abuse; and he certainly would not require them to do anything unbiblical, immoral, or illegal in an attempt to fulfill familial responsibilities. But apart from these exceptions, our faithfulness must not depend on the other members of our households. We are ultimately accountable to the Lord and should fulfill our roles and responsibilities accordingly.

We Must Serve with His Love

In addition to submitting to Christ's leadership, we must also serve with his love. The underlying disposition of his disciples should always be love (John 13:35), while the overarching mindset for his followers should always be service (Matt 20:26-28). Our homes should epitomize both of these convictions as each member of the household adopts a servant's heart of loving devotion to others.

This means that the fulfillment of our duties does not ultimately fulfill our responsibility before the Lord. Apart from love, even our best efforts or perfect checked-box compliance are empty and worthless (1 Cor 13:1-3). As husbands, wives, children, and servants of the Lord, we must operate with love for one another as expressions of our love for Christ. The redeeming love that transforms our hearts must be evident through our kind interaction with one another and in the domestic duties we willingly perform.

When our homes are saturated with loving service, it accomplishes far more than any specific task we complete. The selfless love we share allows our familial relationships to express the intimate devotion they were designed to experience within our covenant relationship with Christ (Eph 5:31-32). Additionally, our loving service provides the evangelistic testimony of God's redemptive love to lost family members as we fulfill our domestic responsibilities and honor Christ (cf. 1 Pet 3:1-2). Ultimately, when our families exhibit this loving service, they also provide a witness to the lost world of the redemptive love of God that is available in Christ. The invitation to be adopted into God's family is extended as we model the truth of the gospel through loving service.

In order to dedicate our homes to the Lord, we must submit to his leadership and serve with his love. God's blueprint for building a home begins with these fundamental steps as the necessary foundation for a godly family.

We Can Dwell with Harmony in the Lord
COLOSSIANS 3:18–4:1

The practical instructions of this passage are directed to the various members of the household. While these guidelines certainly are functional, they are not simply meant to be pragmatic. In other words, the roles and responsibilities he identifies are more than just a how-to success manual. God's design and desire for the home ultimately teach us how to experience some of the most intimate relationships we were meant to share and provide some of the greatest avenues of harmony and happiness we are made to enjoy.

Wives Should Respectfully Lift Up Their Husbands (3:18)

The first two members of the household that Paul addresses relate to the fundamental roles that establish a home. When God instituted marriage in the garden, he asserted that it was "not good for the man to be alone," and therefore, he created "a helper corresponding to him" (Gen 2:18). He provided Adam with Eve and presented her as his wife (Gen 2:22-24). This original design serves as the foundation for a biblical understanding of marriage (Matt 19:5-6) and as the basis for Paul's guidelines in this passage (cf. Eph 5:31).

The household instructions in these verses begin with "wives" who are called to "submit [to their] husbands" (Col 3:18). The term *submit* has been historically misunderstood in a variety of ways. Some interpreters accuse Paul of being a misogynist. They believe the term sanctions abuse, or they use it to validate their dismissal of Scripture as being culturally confined or outdated. Others have adopted and employed the term as a license for domineering leadership in the home that requires obedient servitude by the wife. Both of these extreme views completely misinterpret the meaning of the term and miss the heart of the passage.

"Submit" is used consistently in the New Testament in reference to a wife's responsibility to her husband (cf. Eph 5:22; 1 Pet 3:1). It directly relates to the nature of marriage and the corresponding roles of the husband and wife. Husbands are intended to be the faithful caretakers of their wives, and wives are the loving complements to their husbands. The instruction given to wives is not the same word, "obey," that Paul uses for children and slaves in the authoritarian relationships of this passage. It is also not a term that subordinates the worth of the wife, who is an equal image bearer and coheir with Christ (cf. Gal 3:28; 1 Pet 3:7).

The term describes a voluntary offering of oneself to another in willing support. It reflects the heart of Christ himself who, though he was equal, willingly subjected himself to the Father (Phil 2:5-8). Practically speaking, it means that wives should offer themselves to their husbands with heartfelt respect and admiration in ways that honor them, lift them up, and meet their needs (see 1 Pet 3:4-6). This cooperative spirit is not dependent on the husband's faithfulness to fulfill his role, although it certainly does not obligate a wife to follow immoral or illegal directions or subject herself to abuse. A wife's dignity and devotion to her husband are ultimately expressions of her love for Christ and should be offered as that which "is fitting in the Lord." Dedicating herself to fulfilling her responsibilities will not only bring her contentment and satisfaction; it will affirm and encourage her husband and cultivate a healthy and happy home for her family.

Husbands Should Sacrificially Love Their Wives (3:19)

The role of husband in this passage perfectly complements the wife and includes a twofold command. The positive aspect of Paul's instructions to husbands is to "love [their] wives." The parallel passage in Ephesians elaborates on this imperative by clarifying the essence and extent of this love, "as Christ loved the church and gave himself for her" (Eph 5:25). This characterizes a husband's love for his wife as sacrificial and selfless. He must be willing to set aside his own needs, wants, and desires for the sake of his wife. Like Adam's Eve in the garden, the wife is a gift from God that he entrusts to the care of her husband, who must cherish, protect, and provide for her.

Husbands are responsible for the emotional, physical, and spiritual needs of their wives. They must be devoted to care for them and promote their sanctification by embodying Christ's example in nurturing his church (Eph 5:26-29). In order for this to happen, a husband's love for his wife should derive from his passion for Christ and his unwavering devotion to him. As a result, it is not contingent on the wife's character or conduct. In fact, a love that most reflects Christ's is that which is undeserved yet freely given. Therefore, a husband's love for his bride should reflect the sacrificial and unconditional love of his Savior in such a way that it stimulates a deeper affection for Jesus in her heart.

When a husband faithfully loves his wife, he also will not "be bitter toward" her. This prohibitive aspect of Paul's instructions to husbands not only references their demeanor toward their wives but also describes the potential response it may invoke. To treat a wife harshly will only embitter her toward her husband, toward their marriage, and potentially toward the Lord. This practical description of the appropriate treatment also forbids demeaning leadership that takes advantage of a wife's willing submission. Instead, a husband's submission to Christ's lordship identifies Jesus as the ultimate leader in the home. Therefore, in reverence to Christ, a husband must sacrificially love his wife by honoring her, caring for her with compassion and understanding, and esteeming her worth before the Lord (cf. 1 Pet 3:7).

Children Should Humbly Listen to Their Parents (3:20)

The second relationship within the home that Paul addresses is between "children" and their parents. The instruction in this verse is directed to those who are young and continue to live under the supervision and provision of their earthly parents (Moo, *The Letters*, 304).[1] He specifically instructs sons and daughters to "obey" their parents (v. 20). The term used here is stronger than the term of submission he used previously in reference to wives (Melick, *Philippians, Colossians, Philemon*, 314). Children have an unqualified responsibility to comply with the instruction and guidance of their parents. The comprehensive nature of this responsibility is clarified by the phrase "in everything." While this would not require children to obey unbiblical, immoral, or illegal commands, it does expect a willing submission and obedience that respects the leadership of their parents.

In the parallel passage in Ephesians, Paul echoes this same instruction for children to "obey" their parents and grounds his instruction in the fifth commandment, to "honor . . . father and mother" (Eph 6:1-4; see Exod 20:12). This underlying premise of respect and admiration reveals the intended motivation and disposition of the heart that should characterize the children's compliance to their parents. A heart of honor does not determine obedience based on the parents' merit or performance, and it also does not feign obedience out of obligation. Instead, it shows humble deference to parents in acknowledgment of God's authority. When earthly parents embody godly love and leadership, it should remind sons and daughters that they have a heavenly Father who epitomizes the perfect form of parental guidance and care. When parents fall short in their efforts to love and lead their families perfectly, children can be encouraged that their heavenly Father will never exhibit those same imperfections.

As a result, they can continue to obey their parents in everything, "for this pleases the Lord." This phrase not only means that it brings pleasure *to* him but also that it is pleasing *in* him. Obedience to Christ provides the greatest satisfaction by fulfilling our created purpose of honoring and glorifying him as Lord. Paul has repeatedly exalted Jesus as the preeminent authority over all things (1:15-20) and believers' subsequent responsibility to do all things in his name (3:17). Therefore, the basis for children's responsibility to obey their parents and the

---

[1] The parallel instruction in Ephesians specifically discusses the father's responsibility to "bring them up in the training and instruction of the Lord" (Eph 6:4) and seems to have younger children in mind. Both passages clearly reference those who are assumed to be living within the household.

subsequent joy it provides derive from the lordship of Christ and their ultimate submission to him.

Parents Should Faithfully Lead Their Children (3:21)

As with the other members of the household, Paul addresses the relationship of the children to their father in particular. By defining the relationship of the children to the father, Paul is ultimately emphasizing their submission to their loving heavenly Father. At the same time, this does not negate or minimize the significance of the mother. In fact, his use of the paternal term is inclusive and is intended to address fathers and mothers.

The responsibility of children to obey their parents is intended to offer a teachable spirit that allows parents to fulfill their responsibility. The home was designed by God to cultivate hearts that love Jesus and live for him in order to produce a godly heritage of Christ followers. Paul's succinct instructions to the Colossians focuses on the negative prohibition for the parents, while the parallel passage in Ephesians emphasizes the positive instructions for parents. Collectively, they provide specific guidelines for raising children in a Christian home.

First, in a home that honors Christ, *parents should disciple their children.* Scripture places the responsibility of training children in the truth of God's Word primarily on the shoulders of the parents. They must "bring them up in the training and instruction of the Lord" (Eph 6:4). Paul's directions to the family in the midst of a corporate letter certainly affirm the collective investment it requires from the church. This is particularly true when children have unbelieving parents or do not have the traditional homelife that promotes spiritual growth. But apart from these increasingly common exceptions, parents are intended to be God's primary representatives for their children. They are accountable to model his love, provide for their needs, and teach them what it means to live according to his Word (cf. Deut 6:4-9).

Second, in a home that honors Christ, *parents should discipline their children.* While our culture villainizes parents who admonish their children, Scripture teaches that discipline is one of the most important aspects of parental love (cf. Prov 13:24). Correction is necessary as children learn right from wrong, and it teaches them the reality of consequences for their sinful choices. This certainly is not a license for emotional or physical abuse by parents. We should model the loving discipline of our heavenly Father, remembering that the goal of discipline is primarily formative, not punitive. "The Lord disciplines the one he loves" in order to train him and to produce his righteousness in him (Heb 12:5-11; cf. Prov 3:11-12). Therefore, as parents, we must adopt a mindset that disciplines our children with a goal that is more constructive than corrective. Our discipline should teach them how to respond to the Lord's loving guidance in a way that fosters love, trust, and a desire to follow him.

Finally, in a home that honors Christ, *parents should not discourage their children.* Paul's instructions in this passage caution against a parenting approach that would "exasperate" children (Col 3:21). This term describes an overbearing parental manner that irritates and frustrates. Practically speaking, this involves enforcing a legalistic standard that demands perfection, creates unreasonable expectations, and constantly berates. We must avoid this form of parenting "so that they won't become discouraged" (v. 21). The damaging effects of this type of harsh oversight are cumulative and cause children to question their worth and to become embittered. Tragically, this form of parenting also causes serious misconceptions that children consequently project onto the Lord, believing that he is cruel and that his love must be earned. Instead, we parents must be patient and compassionate toward our children, not shackling them with guilt and shame but encouraging them with kindness, mercy, and understanding. This will promote a healthy relationship between parents and their children that is characterized by mutual love and appreciation.

Believers Should Diligently Labor for Their Master (3:22–4:1)

The final domestic relationship addressed in this passage is between "slaves" and "masters." It is important to note that Paul was certainly not advocating slavery. Some have misunderstood his failure to condemn the institution or his refusal to endorse rebellion against it as an implicit endorsement. But Scripture is clear that discrimination of any kind (social, political, or racial) and inhumane treatment of others is ungodly and unacceptable. Similar to the way Peter addresses unjust suffering and political injustices in his first letter (see 1 Pet 2:13-25), Paul provides practical instruction for a Christian response for those who find themselves in these lamentable situations.

Through the example of Christ, the apostles understood that the greatest means for social and cultural change was a spiritual transformation through the power of the gospel. These verses reveal several important aspects of the gospel and our responsibility to embody it. For example, the gospel meets us in the circumstances where we are, and it teaches how to respond accordingly. Additionally, the gospel redefines social relationships within the context of the spiritual relationship believers share with Christ and one another. This was particularly evident through the situation with the Colossian church leader and his regenerate and repentant servant. Paul appealed to Philemon to regard Onesimus as a brother rather than a bond servant (Phlm 16). Finally, the gospel also reorients the relationship of all believers with God as we are adopted as his children and simultaneously appointed as his servants.

Our view of God as our Master (Col 4:1) recognizes that his purchase of our freedom also established his ownership (1 Cor 6:19-20) and our corresponding obligation to him as slaves to righteousness (Rom 6:17-18). Therefore, Paul's instructions for slaves and masters changed the perspective of their respective positions, focusing on their roles and responsibilities as service to the Lord. His instructions to servants focused on their willing compliance: "Obey your human masters in everything" (Col 3:22), with the assurance that their service would be rewarded by their ultimate Master, "the Lord Christ" (v. 24). Conversely, the "wrongdoer" would be punished accordingly, with "no favoritism" (v. 25).

Beyond their obedience, Paul was also concerned with the condition of their hearts and the faithful discharge of their duties. As Christians, they were directed to work with integrity, not "only while being watched." They were to serve with sincerity, not simply as "people-pleasers," and to labor diligently, "wholeheartedly, fearing the Lord" (v. 22). Likewise, redeemed "masters" were directed to deal "justly and fairly" with their servants in reverence to and in resemblance of their "Master in heaven" (4:1). These guidelines are certainly applicable for contemporary believers since they characterize a Christian work ethic that should be displayed in our vocations.

Paul's instructions for masters and servants in these verses mirror his emphasis for all of the members of the household: "Whatever you do, do it from the heart, as something done for the Lord and not for people" (v. 23). This verse summarizes and reiterates his general directive for all believers in verse 17. It reminds us that *what* we do matters, "whatever you do," *how* we do it matters, "do it from the heart," and *why* we do it matters, "as something done for the Lord." This means that regardless of our circumstances, everything we do—in our homes, in our places of work, and in our churches—should be done for the honor of the Lord as we diligently labor for our Master.

We Should Display Our Hearts for the Lord
COLOSSIANS 3:18–4:1

As we carefully consider God's desire for our marriages and our homes, we must also be careful to preserve his design for them. In this day and age that is becoming increasingly difficult as our culture attempts to reject a biblical view of marriage and redefine it according to contemporary sexual ethics or lifestyle preferences. But Scripture is clear: God designed marriage to be between one man and one woman for one lifetime. The first marriage in the garden established this as an unalterable template (Gen 2:24) that Jesus affirmed (Matt 19:4-6) and that Paul also prescribed (Eph 5:31).

God's design for marriage not only includes this distinct pattern, but it also serves a definitive purpose. Scripture teaches that marriage is ultimately a depiction of the eternal relationship between Christ, the bridegroom, and the church, his bride (Eph 5:32), that one day will be celebrated as part of the consummation of the ages (Rev 19:7; 21:9). As such, it is characterized by his covenant love for his people that is both sacrificial and selfless. Therefore, marriage cannot be altered from its original design; otherwise it distorts the eternal reality it is meant to reflect and undermines the redemptive purpose it is intended to serve.

Marriage is a sacred relationship that is more than a ceremonial tradition, a convenient arrangement, a compatible friendship, or a contractual agreement. Marriage is a covenantal union that can be defined this way: *a sacred and exclusive union performed by God that spiritually joins the husband and the wife with the bonds of sacrificial love and unconditional devotion, reflects the relationship of Christ and his church, and is ceremoniously celebrated and physically consummated before the Lord.*[2]

While we must be faithful to preserve this biblical understanding and advocate nothing less than God's timeless standards, we must do so with compassionate hearts that carefully consider the people of our

---

[2] For a more developed explanation of this definition, see Akin and Pace, *Pastoral Theology*, 264–94.

communities and the members of our churches. We should display our hearts for the Lord by demonstrating sincere love for others through kindness and understanding.

We Must Carefully Consider Different Situations

Anytime the perfect standard of the Scriptures confronts the imperfect lives of people, there is a tension that makes faith necessary and obedience difficult. Therefore, we must teach the truth of God's Word with mercy and grace for those who have been affected by the tragedy of personal heartbreak, family dysfunction, and/or marital misfortune.

Throughout the letter to the Colossians, Paul has focused on God's redemptive love through Christ that is appropriated individually through faith. Christ's sacrifice on the cross provides forgiveness for sins (1:14) and reconciles us to God (1:21-22) by meeting us where we are and redeeming our lives for his purpose and his glory. While Paul is advocating God's ideal standard, he is also mindful that the Colossians were rescued from lives that were previously sticky, messy, and complicated. The practical consequences of their former lives apart from Christ were not immediately reversed or canceled. The Christians were continuing to be refined, and their circumstances were being redeemed as testimonies of his grace.

In the same way, many people we are called to serve—neighbors, friends, coworkers, extended family members—may find themselves buried under the collateral damage of their family histories or the aftermath and rubble of their former situations. Moreover, many of us may struggle with guilt, anger, and shame from our pasts or raw emotions from open wounds and ongoing circumstances. God's standard for the home in this passage does not ignore these realities; instead, it should provide us with hope as it points us to the redemptive remedy for our homes when we live according to his design and his desire. The truths in this passage also encourage us with his redemptive love as we are confronted with our inadequacies, past regrets, and current shortcomings. In Christ, our failures are forgiven, our guilt is cleansed by grace, and our hearts can be healed.

We must also be mindful of those who find themselves in abusive situations. God's Word consistently champions the oppressed and offers refuge and comfort to victims. His intended design for the home does not require them to continue to subject themselves to harm. Therefore, we must come alongside those who find themselves suffering from all forms of abuse—emotional, physical, spiritual—and offer shelter and protection. While we should pray and counsel toward reconciliation, to expose them to ongoing abuse is irresponsible and ungodly. Unfortunate and heartbreaking realities require us to carefully consider different situations.

We Must Prayerfully Consider Difficult Seasons

The perfect standard in this passage also reminds us that no family is perfect. Even when we desire to live according to God's design for our homes, every marriage and every family will experience difficult seasons. Our sinful desires and selfish behaviors can disrupt our lives and cause times of tension and establish patterns of dysfunction. During these seasons, this passage can remind us of our roles and responsibilities in our homes and renew our commitment to the Lord and to our families.

There are particular seasons that are notoriously difficult for households to endure. Hard times and holiday seasons present unique challenges that require prayerful consideration. When our families experience times of emotional grief in the loss of loved ones or situational instability with a job change or relocation, the additional stress and required adjustments can be especially difficult. Additions to the family or parental challenges with children and grandchildren can also result in hard times that require us to renew our devotion to our families and our individual roles and responsibilities.

Holiday seasons can also present periodic challenges for our families. Traveling for the holidays, navigating the expectations and personalities of our extended families, and balancing time between in-laws all create dynamics that are stressful and can be overwhelming. Prayerful preparation in anticipation of these seasons, along with clear communication during them, can help alleviate some of the unavoidable pressure that comes with the holidays.

In the midst of these seasons, maintaining our selfless consideration of one another and operating with hearts of understanding and love can help us endure (and enjoy!) God's design and desire for our homes as we display our love for the Lord.

Conclusion

The assumption in Jesus's parable of the wise and foolish builders is that our homes necessarily have to endure a barrage of torrential storms.

The assurance of his parable is that those who build their homes according to God's blueprint can withstand life's onslaughts. According to Jesus, when we build our homes on the uncertain and unstable sand of the world's principles and philosophies, our houses will collapse. Many of us have witnessed or endured the collateral damage of such tragic family downfalls. But when Christ is the architect and his Word is the foundation, our homes will be established on the immovable rock that will not allow our houses to be destroyed, despite whatever devastating storms we may have to endure.

In these verses Paul outlined the necessary blueprint for building our homes according to God's design and desire. The entire letter to the Colossians has taught them what it means to be adopted into the family of faith through Christ. This particular passage helps us understand the implications of this reality for our domestic families. When our homes are dwellings where the love of Christ is shared within our families, parents can cultivate hearts for Christ and nurture children into mature disciples who live for him. But building our homes according to God's blueprint extends beyond the immediate impact on our families. Jesus taught that there is another intended implication as well.

While his concluding parable describes the consequences of not building our lives and our homes on his Word, it is not the only mention of a house in the Sermon on the Mount. Earlier in his message, Jesus described the impact believers are intended to have on the lost world through the testimony of our transformed lives (Matt 5:13-16). Our identity in Christ distinguishes us from the world and is intended to influence all those around us. In this familiar passage on "salt" and "light," Jesus used the house as an important feature of the analogy.

The assumed use of a "lamp" is that it would give "light" to all who are "in the *house*" (Matt 5:15, emphasis added). This not only impacts those who dwell in the house, but as families are transformed, a community of believers serves as a city on a hill that cannot be hidden. Collectively, the impact of these homes extends beyond their immediate occupants. Redeemed households become beacons of light that shine the gospel to the lost world around us. In this way, God's blueprint for our homes is also part of the game plan for his mission. When we dedicate our homes to the Lord, we can dwell with harmony in him and display our hearts for Christ as a testimony of his redemptive love that is universally available and invites everyone to join his family!

Reflect and Discuss

1. What are some ways the lordship of Christ over our families should work out practically?
2. What does it mean that our household roles are ultimately accountable to the Lord?
3. How should husbands and wives relate to each other according to this passage?
4. How should children relate to their parents according to this passage?
5. How would you address the issues of assault and abuse in light of a passage like this?
6. What are some ways parents can obey the truth of this passage in their parenting?
7. How should we consider different marital and familial situations?
8. How should we consider difficult seasons in family life?
9. How do the truths of the gospel inform the commands in this passage?
10. Why is homelife important for our mission?

When Opportunity Knocks

COLOSSIANS 4:2-6

Main Idea: As believers, we are called to participate in God's redemptive plan through specific prayers for gospel advancement and strategic plans for personal engagement.

I. **We must pray for witnessing opportunities (4:2-4).**
 A. God will open the doors (4:2-3).
 B. God will open our hearts (4:3-4).
II. **We must pray for wisdom in opportunities (4:4-6).**
 A. We must be wise in our speech (4:4-5).
 B. We must be wise to our surroundings (4:5-6).
III. **Points of Application (4:5-6)**
 A. We cannot be argumentative.
  1. We can compel, but we ultimately cannot convince.
  2. We can contend, but we ultimately cannot convict.
 B. We cannot be ashamed.
  1. The testimony of our lives must show the gospel.
  2. The testimony of our love must spread the gospel.
  3. The testimony of our lips must share the gospel.

In the early morning hours of March 13, 1964, a young lady named Kitty Genovese was brutally assaulted and stabbed to death. She was returning home from work to her apartment in Kew Gardens, a local section of Queens, New York, when her attacker assaulted her in the shadows of the night. The twenty-eight-year-old woman screamed for help and, according to the *New York Times*, at least thirty-eight of her neighbors heard her cries or witnessed some aspect of the attack. As they turned on their lights to see what was happening, their awareness initially frightened the assailant away. Nevertheless, he returned to her helpless form and finished his heinous crime. In spite of the extended attack, tragically none of her neighbors notified the authorities or offered assistance ("37 Who Saw Murder").

The neighbors' negligence prompted scrutiny and curiosity, leading two young psychologists, Darly and Latane, to explore the reasons that prevent people from helping out in an emergency. The results of their study determined that the more witnesses are present or observe an incident, the less likely they are to be involved. Essentially, in the case of an emergency, the responsibility is diffused as everyone expects someone else to intervene. This phenomenon became known as the "bystander effect" ("The Bystander Effect").

This tragedy and the resulting study demonstrated the necessity for a concerted effort to watch out for fellow members of one's community and led to the launching of the Neighborhood Watch program. And while it is obvious how neighborly cooperation can help save lives, sadly a similar need exists within the church today. All too often we continue to ignore the tremendous need for salvation in our communities as we diffuse responsibility and expect others to intervene and engage people with the gospel. While we celebrate God's grace to us in Christ, opportunity is knocking all around us, yet we often continue to dismiss the severity of others' needs and disregard our responsibility to help.

The Colossians faced similar circumstances in their community, and Paul recognized the gravity of their situation and the importance of the gospel mission. The majority of Paul's instruction has been focused on inward issues related to living under the lordship of Christ within the community of faith. He has exhorted them regarding the false teaching (2:8-23), encouraged them in their daily walks and mutual service for Christ (3:1-17), and established the paradigm and practices for godly households (3:18–4:1). The verses in this passage shift the focus from life within the body toward an outward perspective that considers believers' cultural engagement with the gospel and begins with strategic intercession (Moo, *The Letters*, 318).

Structurally, this passage breaks down into two distinct segments that parallel each other in several ways: an initial command, "Devote yourselves to prayer" (v. 2), and "Act wisely toward outsiders" (v. 5); evangelism, both in Paul's mission (v. 3) and in the Colossians' ministry (vv. 5-6); how the gospel "should" be shared in each context (vv. 4,6); and the centrality of the gospel message through "the word" (v. 3) and in their words (v. 6; Beale, *Colossians and Philemon*, 333). That is, the missional-oriented prayers Paul desires for his own ministry are meant to inspire and instruct the Colossians in their participation in the gospel mission.

These verses signify the conclusion of Paul's practical instruction[1] as his letter crescendos into the ultimate outworking of our faith. According to the truth of this passage, we, as believers, are called to participate in God's redemptive plan through specific prayers for gospel advancement and strategic plans for personal engagement.

We Must Pray for Witnessing Opportunities
COLOSSIANS 4:2-4

Paul begins and ends his letter with an emphasis on prayer. The opening of the letter modeled prayer through his intercession on behalf of the Colossians and his petition for them to know and fulfill God's missional purpose for their lives (1:3-14). The conclusion invites them to join him in prayer, interceding on his behalf in the same way—with a missional purpose in mind.

In 4:2, Paul challenges the Colossians, "devote yourselves" to persistent and ongoing prayer. This term describes continual intercession that perseveres in prayer according to Jesus's instructions (Luke 18:1-8). It also reflects the earliest practices of Christ's followers (Acts 1:14) and parallels Paul's commendations in other letters (e.g., Rom 12:12). This commitment to pray also mirrors the ongoing nature of Paul's continued prayers for the Colossians that he "always" (Col 1:3) offered on their behalf and that "haven't stopped" (1:9; Beale, *Colossians and Philemon*, 334).

The specific command to pray is modified by two complementary phrases that describe the careful discernment of our minds and grateful disposition of our hearts. To "stay alert" in prayer echoes Jesus's words to his disciples in the garden prior to his betrayal that involved guarding themselves, staying wakeful in prayer (Mark 14:38). For the Colossians, this would remind them of their need to "be careful" regarding the false teachers (Col 2:8; cf. Acts 20:29-31). But more specifically in this context, this term includes an alertness with a missional connotation. It describes an awareness that stays "in tune with the times" and is mindful of the cultural circumstances, particularly as they relate to the spread of the gospel (Melick, *Philippians, Colossians, Philemon*, 321–22).

Our devotion to prayer should also be done "with thanksgiving." Paul's repeated emphasis on this grateful disposition throughout the

---

[1] O'Brien recognizes similar concluding exhortations in several of Paul's letters, including Gal 5:25–6:6; Phil 4:8-9; and 1 Thess 5:12-22 (*Colossians, Philemon*, 235).

letter (Col 1:12; 2:7; 3:15,16,17; 4:2) flows from the hearts of those who have been rescued (1:13), redeemed (1:14), reconciled (1:22), and regenerated (2:13). Beyond our own salvation, thanksgiving also overflows when we are humbly aware of our unworthiness to participate in God's plan, and yet we see his grace to include us in his redemptive work. A heart of gratitude is one that possesses and maintains a proper perspective. With the mission in mind, that heart is not deterred by obstacles or opposition but operates with faith in the lordship and leadership of Christ.

The responsibility to pray constantly is a timeless imperative for all believers (cf. 1 Thess 5:17). God has established prayer as his necessary means to work in and through our lives, and we must devote ourselves to interceding with an informed perspective that is grateful for the privilege to participate in his mission. Through Paul's request for their prayers, we also learn specific ways we should pray for witnessing opportunities.

God Will Open the Doors (4:2-3)

Paul's admonition for the Colossians to pray is supplemented by specific requests, "at the same time," that he entreats them to make on his behalf. His plea, "pray also for us," is not focused primarily on his personal misfortune or his physical needs. Instead, it is centered on his missional purpose and the gospel message. His use of "us" (v. 3) likely includes Timothy (1:1) and Epaphras (1:7; 4:12) as partners in his current endeavors and acknowledges his humble recognition that the mission is larger than any one individual, including himself. His focus is on "the word," the "mystery of Christ," and its reception through a "door" that only God can "open" (v. 3).

The metaphor of an open door is used repeatedly throughout the New Testament to describe opportunities for evangelistic outreach. Luke used it to describe God's work through Paul and Barnabas that "opened the door of faith to the Gentiles" (Acts 14:27). Paul used it in reference to his missional opportunities in Ephesus, testifying that "a wide door for effective ministry has opened" (1 Cor 16:9; cf. 2 Cor 2:12). Likewise, John used it in reference to God's missional intention for the church in Philadelphia: "I have placed before you an open door that no one can close" (Rev 3:8).

In all of these instances, it is important to note that God is the one who opens the door in each circumstance. This is consistent with Paul's request for prayer and the Colossians' appeal "that God may open a door." In addition, the prayer is not for his release, which could have easily been misunderstood through the "open door" metaphor. Instead, it is a prayer for a pathway for "the word" (cf. Col 1:5-6,25), which is "the mystery of Christ" (cf. 1:26-27). While he could be restrained, "I am in chains," the good news of Jesus could not be imprisoned.

According to Paul's petition for prayer, we can recognize the specific way we should pray for witnessing opportunities. As we appeal to the Lord, we must trust him to prepare the way for the gospel to go forward and to open the hearts of the lost to receive it. We do not have to force conversations, intimidate people, or try to coerce them to believe. Instead, we must simply be faithful to look for the open doors and to share the gospel when he provides the opportunity.

God Will Open Our Hearts (4:3-4)

Praying for witnessing opportunities trusts the Lord to open the doors, but he also uses these prayers to open our hearts. The shift in pronouns from "us" to "I" (vv. 3-4) expresses a reflective awareness in Paul's heart that viewed the circumstances of his imprisonment through the lens of opportunity. He explained to the Philippians that his arrest had "actually advanced the gospel" through his testimony among the guards and other prisoners. His situation instilled "confidence in the Lord," and his suffering had inspired other believers with greater courage "to speak the word fearlessly" (Phil 1:12-14).

Paul did not view his imprisonment as a hindrance to the gospel but as a platform. He understood that the gospel was the reason "for which [he was] in chains" (Col 4:3). In other words, not only was the gospel *the cause* of his imprisonment, his imprisonment became the platform for *the cause* of the gospel. This eternal and missional perspective was motivated by his own conversion, his compassion for others, and the conviction of his calling to proclaim "the mystery of Christ" to the nations (v. 3; cf. 1:25). Therefore, he asked the Colossians to pray that he would "make it known as [he] should" (v. 4).

In light of these verses, there are several principles for us to consider as we pray for witnessing opportunities. First, we must devote ourselves to specific prayer that trusts the Lord to open doors. We should be consistent and persistent in our prayers for all of God's people with a burdened plea for the gospel mission, both for faithful workers and for receptive hearers (cf. Matt 9:36-38; Eph 6:18-20).

In addition, we must recognize that by opening doors, God not only gives us a *chance* to share the gospel, but he also gives us a *choice* to share the gospel. Our prayers for opportunities must be supplemented by a willingness and an intentionality to bear testimony to the good news of Christ. Our prayers for witnessing opportunities should cultivate a missional mindset that gives us the necessary discernment to recognize divine appointments the Lord brings across our paths or impresses on our hearts. They should also embolden us with courage to walk through the open doors, believing the Lord will honor his Word and our faithfulness.

Finally, these prayers should also generate compassion for the lost people around us and their desperate need for Christ. In light of our own salvation and the underserved mercy God has extended to us, we must pray that the Lord would give us a burden for the nations. And while we long for their redemption, our prayers should also be motivated by a desire for the name of Christ to be magnified and for God to be glorified through their salvation. May the Lord impress on us the need to pray strategically for witnessing opportunities, that he might open doors for the gospel as he opens our hearts for people!

We Must Pray for Wisdom in Opportunities
COLOSSIANS 4:4-6

Paul's request for intercession on behalf of his evangelistic efforts invited the Colossians to be involved in the global mission of Christ. But their participation was not intended to be limited to the vital role of prayerful support for his ministry. It also included their active cultural engagement through missional efforts of their own. His repeated cautions throughout the letter to avoid the false teachers could easily become a license to avoid nonbelievers and retreat in the gospel mission (Moo, *The Letters*, 319). Therefore, he makes their missional responsibility explicit by addressing how they should engage "outsiders." This term was not a reference to those who had infiltrated the church with errant teaching; it focused on the unbelieving members of their surrounding community in general (Beale, *Colossians and Philemon*, 341).[2]

---

[2] Moo notes that Paul uses this same phrase as "a general reference to non-Christians" in several other passages (1 Cor 5:12,13; 1 Thess 4:12; cf. Mark 4:11) (*The Letters*, 326).

For the Colossians, and for all of us as believers, taking personal responsibility to share the gospel requires us to consider some important principles of contextualization. In order to navigate the various contours of our cultural terrain, we must "act wisely toward outsiders" (v. 5). So in addition to his missional exhortation, Paul also provides some practical guidelines for us to follow. The specific prayers he requests for gospel advancement (vv. 2-4) parallel the intentional and strategic instructions he provides for their personal engagement (vv. 5-6).

We Must Be Wise in Our Speech (4:4-5)

The apostle's prayer affirmed the Lord's providence in orchestrating witnessing encounters, but Paul also recognized the wisdom these opportunities would require. The specific prayers he requested the Colossians offer up, "that [he] may make it known" (v. 4), affirmed the divine responsibility he felt as a faithful follower of Jesus to declare "the mystery of Christ" (v. 3) and "to make the word of God fully known" (1:25). The apostle understood his personal witness as a delightful duty and was compelled by necessity to preach the gospel (1 Cor 9:16). Therefore, he urged them to pray that he would proclaim it according to this responsibility, "as [he] should" (4:4).

When combined with the concept of making known the mystery of Christ, this phrase, "as I should," also describes the manner in which Paul explained the gospel.[3] He desired that his teaching would not be misunderstood or misinterpreted. The message needed to be *clear* so that it would be distinct from the misleading doctrines and confusing practices of the false teachers and the beliefs of the surrounding culture (cf. 2:8). Therefore, his prayer request expressed this burden and acknowledged this need as well—that clarity would be a distinguishing mark of his message.

In the same way, he instructed the Colossians regarding their "speech," that they would "know how [they] should answer each person" (v. 6). The phrasing of this verse parallels the description of Paul's own ministry (vv. 3-4) and communicates a divinely commissioned responsibility to share the gospel that all believers are called to embrace. The

---

[3] Some translations include a clarifying connotation for this reason. For example, the ESV translates it, "that I may make it clear, which is how I ought to speak." Likewise, the NASB, NRSV, and NIV all translate it according to the manner of Paul's declaration and explanation of the mystery, that he would do so "clearly."

corresponding verbiage also reinforces our need to declare the good news clearly, according to the specific context and conversation. Paul's prayer and instruction remind us of the need we have for wisdom in our speech. Sometimes our message is confusing because we struggle to find the right words. But perhaps more often we muddy the waters of the gospel with social, political, or personal issues as we unintentionally or indiscriminately mingle these elements into a gospel conversation. This can make it difficult for our message to be deciphered. Therefore, we must carefully disentangle the gospel from the cultural battles that would define it according to worldly philosophies, principles, and practices. Knowing what to say, how to say it, when to say it, and whom to say it to are all included in the Spirit-led guidance that witnessing opportunities require.

We Must Be Wise to Our Surroundings (4:5-6)

In addition to our speech, we must also be wise to our surroundings. Paul was painfully aware of his culture and its hostility toward the gospel as his efforts to proclaim Christ had resulted "in chains" (v. 3). Therefore, he counseled the Colossians to "act wisely" and to live with wisdom in their interaction with "outsiders" (v. 5). These terms are not limited to a specific encounter as much as they refer to a lifestyle and pattern for how believers should "act" (lit. "walk"; cf. 2:6).

His clarifying instruction, "making the most of the time," reinforces this understanding since they are intended to be discerning within their context and culture (v. 5; cf. Eph 5:16). To redeem or buy back the time recognizes the fleeting nature of this life and the limited season of opportunity that is available for salvation (see 2 Pet 3:8-10). This understanding also magnifies the significance of every individual encounter and our urgency in leveraging every open door of opportunity for the gospel.

In order to do so, an informed understanding of our surroundings is even more paramount. Paul focuses the practical wisdom of our everyday lifestyle on the specific importance of our "speech." The particular wisdom associated with our words is informed by our careful discernment of our context. Paul instructs them that their conversations should "always be gracious" (v. 6). This phrase alludes to the essence of the gospel and our responsibility to infuse our speech with the message of grace. But it also describes the manner in which we are intended to communicate. He uses a word picture, "seasoned with salt," to describe the winsome nature of our speech that distinguishes us from the world (cf. Matt 5:13) while inviting others to "taste and see that the LORD is good" (Ps 34:8).

The importance of contextualization is also emphasized by the final phrase, "that you may know how you should answer each person" (Col 4:6). Unique backgrounds and experiences, along with individual perspectives and beliefs, require the use of wisdom as we engage various people in different places along their spiritual journey. We must also be mindful of their disposition, perhaps even their resistance toward the gospel, and balance what Christ perfectly embodied, "grace and truth" (John 1:14). This requires us to adopt the blended approach Jesus endorsed in sending out his disciples, to "be as shrewd as serpents and as innocent as doves" (Matt 10:16).

Being wise to our surroundings is not a license to become cultural critics and cynics. In the midst of a culture that is volatile and hostile, the gospel of grace should be reinforced through the kind and compassionate tone in which we communicate. With sincere and sympathetic hearts, we must be "ready at any time to give a defense to anyone who asks [us] for a reason for the hope that is in [us]" (1 Pet 3:15).

Points of Application
COLOSSIANS 4:5-6

As we consider how to prayerfully and carefully engage the world around us with the gospel, it is important for us to keep some practical guidelines in mind. God provides us with several biblical and theological principles to help us navigate the cultural and relational dynamics of strategic engagement with wisdom.

We Cannot Be Argumentative

As believers, the truth of the gospel is at the heart of our strongest convictions and deepest passions. Understandably, this often results in emotional conversations with those who disagree with or reject our foundational beliefs. People who hold different views from our own will often be equally devoted to their own perspectives, which can result in combustible or contentious interaction.

In a culture that thrives on polarizing dissent, the exclusive nature of the gospel will be controversial, yet it requires us to maintain our doctrinal conviction. At the same time, in a culture that is broken and hurting, the compassionate nature of the gospel will be compelling, yet it requires us to maintain our relational courtesy. In all instances, as we share our faith, we must do so "with gentleness and reverence, keeping a clear conscience" (1 Pet 3:16). This diplomatic balance can only be achieved when we embrace two important biblical principles as we share the gospel.

First, we must keep in mind that *we can compel, but we ultimately cannot convince.* Scripture teaches us that we should share the gospel with urgency because of the desperate nature of the sinful condition and the tragic reality of eternal punishment. And while we may plead with people, we are not ultimately responsible to persuade them. Scripture is clear: the gospel of Christ is foolishness to those who are perishing, and the absurdity of grace and the cross actually confound the intellectual understanding of those who are lost (1 Cor 1:18-25). Their hearts and minds have been hardened and will remain veiled until the truth of the gospel penetrates and illuminates their understanding (see 2 Cor 3:14-16; 4:3-6).

Therefore, we must share Christ with passionate and persuasive zeal, but our hope and confidence must remain in the power of the gospel to ultimately convince others of its truth. This liberates us from the misleading feeling of guilt when some reject Christ and the misplaced pressure of expectation to convert anyone. Our hearts should grieve over their lack of understanding and their hopeless condition apart from Christ. But we can also rejoice in the faithfulness of God to bring spiritual growth from our humble efforts to plant and water gospel seeds (1 Cor 3:6; cf. Matt 13:1-9).

In the same way, we must also remember that *we can contend, but we ultimately cannot convict.* Salvation is not merely an intellectual decision; it is a spiritual conversion. The reality of the holiness of God, the sinfulness of man, and the forgiveness of Christ are spiritual convictions that we have no ability to coerce. The penetrating power of the gospel is accompanied by the regenerating work of the Spirit to "convict the world about sin, righteousness, and judgment" (John 16:8).

We are responsible to "contend for the faith" (Jude 3) by standing up for truth, standing against moral and social evils, and standing for those who are unable to speak up for themselves. Yet we must also recognize that emphatic disagreements, a contentious spirit, or even a persuasive argument cannot ultimately produce spiritual conversion. Faith toward God is ultimately expressed through genuine repentance that results from godly sorrow over sin and leads to salvation (2 Cor 7:10; cf. Acts 20:21). Confrontation and condemnation do not lead people to repentance, but compassion exposes them to the undeserved kindness of God (Rom 2:4).

As we exhibit the love that is epitomized in Christ, we can compel others and contend for the gospel while recognizing our ultimate inability to convince or convict them of their sinful condition and need for a Savior.

We Cannot Be Ashamed

In our attempts to avoid being argumentative, we must not resort to the opposite extreme of avoiding gospel engagement altogether. Because of our confidence in the power of the gospel, we have assurance and do not have to be ashamed of the good news (Rom 1:16). God has graciously included us in his divine plan for redemption, and we have been commanded and commissioned to make disciples (Matt 28:18-20). This sacred responsibility includes several aspects of intentionality that are each necessary and collectively work together as we live on mission. Ours is a multidimensional testimony. Scripture describes visible, tangible, and verbal expressions of the gospel that we as God's people must consider.

The visible aspect of sharing the gospel means that *the testimony of our lives must show the gospel*. Paul instructed the Colossians to "act wisely toward outsiders" (Col 4:5). Jesus described this "walk" as a lifestyle that corresponds with our identity in him and distinguishes us from the rest of the world. We are called to live as "salt" and "light" in a world that is decaying and dark (Matt 5:13-16; cf. Eph 5:8). Because we are God's children, our lives are meant to be "blameless and pure" as we stand out as "faultless in a crooked and perverse generation" so that we might "shine like stars in the world" (Phil 2:15).

On a practical level this influences the ways we differentiate ourselves from the values, morals, and behaviors of our culture. We must be careful not to camouflage ourselves by adopting its principles or patterns. Instead, we should conduct ourselves "honorably" so that others see our "good works" and "will glorify God" (1 Pet 2:12). In other words, our lives must bear a family resemblance to the holiness of our heavenly Father so that they recognize his greatness and glory.

In addition to the visible dimension of our testimony, there is a tangible dimension as well. *The testimony of our love must spread the gospel.* Acting "wisely toward outsiders" with speech that is "gracious" (Col 4:5-6) describes our attitudes and our actions that ultimately reflect the deeper reality of our salvation. Genuine faith will be evidenced by our willingness to extend kindness to others (Jas 2:14-17). Likewise, God's love will be observed by our disposition and demeanor toward others as a testimony of his universal love for all people (John 13:35).

This love becomes tangible and extends beyond attitudes of compassion when it expands into acts of kindness. Our charitable efforts to serve others, our willingness to sacrificially invest in the lives of others, and our attempts to graciously help others are not simply humanitarian acts of philanthropy or manipulative attempts of persuasion. Our loving actions toward others are an expression of the gospel in an effort to display God's love that is made available to all people in Christ (1 John 4:10-11).

Finally, the visible and tangible expressions are complemented by the verbal dimension of our testimony. Our lives and our love are powerful tools that are ultimately limited in their ability to offer salvation to others. Paul challenges the Colossians to consider the missional importance of their "speech" as they consider how to "answer each person" (Col 4:6). Apart from a clear explanation of the gospel, people may be inspired to lead more upstanding lives, but heart change can only occur as a response to the good news. As Paul explained, "Faith comes from what is heard, and what is heard comes through the message about Christ" (Rom 10:17).

Therefore, *the testimony of our lips must share the gospel.* We must be willing to speak up and speak out in a culture that attempts to mute and muffle the message of Christ. If we remain silent, we are simply refusing to answer the door when opportunity knocks. Our responsibility to tell others about Christ requires us to clearly explain the core components of the gospel. These foundational elements include the truth about God—his holiness and love (Rom 5:8); the truth about man—our sinfulness and need for redemption (Rom 3:23); and the truth about Christ—forgiveness comes through his substitutionary death and his bodily resurrection (Rom 6:23). Salvation is received by grace through personal faith (Eph 2:8-9) that surrenders to the lordship of Christ (Rom 10:9-10).

Collectively, our visible, tangible, and verbal testimony should show, spread, and share the gospel with others. This all-encompassing approach reinforces the missional essence of who we are as God's children and ambassadors.

Conclusion

We began by considering the tragic death of Kitty Genovese and the abdicated responsibility of those who could have possibly helped. Following the tragedy, those in the community expressed a desire to intentionally help their neighbors, but sadly their follow-through was short-lived. Roughly ten years later on Christmas Day, another murder occurred in an apartment that overlooked where Genovese's death occurred. Another young woman, Sandra Zahler, was killed, and she had cried for help during her attack. While it was reported that her neighbors heard screams and struggles, once again they did nothing (McFadden, "A Model's Dying Screams").

As the church—those who are redeemed and have been saved from the grasp of impending death—we cannot continue to stand back as others suffer and ultimately perish without Christ. We cannot read this passage, affirm its truth, and roll back over to hit the spiritual snooze button. We *must* pray for witnessing opportunities and trust the Lord to open doors to share the gospel and to open our hearts with a burden and compassion for the lost. We must also pray for wisdom in these opportunities as we contextualize our engagement with a diplomatic approach in our speech and a discerning awareness of our surroundings.

When we are faithful to share the good news, both in word and witness, we can trust the Lord of the harvest to ripen the spiritual fruit and graciously draw people into a loving relationship with him. Paul's instruction in this passage is predicated on Jesus's commission to make disciples, his compassion for the lost, his assurance of the abundant redemption that awaits, and his instruction to his disciples. Jesus implored them: "Pray to the Lord of the harvest to send out workers into his harvest" (Matt 9:36-38). What is wonderful about this prayer is that we not only have the privilege of interceding, but we also have the opportunity to participate as part of God's answer by engaging as laborers in the mission!

Reflect and Discuss

1. In what ways have you been tempted to be a bystander when it comes to engaging the world with the gospel?
2. Why is prayer so important to the further spread of the gospel among us?
3. The passage teaches us to pray for witnessing opportunities. What does it say we should pray for specifically?
4. How does this passage encourage us to pray for wisdom in our witnessing opportunities?
5. Why is wisdom in speech important for our evangelistic efforts?
6. Why is wisdom in contextualization important for our evangelistic efforts?
7. Why should we not be argumentative when sharing the gospel?
8. Why should we not be ashamed when sharing the gospel?
9. What are some ways we might entangle our gospel presentations with things that distract from the gospel?
10. How does this passage encourage you to participate in the work of evangelism?

How to Invest in God's Kingdom

COLOSSIANS 4:7-18

Main Idea: As members of the body of Christ, we are called to cooperate and collaborate as we serve Jesus and partner with others to fulfill his mission and build his kingdom.

I. **We Should Enlist Others to Serve Christ (4:7-9).**
   A. Enlist others to be ministers of Christ (4:7-9).
   B. Enlist others to be messengers for Christ (4:8-9).
II. **We Should Encourage Others to Serve Christ (4:10-14).**
   A. We must support one another (4:10-14).
   B. We must strengthen one another (4:12-14).
III. **We Should Empower Others to Serve Christ (4:15-18).**
   A. We must be faithful to the ministry of the church (4:15-16).
   B. We must fulfill the ministry of our calling (4:17-18).

Over the years our nation's investment market has demonstrated its volatility through several notable downturns. Historical references like "Black Thursday," with regard to the stock market crash of 1929 that spawned the Great Depression, or "Black Monday," in 1987 when the global economy suffered massive losses, are reminders of its instability and unreliable nature. Other significant occurrences, like the "dot-com" setback of 2000, the economy collapse in 2008, and even the major losses due to the coronavirus pandemic provide more recent examples of the ephemeral nature of earthly investments.

While cautionary reminders of the fleeting nature of wealth and the importance of wise financial planning are appropriate, perhaps there is a more significant investment strategy to consider. In God's economy the foundational principle of reaping and sowing is as reliable as the law of gravity (Gal 6:7-9). Concepts like *return on investment* are not random or theoretical (2 Cor 9:6), and God provides the ultimate *investment protection* from the unforeseen and unfortunate circumstances of this life (Matt 6:19-20). Beyond these important distinctions, perhaps the greatest differences are the commodities and measure of success in God's economy. Instead of investing in products, we are called to invest in people. We are not building a company; we are building a kingdom. Rather than marketing to recruit people, we are mobilizing to rescue people. And instead of yielding earthly revenue, we are harvesting an eternal return!

As in the case of the stock market in our country, many people are aware of God's economy but are not exactly sure how to maximize their investments. Paul's letter to the Colossians offers some insight since it represents a deposit of spiritual capital into their personal growth fund. The concluding passage essentially provides the strategic model for success as they learn how to invest in others to produce fruitful returns.

The primary thrust of the passage, in both style and substance, is summarized by Paul's "purpose" for sending Tychicus, "that he may encourage your hearts" (v. 8). Paul's tone is uplifting and motivating, and the content of what he shares is a clear expression of sincere love and support. The evidence of his pastoral concern would provide the Colossians with the inspiration they needed to denounce the heresy of the false teachers and to affirm their loyalty to the lordship of Christ. His pastoral instruction would ensure their continued growth and success as they learned to invest in others the way he and his ministry team invested in them.

Structurally, the passage has four primary components that sequentially flow together to form the conclusion: an introduction of the messengers (vv. 7-9); greetings from Paul's coworkers (vv. 10-14); instructions and greetings to others (vv. 15-17); and a final salutation (v. 18; O'Brien, *Colossians, Philemon*, 246). In total Paul mentions nine names,[1] and each segment includes multiple individuals that occupy a particular role. These verses follow the typical closing pattern of personal salutations in a biblical letter while also accomplishing a final instructional purpose.

While his attention is directed toward others, Paul begins and ends this concluding section of his letter with a reference to his imprisonment (vv. 7,9,18). The apostle simultaneously provides an update for the Colossians on his circumstances and delivers one last word of exhortation. By way of example, Paul's life and ministry reflect a selfless heart through his sincere concern for them, provide a tangible invitation for

---

[1] Melick observes that the list of names in Colossians is longer than most and includes more details about the individuals. He notes some similarities to Romans in the size of the list and attributes it to the common fact that Paul had never met either church in person (*Philippians, Colossians, Philemon*, 326).

the church to join him in suffering for the cause, and offer them assurance of Christ's faithfulness no matter what lies in store for them.

In addition, his affirmation of others establishes the paradigm for personal investment that God desires each of us to follow. As members of the body of Christ, we are called to cooperate and collaborate as we serve Jesus and partner with others to fulfill his mission and build his kingdom.

We Should Enlist Others to Serve Christ
COLOSSIANS 4:7-9

The sign of any good leader is knowing how to motivate and mobilize others. It requires an organized understanding of the mission, an insightful awareness of the people around you, and the character credibility to lead them. Paul's dedication to the mission and his personal investment in others attracted willing servants who partnered with him in a variety of ways.

In these verses Paul specifically mentions two such partners whom he enlisted to serve Christ—Tychicus and Onesimus. Their descriptions parallel each other as he identifies three attributes of each that affirm their value and endorse their acceptance. In addition, their shared responsibility to update the Colossians on Paul's situation highlights their significance and bookends the passage (vv. 7,9). For contemporary believers, his endorsement of these two "faithful" brothers underscores the importance of our responsibility to enlist others to serve Christ.

Enlist Others to Be Ministers of Christ (4:7-9)

The Great Commission is the primary marching order from King Jesus for every Christian (Matt 28:18-20). While this command is most commonly associated with our evangelistic efforts, the responsibility to "make disciples" cannot be reduced to sharing Christ and inviting others to respond. Jesus's invitation to those he encountered began with a spiritual conversion (John 3:3) that resulted in a call to "follow [him]" through a pattern of service (Matt 20:26-28) and personal surrender (Matt 16:24-27).

Paul helped Tychicus and Onesimus understand the practical outworking of their salvation by enlisting them to serve as ministers for Christ. Tychicus was from Asia and accompanied Paul on his third missionary journey (Acts 20:4). He spent considerable time with Paul during his Roman imprisonment and was a close enough associate to be able to "tell . . . all the news about [him]" (Col 4:7). Paul's description of him as a "dearly loved brother" communicated his personal affection for him and the familial depth of their relationship as siblings in the Lord. Most importantly, it commended his status to them as an adopted member of God's family (cf. 1:2) and co-laborer in Christ.

He also characterizes Tychicus as a "faithful minister" and "fellow servant in the Lord" (v. 7). These phrases describe his tireless devotion and dedication to the cause of Christ as Paul enlisted him as a helpful partner in various ministry contexts (2 Tim 4:12; Titus 3:12). Through his almost identical description to the Ephesian church (Eph 6:21-22), along with a description that paralleled the founder of the Colossian church, Epaphrus (cf. Col 1:7), Paul's endorsement validated Tychicus as a trustworthy leader. Beyond simply updating them with Paul's situation, he was also sent to "encourage [their] hearts" (Col 4:8). This ministerial purpose speaks to his abilities beyond delivering a letter. His servant heart and accompanying gifts would be evident to the Colossians and were being employed as Paul enlisted him as a minister of Christ.

Onesimus had previously lived in Colossae and accompanied Tychicus to deliver the letter. Paul's parallel inclusion and honorable description of Onesimus is especially significant given his prior status as a bondslave. As the former servant of Philemon, the Colossian church host, Onesimus unlawfully fled from his domestic role. Upon meeting Paul in prison, he became a follower of Christ (Phlm 10) and was sent back to Philemon, "no longer as a slave, but . . . as a dearly loved brother" (Phlm 16). His redeemed identity made him "useful"[2] in a new and more valuable way (Phlm 11).

In his description of Onesimus, Paul most likely avoided using servant/slave terminology to describe him in order to avoid any unintended confusion. Instead of describing him in terms of his previous status, he focuses on his redeemed character and his confirmed position in Christ, "a faithful and dearly loved brother," while also identifying him as "one of [them]" (Col 4:9). His salvation had redefined him as a "brother" (cf. 3:11), and his new identity provided the basis for his restoration as a member of their local community. This would enable

---

[2] The name *Onesimus* means "useful" (O'Brien, *Colossians, Philemon*, 248).

him not only to serve according to a domestic role but also to minister as a servant for Christ (3:22-25).

In many ways Paul's letter to the Colossians is a manual for discipleship. His goal was to emphasize the practical implications of living under the lordship of Christ and the Colossians' continued growth in him (2:6). Paul had identified his own role as one of a "minister" (1:23,25 ESV), and by sending Onesimus and Tychicus to them, he was encouraging the Colossians to adopt the same mindset and enlist others to be ministers for Christ.

Enlist Others to Be Messengers for Christ (4:8-9)

Letters as the primary form of correspondence in the first century required couriers who would deliver an epistle to the intended audience. Tychicus was a coworker and frequent companion of Paul who was authorized to deliver multiple letters for the apostle. In addition to the letter to the Colossians (v. 7), he most likely carried the letter to Philemon (v. 9) and to the Laodiceans (v. 16), to the Ephesians (Eph 6:21), to Titus (Titus 3:12), and Paul's final letter to Timothy (2 Tim 4:12).

In the first century messengers were more than mail carriers; they were personal emissaries who also served as official representatives of the senders. Their role included delivering the letter, publicly reading the message (1 Thess 5:27), and providing oral commentary on behalf of the author (Pao, *Colossians and Philemon*, 309). Paul deputized them in this way by noting, "[Tychicus] will tell you all the news about me" (Col 4:7), and together with Onesimus, "they will tell you about everything here" (v. 9).

In addition to carrying the mail and serving as personal representatives of Paul, these particular disciples of Christ also doubled as messengers of Jesus. The Colossians had received the gospel, and it continued to spread throughout the world (cf. 1:5-6). Just as they were invited to participate in God's global mission, the Lord commissions all believers as "ambassadors for Christ" to carry "the message of reconciliation" (2 Cor 5:19-20). We have been entrusted to deliver the good news of Jesus to a world in desperate need of him. And as the Spirit of God leads people to place their faith in Christ, we must enlist them as fellow messengers who participate in his mission.

We Should Encourage Others to Serve Christ
COLOSSIANS 4:10-14

In addition to enlisting others to trust Christ, we should also encourage others to serve Christ. Long-distance relationships, difficult circumstances, and uncertain outcomes were all part of Paul's situation as he was writing to the Colossians. As a church they were continuing to wrestle with the implications of their new faith and also dealing with the overbearing false teachers. The combination of all of these factors would have been a recipe for division and discouragement. So Paul sent ministers and messengers to "encourage" the Colossians (v. 8). Within the letter he attempts to bolster their faith further by sharing personal greetings and testimonies from other faithful servants. In these verses Paul's focus shifts from those he is sending to them to those who were staying with him.

We Must Support One Another (4:10-14)

Paul's letter to the Colossians is an effort to affirm his support for them. He writes with an encouraging tone throughout, and as he concludes his letter, he broadens their support network through the affirming acknowledgments of six additional co-laborers for Christ. The first three associates Paul mentions—Aristarchus, Mark, and Justus (vv. 10-11)—are identified as Jews; they are "of the circumcised" (4:11). The second set of three—Epaphras, Luke, and Demas (vv. 12-14)—by lack of designation are understood to be Gentiles (Pao, *Colossians and Philemon*, 302). These two parallel lists are deliberately chosen to make several intentional points by Paul.

First, Paul commends the intrinsic value of each individual by including them in this group that includes persons of high standing and prominent connections. Aristarchus was a Jew from Thessalonica and a traveling companion of Paul who helped deliver the collection for the Jerusalem offering (Acts 19:29; 20:4). Mark, "Barnabas's cousin" (Col 4:10), certainly was noteworthy as he accompanied Paul on his first missionary journey (Mark was called John in Acts 13:5). He also served with Peter (1 Pet 5:13), and, at the end of his life, Paul would personally request his presence (2 Tim 4:11). By contrast, this is the only place where Justus (Col 4:11) is mentioned in the New Testament, and the text does not include any additional commentary.

In the second set of co-laborers, Epaphras most likely helped establish the Colossian church (vv. 12-13; cf. 1:7) and was sent by them to be a supportive encourager for Paul. Luke, "the dearly loved physician" (4:14), was clearly known as an integral part of the early church. He accompanied Paul at various times on his missionary journeys throughout Acts and awaited his final trial with him (2 Tim 4:11). Conversely, like Justus in the previous list, "Demas" (Col 4:14) was far less recognizable and possibly abandoned the faith later (cf. 2 Tim 4:10). Still, they are mingled into the list and thereby equated in essence and value to Paul. By contrast, we live in a culture where celebrity status is acclaimed and famous people are elevated. But in Christ and in the local church, we should affirm that every believer is significant in God's kingdom and plays an important role within his plan.

In addition, their diversity emphasizes the unity that is possible through the gospel when formed around its mission. Ethnically they were different. The inclusion of Jews and Gentiles conquered the greatest barrier for discrimination. Socially and economically they also differed. But the assumed affluence of Epaphras and Luke did not elevate them above the other partners. And spiritually they also exhibited different gifts and levels of maturity (i.e., the noted diligence and devotion of Epaphras; Col 4:12-13). In the same way, because of Christ's work on the cross, the superficial distinctions that divide us have been demolished, and we have been established as one family and one spiritual army in Christ (cf. 3:11).

These realities and the people mentioned in these verses are the perfect expression of the body of Christ that Paul has repeatedly referenced throughout his letter. As the church, Christ is our "head" and we are his "body" (1:18,24); and as members of the body of Christ, we are united to him, "nourished and held together" by the supporting "ligaments and tendons" of one another (2:19). As Paul's partners with all of their diversity were demonstrating, we are called to operate and support one another as "one body" (3:15).

Support for one another may come in a variety of forms—spiritual, relational, emotional, physical, or financial. What is amazing about these dynamics is that the same categories used by the world for segregation actually become useful to the Lord for affirmation. In other words, those things that would otherwise divide us, God uses to unite us. It is through the diversity of the body of Christ in these various areas that we are able to build one another up.

Therefore, if we are going to support one another in the mission, we cannot allow any form of preferential or prejudicial treatment to interfere with our cooperation and collaboration. In addition, we must also recognize that the individual distinctions that make us unique are strategically organized and used by the Lord to accomplish his plan. Unity with diversity models the universal availability of the gospel to everyone, the equal essence we all share in Christ, and God's desire to use each one of us for a particular purpose as a member of the body.

We Must Strengthen One Another (4:12-14)

In addition to the church members' mutual support for one another, Paul also describes their responsibility to strengthen one another. In particular he elaborates on Epaphras and his ministry. The previous mention in the letter identified him as a "dearly loved fellow servant" and "faithful minister of Christ" (1:7). His abbreviated description here references his Colossian roots, "who is one of you," and reinforces his character and value as "a servant of Christ Jesus" (4:12). Like the other coworkers in the passage, he sends his "greetings," but Paul also describes his additional efforts.

Even though he had been sent by the church for the purpose of supporting Paul, Epaphras was continuing to serve the Colossians through the strengthening work of prayer. His diligence and persistence are communicated by Paul's description of his intercession as "always wrestling for [them] in his prayers" (v. 12). His commitment to the discipline of prayer reflects both the strength of his faith in God and the depth of his love for the Colossians.

His affection for them compelled him to pray based on the severity of the issues he knew they were facing. Because of the cultural challenges and the false teachers, Epaphras prayed so that they could "stand mature" and be "fully assured in everything God wills" (v. 12). His prayer reflects elements of Paul's intercession for them, particularly with regard to divine strength for perseverance (1:11) and for their complete understanding of God's plan for them (1:9). In addition, based on Paul's stated ministry goal of presenting "everyone mature in Christ" (1:28) and his challenge for the Colossians to continue to be "rooted . . . built up . . . and established in the faith" (2:7), Epaphras's prayers were likewise focused on the firmness and fullness of their faith.

In addition to his spiritual labor in prayer, Epaphras also exerted himself through physical labor on their behalf. Colossae was in close geographical proximity to "Laodicea" (cf. 2:1) and to "Hierapolis," and those cities shared many of the same cultural and commercial characteristics. Epaphras was likely instrumental in establishing all three congregations and probably continued to exercise some level of pastoral oversight over each (Moo, *The Letters*, 347). He adopted Paul's work ethic and philosophy of ministry as he toiled and "work[ed] hard" for their sake (4:13; cf. 1:29–2:1). This phrase speaks to the strength and energy he was exerting in his ministerial efforts, but it indicates much more. Epaphras's level of physical sacrifice revealed the extent of their personal value to him, his passionate zeal for the gospel, and his total reliance on divine strength to serve.

As we strengthen one another, we must learn to rely on these same driving forces. We must allow our sincere care for others and for Christ's church to be a true labor of love (1:24). In addition, the transforming power of the gospel and the glory of Christ must serve as the ultimate motivation for our sacrifice (1:25-27). And our faith must be totally dependent on his strength that allows us to accomplish more than what we are capable of on our own (1:29). These motivating factors will not only enable us to serve Christ; they will also encourage others to do the same.

We Should Empower Others to Serve Christ
COLOSSIANS 4:15-18

In addition to enlisting and encouraging others to serve Christ, Paul also demonstrates the responsibility we have to help empower others to serve Christ. These final verses conclude with a personal statement and signature that authorize and authenticate the letter in its entirety (v. 18). This not only certifies the doctrinal convictions and practical instructions he asserts throughout the epistle, but his personal autograph also doubled as an official endorsement of these young believers. The apostle's handwritten greeting was a personal validation to inspire them to the end, and it serves a similar purpose for us as well. In these final verses, by way of example and instruction, Paul models for all believers the importance of empowering others to serve Christ.

We Must Be Faithful to the Ministry of the Church (4:15-16)

After sending messengers to the church (vv. 7-9) and conveying greetings from his coworkers in Rome (vv. 10-14), Paul extends his own personal acknowledgments to members of the surrounding community and the church in Laodicea (vv. 15-16). The integral connection between the Colossians and Laodiceans is obvious through their common association in the letter (2:1; 4:13). His personal request for the Colossians to share his "greetings" with those in Laodicea (v. 15) assumed collaboration between the churches in neighboring communities. He also extended a personal greeting to "Nympha and the church in her home" (v. 15).[3] To ensure their interaction, Paul further instructed them to read their letter to "the church of the Laodiceans" and for the Colossians to "read the letter from Laodicea" (v. 16).

Paul's intentionality to foster cooperation between the congregations exhibits several important aspects of his empowering efforts and the ministry of the church. For example, his instruction for them to read each other's letters demonstrates a relevance that was not limited to a specific context. Instead, the content of the letters included timeless truth that was empowering and applicable for both congregations. At the same time, the desired collaboration also assumes a common experience for the believers in both communities even if their situations were not identical. God's people may face various forms of opposition (e.g., false teachers, cultural hostility, etc.), but the supremacy of Christ is universal and can empower all Christians to overcome every obstacle (John 16:33).

Perhaps most importantly, Paul's directed cooperation between the churches reinforces their collective need for mutual support and encouragement. While he references Nympha as an example of an individual leveraging her resources for the church as a whole, his ultimate emphasis is intended to be congregational. The churches in Laodicea and Hierapolis (Col 4:13), along with the Colossians, needed each of their individual members to be faithful to the ministry of the church at large. Their cooperation with other congregations would help remind them that the gospel mission is a global mission (1:6-7) that extended beyond their community. Paul maintained this mindset throughout his ministry, and he desired for them to adopt the same mentality. His

---

[3] There is some ambiguity regarding the gender of the name *Nympha* and whether this was an additional faith community in Laodicea or the primary congregation. Moo provides a helpful and concise summary of the related issues and concludes that Nympha was most likely a wealthy widow who hosted a house church in her home as one of several domestic congregations in Laodicea (*The Letters*, 349–50).

devotion to individual congregations like the Laodiceans and Colossians (2:1-5) was always part of a much broader understanding of his ministry to the church (1:24-29).

The emphasis throughout the letter has been on the corporate and universal body of believers. From the earliest verses, God's people are defined as a spiritual family (1:1-2) that has been established as redeemed citizens of Christ's kingdom (1:13). As the church, we are members of his body (1:18; 2:19), and we are called to dwell in unity under his lordship and leadership (3:15). The reality of our individual memberships within the broader corporate identity of believers only serves to emphasize the privilege and personal responsibility we have to participate in God's redemptive plan. Our personal value and worth as contributing coworkers in the global purpose of God should empower us to serve Christ by being faithful to the ministry of the church.

We Must Fulfill the Ministry of Our Calling (4:17-18)

The individual responsibility of every believer to the church at large is highlighted in Paul's final words of commendation. He directs an admonition to Archippus that could easily be addressed to every believer: "Pay attention to the ministry you have received in the Lord, so that you can accomplish it" (v. 17). While Archippus is identified as a "fellow soldier" and recipient of the letter to Philemon (Phlm 2), there is no other textual evidence that indicates the specific nature of his calling. The term used for "ministry" does not designate it as a reference to any official capacity, but perhaps the general understanding of Christian service actually serves the enduring purpose of the Scripture even more.

While Archippus would have certainly had a specific task that Paul was referencing, the ministry he had received was ultimately the same role of service that all believers are assigned "in the Lord." The personal role may be particular to an individual, but all Christians are called to serve Christ in a given capacity to further the gospel mission. Paul had reflected on his personal calling (1:23,25), and he had encouraged the Colossians with the assurance of God's will for each of them (1:9). Similarly, he instructed Timothy, "fulfill your ministry," while also exhibiting his unwavering commitment to complete his own "race" (2 Tim 4:5-7).

Paul's concluding autograph in this letter is a further demonstration of this same devotion as he entreats them, "Remember my chains"

(Col 4:18). This expression was undoubtedly meant to prompt them with a prayer reminder, but it also served several other purposes as well. His chains were a tangible example of what was involved in fulfilling the ministry entrusted to him. For the Colossians, their devotion would certainly be tested, and Paul wanted them to be empowered to remain faithful. In addition, his chains signified the partnership they shared as fellow servants of Christ. While their callings may have been different, their involvement in the same gospel mission qualified them as fellow participants in his suffering for Christ. And finally, his chains were also a testimony of the depth of his love for Jesus and for them. God's unfailing love epitomized in the gospel ultimately constrained Paul to sacrifice himself for the mission (cf. 2 Cor 5:14), and it was the reason for his imprisonment (Col 4:3). But he also recognized his suffering as a sacrifice he willingly made on behalf of the church (1:24). The simple phrase, "Remember my chains," would have served as an empowering refrain as they sought to fulfill their own ministry.

Paul concludes his letter with a benedictory blessing: "Grace be with you" (v. 18). This phrase is consistent with his typical closing and perfectly completes his letter that began by commending them to "grace" from "God our Father" (1:2). But the empowering nature of God's grace (cf. 2 Tim 2:1) would be particularly important for their continued growth in the knowledge of the Lord (Col 1:10; 2:6; cf. 2 Pet 3:18). As they endeavored to fulfill the ministry of their callings, it would only be possible by the saving and sanctifying grace of God that had done the same for Paul (1 Cor 15:10).

Like the Colossians, we must empower others to serve Christ by exhorting one another to fulfill the ministry of our callings. The echo of Paul's challenge to Archippus must resound within our own hearts as we pursue God's will for our lives. In addition, the reminder of Paul's chains should empower us as fellow participants in the gospel who are motivated by Christ's love to fully devote ourselves to his people through sacrificial service. Finally, the preeminence of Christ throughout the entire letter points us to the source of divine grace that we desperately need in order to fulfill the ministry of our callings.

Conclusion

The entirety of Paul's farewell is saturated with an others-focused mentality. While he may be suffering in chains, he makes every effort in each aspect of his conclusion to equip the Colossians to succeed in their service to Christ. He sends others to encourage them (vv. 7-10), he shares greetings from those they know (vv. 10-14), he instructs them to mutually build others up through edification and exhortation (vv. 15-17), and he commends them with God's grace (v. 18; Beale, *Colossians and Philemon*, 349–50). In other words, Paul embodies and exemplifies his concluding message to the Colossians through his own efforts to enlist, encourage, and empower them to serve Christ.

The pattern of Paul's model and the approach he endorses for us ultimately follow the strategy established by Jesus himself. Throughout his earthly ministry, Jesus enlisted others to serve him. From his initial apostles to improbable outcasts, Jesus issued personal invitations to follow him (Matt 4:18-22; Luke 19:10). As he enlisted others to serve him, he commissioned them as his ministers and his messengers so that they might enlist others to be his followers (Matt 16:24; 28:18-20). The ministry of Jesus and his disciples was never one of passive observation; it was always one of active obedience.

In addition to enlisting others to serve him, Jesus also encouraged others to serve him. The incarnation of Christ was the ultimate display of sacrificial service and epitomized the humble demeanor we are called to adopt (Phil 2:3-11). Jesus's invitation to follow him included embracing this same disposition of meekness (Matt 11:28-30). His attitude extended into his actions; and as he washed the disciples' feet, he commended to them a lifestyle of serving others (John 13:13-15). Ultimately, acts of service should be a distinguishing mark of Christ's followers as we encourage others to serve him through intentional efforts to support and strengthen one another (Matt 20:26-28).

Finally, Jesus also empowered others to serve him. As Peter and the disciples were beginning to understand the truth about Jesus's identity, he introduced them to his plan to establish the church as his covenant community (Matt 16:18). The assurance of its victory through his death and resurrection provided them with confidence to overcome every form of opposition and fulfill his mission. But he also empowered them with the promise of his abiding presence through the person of the Holy Spirit (Acts 1:8). His power would enable them to be faithful to the ministry of the church and to fulfill the ministry of their callings.

Our confidence is found in these same assurances—that Christ continues to enlist, encourage, and empower his followers to serve him. As his ambassadors, we can adopt this same approach as the investment strategy that pays spiritual dividends in the lives of others and ultimately builds God's kingdom.

Reflect and Discuss

1. Why are collaboration and cooperation so important to fulfilling the mission God has given us?
2. Why is enlisting others to serve Christ necessary for the fulfillment of the Great Commission?
3. How does Paul serve as an example in enlisting others to serve Christ?
4. What are some ways we should encourage others to serve Christ that are modeled in this passage?
5. How might Paul's discussion of Epaphras's model strengthen others to serve Christ?
6. What can we learn from Epaphras's ministry in this passage?
7. How does this passage encourage collaboration among local churches?
8. How can we help one another fulfill the ministries of our callings?
9. How does Paul serve as an example in empowering others to serve Christ?
10. How does Jesus perfectly model empowering others in ministry?

Philemon

We Are Family

PHILEMON 1-3

Main Idea: Those who are in Christ are brought into a spiritual family by God's grace and are called to participate in his work.

I. **We Serve by Divine Appointment (1).**
    A. Know who you are.
    B. Know whom you please.
II. **We Serve with Dedicated Partners (1-2).**
    A. We serve with brothers (1).
    B. We serve with fellow workers (2).
    C. We serve with sisters (2).
    D. We serve with fellow soldiers (2).
    E. We serve with a community of believers (2).
III. **We Serve by Divine Enablement (3).**
    A. We are divinely enabled by our Father.
    B. We are divinely enabled by our Savior.

In 1979, when Charlotte and I (Danny) had been married for one year, the singing group Sister Sledge released a dance hit entitled, "We Are Family." It would eventually go gold, rise to be the number one R&B song on the US charts, and become the theme song for the 1979 World Series Champion Pittsburgh Pirates.

The catchy song boldly asserts the following:

> All of the people around us they say
> Can they be that close
> Just let me state for the record
> We're giving love in a family dose.

"We're giving love in a family dose!" Could that not be—*should* that not be—a style of living that characterizes the family of God? The apostle Paul, in his shortest letter in the New Testament, shows us the answer is yes. In this letter, one we call the epistle to Philemon, we see this ideal lived out in a real-world situation, one that apparently involved betrayal, theft, slavery, God's providence, and gospel reconciliation.

Philemon is a letter Paul wrote while he was a prisoner under house arrest (vv. 1,9), during what is called his first Roman imprisonment (see Acts 28:30-31). The date of the letter would fall somewhere between AD 60 and 63, which is the same time frame during which he wrote Ephesians, Philippians, and Colossians. Some have referred to Philemon and Colossians as "sister epistles," since Philemon apparently lived in Colossae and the two letters probably arrived at the same time.

This brief, twenty-five-verse letter is unique in the writings of Paul. Though addressed to Philemon of Colossae, it is not, strictly speaking, a private letter, as its content reveals. Yet it is occasioned by a personal problem the apostle hopes to resolve. The letter provides an interesting glimpse into the apostle Paul's strategy in handling personal issues as they impact the lives of his converts in the family of God. Philemon is one of the five one-chapter books of the Bible, the other four being Obadiah, 2 and 3 John, and Jude.

The book references a slave (Onesimus) who ran away from his master (Philemon). Onesimus ran to Rome where he providentially came in contact with Paul and was converted (v. 10). Paul then sent Onesimus back to Philemon with this letter, which asks the master to forgive his former slave—now his brother in Christ (v. 16).

This epistle, then, is a family letter and personal appeal by Paul to Philemon asking him to unconditionally forgive and receive back his slave Onesimus without penalty (v. 17). Before, he was a slave, but now he is a beloved brother (v. 16). Before, he was useless, but now he is useful to all (v. 11). Paul is so passionate that they be reconciled that he states he will personally be responsible for any debts Onesimus has incurred (v. 18). We do not know why Onesimus ran away or if he took anything from his master (though it sounds like he did). All we really know about are Onesimus's conversion and Paul's appeal. Since a slave was subject to severe discipline or even death for running away, Paul's appeal is a kind and gracious act on behalf of Onesimus.

Because it deals with a problem arising out of a slavery situation, this letter has figured prominently in the debates surrounding that institution. It has been confidently appealed to by both those who sanctioned slavery and those who advocated its abolition. While it is true that the words of the apostle here cannot be construed to advocate the abolition of slavery, the spirit of the epistle has definitely supported that position. The manner in which Paul treats the problem of Onesimus indicates the way Christianity confronted the evils of human society. To have directly denounced the institution of human slavery would have been problematic. It would have precipitated an immediate conflict between Rome and Christianity. It would have marked Christianity as being antisocial and would have turned all the powers of the empire against it. Instead of making a frontal attack on the institution of slavery, Christianity inculcated a spirit of love, grace, compassion, and consideration that ultimately meant the death knell of that evil institution. That anyone claiming the name of Jesus Christ could advocate slavery of any kind is simply another indictment of our depravity and wickedness.

Philemon is a marvelous example of the use of mitigated exhortation, what we might call "gentle arm twisting"! Indeed, as a type of hortatory discourse, it contains the three salient components of problem, command, and motivation. However, Paul moves the command to the final position of the text. This is borne out by the fact that there is not a single imperative in verses 1-16, but in verse 17-20 three imperatives rapidly follow one another (a fourth is in verse 22). Verse 17, therefore, is the key to the book. There Paul says to Philemon, "Welcome [Onesimus] as you would me." Paul employs psychological and spiritual tact while at the same time not sacrificing his apostolic authority. He also grounds his request in the gospel, as we will see in verses 17-20. In fact, the analogy is too obvious to miss!

Philemon is an insightful guide as to how believers might go about the task of mediating conflicts within the family of God. As an instruction manual in resolving personal difficulties between Christians, this short letter is of great value. As Onesimus returned from his time with Paul, Tychicus probably accompanied him back to Philemon while carrying the letter to the Colossians (cf. Col 4:7-9). The family has an important issue it must deal with. Let's see how Paul gets the conversation stated.

We Serve by Divine Appointment
PHILEMON 1

Christians are new creations in Christ (2 Cor 5:17). Saved by grace through faith in the perfect atoning work of Jesus, we have a new identity. This new identity impacts both our position and our posture. Both are given to us by Christ. All who follow Jesus are his children (position), but we remember that we are saved for service (posture). Our standing is the same: we all are adopted children into one family (Rom 8:16-17; Gal 4:5-7). However, our service is specific and particular, taking different forms. It is by divine appointment and providence. We should as readily embrace it, and we enjoy the former.

Know Who You Are

It is interesting and instructive to see how Paul designates himself in his letters. Nine times he says he is an apostle (Rom 1:1; 1 Cor 1:1; 2 Cor 1:1; Gal 1:1; Eph 1:1; Col 1:1; 1 Tim 1:1; 2 Tim 1:1; Titus 1:1). Three times he calls himself a servant (Rom 1:1; Phil 1:1; Titus 1:1). He was a happy spiritual slave sent with delegated authority by his Master, King Jesus. However, here in Philemon, he does something totally different.

Paul self-identifies as a "prisoner." It is only in Philemon that he begins a letter in this way, though there are other places in his letters where he makes his incarceration known (cf. Phlm 9,10,13,23; Eph 3:1; 4:1; Phil 1:7,13,14; Col 4:18; Garland, *Colossians and Philemon*, 315). Also interesting is whose prisoner he is. He is a prisoner of or "for" (ESV) Christ Jesus. Paul may appear to be a prisoner of Nero (AD 54–68), but he is, in a deeper sense, a prisoner of Messiah, King Jesus (Moo, *The Letters*, 380). Paul is here, under house arrest awaiting trial, by divine appointment and providence. It is no accident. It is not an unfortunate circumstance of life. It is not bad luck. He knows *who* he is and *whose* he is. He is where he is "for the gospel" (Phlm 13). The political powers of the day might deceive themselves into thinking they are in control, but they are not. William Hendriksen says it beautifully:

> All the details of the imprisonment as well as its outcome,
> whether it be the death sentence or acquittal, are in the hands
> that were pierced for this prisoner, those very hands that
> now control the entire universe in the interest of the church
> (Eph 1:22). (*Exposition*, 209)

Know Whom You Please

Paul is a prisoner for "Christ Jesus." He was not a prisoner for just anyone. He was a prisoner for this one, his Messiah Savior. Having been purchased, redeemed by his blood (Rom 3:24-25; Eph 1:7), he knew who his Master was. He knew who his King was.

Life can get terribly complicated and confusing if we lose sight of whom we must strive to please. This is especially true for those in ministry, but it is also true for those in politics, business, and athletics. Divided allegiances can easily entrap us, leading us away from our Savior. Paul's singular devotion reminds us of Jesus's warning about money:

> *"No one can serve two masters, since either he will hate one and love the other, or he will be devoted to one and despise the other. You cannot serve both God and money."* (Matt 6:24)

The same general rule applies to anything that tends to distract our affections away from the Lord Jesus. And added to the spiritual danger, following these competing loves is often accompanied by anxiety, high blood pressure, and ulcers! Therefore, settle in your heart and in your soul, once and for all, that you will live by a simple life principle: "All that truly matters in life is that I please Jesus." The fact is, you cannot please everybody, so stop trying. Do not try to please everybody. Strive to please Somebody! And make sure that Somebody is Jesus (cf. Gal 1:10).

We Serve with Dedicated Partners
PHILEMON 1-2

Paul had a gift for describing the members of the family of God. His descriptions are varied and sometimes colorful. They are also insightful concerning what God does in us through the gospel of Jesus Christ. When our God saves an individual from sin, he does so for a purpose. For some of us, his plan is quite simple. There is nothing all that spectacular or unusual (see, for example, the straightforward narrative of the book of Ruth). For others the assignment God has is more public, visible, and extraordinary. Still others are called to lives of very hard work and even danger. All of this comes at God's choosing, not ours. What we can do, whether in the mundane or the miraculous, is rejoice to know that there are dedicated partners within the family of God; with them we work side by side for the expansion of the gospel across the globe. In verses 1 and 2, Paul gives us a snapshot of some of those partners.

We Serve with Brothers (1)

Paul informs Philemon that Timothy, his son in the faith (cf. 1 Tim 1:2; 2 Tim 1:2), is with him. The inclusion of his name would indicate his support of Paul in the Onesimus affair. Further, it is likely Timothy knows Philemon. Some think Timothy, though not the author of Philemon, may have served as Paul's amanuensis or secretary for the letter. That is possible but not certain.

Paul simply calls Timothy "our brother" (lit. "the brother"). He, through Christ, is part of the family. D. Edmond Hiebert notes,

> The designation of Timothy as "brother" would also remind Philemon of that great brotherhood of all believers into which he himself had been brought at his own conversion. It was this very spirit of brotherhood, engendered by faith in Christ, which Paul confidently expected to work a kindly reception for Onesimus in the heart of Philemon. (*Titus and Philemon*, 89)

We Serve with Fellow Workers (2)

Philemon, whose name means "the loving one" or "affectionate," is the primary recipient of this letter. He appears to have been a resident of the small town of Colossae, based on Colossians 4:9. He was wealthy enough to have slaves and a house in which the church could meet, having come to Christ through the ministry of Paul (Phlm 19).

Paul describes him as a "dear friend and coworker." The words translated "dear friend" are literally "beloved." Philemon was both a much-loved brother in Christ and a fellow laborer for the gospel. Doug Moo points out:

> Paul can use "fellow worker" to denote Christians in general (2 Cor 1:24) but generally applies this designation only to people who have worked closely with him in significant ministry (Rom 16:3,9,21; 1 Cor 3:9; 2 Cor 8:23; Phil 2:25; 4:3; Col 4:11; 1 Thess 3:2; Phlm 24). (*The Letters*, 381)

It is obvious the family of God needs a lot of fellow workers if it is to function and work effectively. We need a lot of Philemons!

We Serve with Sisters (2)

Apphia was probably Philemon's wife. Her name means "endearment." It is easy to think she had been active in serving Jesus alongside her husband. I envision her as a Titus 2 woman mentoring younger women to grow in grace and maturity in the Lord. Interestingly, church tradition says she was stoned to death for her faith in Jesus, along with her husband, during the reign of Nero.

We Serve with Fellow Soldiers (2)

The Bible does not shy away from using military images to describe the Christian life. We are in a war "against the rulers, against the authorities, against the cosmic powers of this darkness, against evil, spiritual forces in the heavens" (Eph 6:12). We must think and live as those in death-and-life warfare for the souls of men and women.

Paul, therefore, refers to Archippus as "our fellow soldier." The only other person Paul calls a "fellow soldier" is Epaphroditus (Phil 2:25). Archippus was a spiritual military man, a Green Beret for the gospel. He also was probably the son of Philemon and Apphia. He is mentioned in Colossians 4:17 where he is challenged, "Pay attention to the ministry you have received in the Lord, so that you can accomplish it." Those who follow King Jesus as commander in chief are called to be soldiers, not civilians. We are warriors for his glory, not spectators sitting on the sidelines of the battlefield.

Church tradition says this valiant warrior for Christ was stabbed to death by a mob during the time of Nero. Like many soldiers of the cross, he apparently died on the battlefield of faith.

We Serve with a Community of Believers (2)

Paul concludes verse 2 by noting "the church that meets in your home." It is interesting to discover that there is no evidence for church buildings of any magnitude until the third century. Apparently, the early church turned the world upside down without elaborate buildings, budgets, and programs. The New Testament provides numerous references to house churches and their hosts:

- Gaius at Rome (Rom 16:23)
- Nympha at Laodicia (Col 4:15)
- Aquila and Priscilla at Ephesus (1 Cor 16:19)
- Philemon at Colossae (Phlm 2)
- Aquila and Priscilla at Rome (Rom 16:3,5)
- Mary at Jerusalem (Acts 12:12)
- Lydia at Philippi (Acts 16:15,40)
- Jason at Thessalonica (Acts 17:5-6)

Tim Keller points out that Christianity spread in the first century through extended household evangelism done informally by Christians. He writes,

The home could be used for systematic teaching and
instruction (Acts 5:42), planned presentations of the Gospel
to friends and neighbors (Acts 10:22), prayer meetings
(Acts 12:12), impromptu evangelistic gatherings (Acts 16:32),
follow-up sessions with inquiries (Acts 18:26), evenings
devoted to instruction and prayer (Acts 20:7), and fellowship
(Acts 21:7). (*Center Church*, 278)

Apparently the early church, like many congregations around the world
today, did just fine with simple, basic essentials—just like a healthy family
today can.

We Serve by Divine Enablement
PHILEMON 3

For those acquainted with the letters of Paul, verse 3 has a familiar ring.
That familiarity can cause us to lose the wonder and miss the impact of
what he writes. Grace, peace, a God who is Father—these were radical
ideas in Paul's day. They are becoming increasingly radical ideas in our
own. The same, sadly, can be said for Jesus as Lord and Christ. First
Corinthians 1:23 says, "We preach Christ crucified, a stumbling block
to the Jews and foolishness to the Gentiles." Things have not changed
much in almost two thousand years. Nevertheless, we faithfully keep on
preaching this message, for it alone is the power of God for salvation
(Rom 1:16).

Verse 3 provides a double blessing from a twin source. Here is the
source of supernatural enablement for the family of God.

We Are Divinely Enabled by Our Father

Grace, God's unmerited and undeserved favor, and peace (Gk *eirēnē*;
Hb *shalom*), God's gift of wholeness and well-being, flow equally from
God who is our Father and Jesus Christ who is our Lord (Phil 2:9-11).
Doug Moo's explanation of these important terms is especially helpful:

Grace and peace both touch on a central gospel truth. While
grace was of course hardly absent from God's dealings with his
old covenant people, it especially marks the extraordinary free
and unmerited gift of his Son that stands at the center of the
gospel (e.g., John 1:16; Rom 3:24; 4:4-5; 5:2; 2 Cor 8:9; Gal 5:4;

Eph 1:6-7). "Peace," on the other hand, has deeper Old Testament roots, used by the prophets as a way of summarizing the universal "well-being" (*shalom*) that God would establish in the last days (see esp. Isa 52:7; 55:12; 66:12; Jer 30:10; 33:6; 46:27; Ezek 34:25; 37:26; Hag 2:9; Zech 9:10). This "peace" has been established by God through the work of his Son (cf. Eph 2:14-17; Col. 1:20), and so it is appropriate that Paul traces the source of both this peace and grace to God our Father and the Lord Jesus Christ. This, too, is the common pattern of Paul's salutations, and it implies that Paul puts Christ on the same level with God the Father. (*The Letters*, 384)

Never forget that our God is a God who has revealed himself as Father. He is a good Father, a great Father, a perfect Father. And because there is only one Father, there is only one family.

We Are Divinely Enabled by Our Savior

I love what is called "the full majestic title" of our Savior! He is the Lord Jesus Christ. That he is "Lord" focuses on his deity and sovereign rule (Matt 28:18-20). His name "Jesus," received at the incarnation, focuses on his humanity. There was a time when Jesus was not, but there never was a time when the Son was not. He is also "Christ." He is the Messiah, the anointed and promised One of the Old Testament.

Interestingly, Paul both begins and ends the book using the full majestic title (Phlm 25). The blessings that are ours in the family of God flow fully and equally from our Father and our Lord. Those whom our God is redeeming and rescuing out of every tribe, tongue, people, and nation have the same Father, serve the same Lord, and are indwelt by the same Spirit. Our triune God truly gives love as it should be in a family.

Conclusion

The church, the body and bride of Christ, is not made up of impressive people. Not really. But it is an impressive family with an impressive Father and Lord. In AD 125, a man named Aristides wrote a letter to the emperor, Hadrian, describing this not-so-impressive ragtag band of brothers and sisters called the church. His words were insightful in the second century. They are instructive in the twenty-first:

But the Christians, O King . . . have found the truth. . . . For
they know and trust in God, the Creator of heaven and of
earth, in whom and from whom are all things, to whom there
is no other god as companion, from whom they received
commandments which they engraved upon their minds and
observe in hope and expectation of the world which is to
come. Wherefore they do not commit adultery nor fornication,
nor bear false witness, nor embezzle what is held in pledge,
nor covet what is not theirs. They honour father and mother,
and show kindness to those near to them; and whenever they
are judges, they judge uprightly. . . . And their oppressors they
comfort and make them their friends; they do good to their
enemies; and their women, O King, are pure as virgins, and
their daughters are modest; and their men keep themselves
from every unlawful union and from all uncleanness, in the
hope of a recompense to come in the other world. Further,
if one or other of them have bondmen and bondwomen or
children, through love towards them they persuade them to
become Christians, and when they have done so, they call
them brethren without distinction. They do not worship
strange gods, and they go their way in all modesty and
cheerfulness. Falsehood is not found among them; and they
love one another, and from widows they do not turn away their
esteem; and they deliver the orphan from him who treats him
harshly. And he, who has, gives to him who has not, without
boasting. And when they see a stranger, they take him in to
their homes and rejoice over him as a very brother; for they
do not call them brethren after the flesh, but brethren after
the spirit and in God. And whenever one of their poor passes
from the world, each one of them according to his ability gives
heed to him and carefully sees to his burial. And if they hear
that one of their number is imprisoned or afflicted on account
of the name of their Messiah, all of them anxiously minister to
his necessity, and if it is possible to redeem him they set him
free. And if there is among them any that is poor and needy,
and if they have no spare food, they fast two or three days in
order to supply to the needy their lack of food. They observe
the precepts of their Messiah with much care, living justly and
soberly as the Lord their God commanded them . . . such, O

King, is the commandment of the law of the Christians, and such is their manner of life. (Aristides, "The Apology")

As it was for them, by God's grace, may it be for us!

Reflect and Discuss

1. How might someone use Philemon to argue that Christianity *endorses* the institution of slavery? How does Paul's letter actually *undermine* the institution of slavery?
2. In what ways can Philemon serve as a manual for addressing interpersonal conflict among Christians?
3. Whom are you tempted to try to please more than Jesus?
4. Who are some of the "fellow workers" with whom you have labored in the gospel?
5. Why is it important to remember that Christians are called to be soldiers for Jesus Christ? How do we fight?
6. Why is it significant that the early church met in homes rather than church buildings? What are some other things about contemporary Western Christianity that, though not wrong, can sometimes be seen as more essential than they really are?
7. Why is it important that God is Father as he gives us his enablement for life and ministry?
8. How do each of the terms used to identify Jesus in these verses contribute to our understanding of his person and work?
9. What most stands out to you about the quote from Aristides? What are some areas in which your church can grow to better fit this description?
10. Why is family imagery often used in the Scriptures to describe Christians? How should this picture affect the way we view and treat one another?

How to Pray for the Family of God

PHILEMON 4-7

Main Idea: Though Christians may experience trials and conflicts with one another, because of their shared faith in Christ, they can lift one another up in prayer and encourage one another with love.

I. **Thank God for the Good Things You Hear (4-5).**
   A. We honor God by our love for one another.
   B. We honor God by our faith in his Son.

II. **Ask God to Help Them Grow in the Knowledge of All We Have in Christ (6).**
   A. We grow as we participate in our common faith.
   B. We grow as we do good things for Christ.

III. **Rejoice in Their Acts of Love that Bless Others (7).**
   A. Be a source of joy.
   B. Be a source of encouragement.
   C. Be a source of refreshment.

In 1 Thessalonians 5:17, the apostle Paul writes simply, "Pray constantly" (ESV, "without ceasing"). This is excellent counsel at any time. It is, however, outstanding counsel when there is a problem in the covenant community that requires wisdom, careful consideration, and godly action.

Paul often begins his letters with a prayer for his recipients. That he does so here is not surprising at all given the issue he is about to address: the return of a runaway slave to his master. Paul's prayer, no doubt, is genuine and authentic as he praises Philemon for his love and faith (v. 4-5). He is grateful for a brother who is a great source of joy, comfort, and refreshment (v. 7). At the same time, what he says is a marvelous example of tact and wisdom as he sets the table for his request on behalf of Onesimus (v. 10). Paul wants to say the *right thing*, but he wants to do so in the *right way*. Beginning with prayer is seldom a foolish or unwise strategy.

Paul's prayer provides a worthy model and pattern for us. We can learn and see the kinds of things we should pray for in the church. Paul rightly begins with God, but he also looks to the life of Philemon and identifies several character traits for which he can praise and thank God. This is the atmosphere and context he wants to establish before confronting the important issue that must be faced.

There is a story (or legend!) about the famous New Testament scholar A. T. Robertson deeply offending a Tennessee mountain man one day in class. Robertson indeed had a reputation for being brutal and rigorous with his students. After class this mountain man, who was a mountain of a man himself, went to Robertson's office and told the great scholar he was there to whip him for embarrassing him in class. Robertson said he understood but had one request before this important event took place: might they pray first before the whipping commenced? His student agreed, and so they got on their knees, and Robertson began to pray . . . and pray . . . and pray! It is said he prayed for an hour! Eventually the anger of his student withered away. Robertson apologized, agreed not to embarrass him again, and spared himself a whipping!

Prayer should always precede important and difficult decisions. Robertson understood this! So did Paul. How, then, did Paul pray for Philemon as the moment of truth for Onesimus neared?

Thank God for the Good Things You Hear
PHILEMON 4-5

In these verses Paul is extremely personal. He addresses God as "my God" in what he calls "my prayers." And he helps us understand what it means to pray without ceasing, at least in part. He "always" thanks God for Philemon each and every time he goes to the Lord in prayer. It was not hard to pray for his "dear friend and coworker" (v. 1) because he was a faithful brother who was a constant blessing to everyone (vv. 5,7). In anticipation of his request for Onesimus, Paul wants Philemon to know that he is aware of all the good things he is doing.

Because of Philemon's "love" for his spiritual family and his "faith" in his Lord (cf. Eph 1:15; Col 1:4), the apostle Paul is *hopeful* for a positive response to the Onesimus affair. Paul is hearing good things, and he is hoping for even better things from this man of God.

We Honor God by Our Love for One Another

Philemon was known as a "lovin' man"! His love was not narrow or
restrictive. It was broad and encompassing. It was for "all the saints."
Philemon's love must have been multifaceted, as Christian love always
is (see 1 Cor 13:4-8). It brought joy, encouragement, refreshment
(Phlm 7), and much more to everyone. Real love flowing from Christ in
us to others always does!

In a simple one-page article entitled, "Love Is . . . ," Allen Rae identifies twenty-four "Practical Manifestations of Love from the Epistle to
Philemon." Asking God to cultivate and manifest these characteristics
within the body of Christ goes a long way in building a healthy spiritual
family. Here is his list:

LOVE IS . . .

1. Respectful—"Timothy, our brother"; "Philemon, our dear
   friend [beloved]" (v. 1).
2. Humble—"Archippus . . . fellow soldier; Mark, Aristarchus,
   Demas, and Luke . . . coworkers" (vv. 2,24).
3. Appreciative—"I always thank my God" (v. 4a).
4. Constant—"I mention you [always] in my prayers" (v. 4b).
5. Responsive—"I hear of your love for all the saints and the faith
   toward the Lord Jesus" (v. 5).
6. Benevolent—"Knowing every good thing that is in us" (v. 6b).
7. Fulfilling—"I have great joy and encouragement from your
   love" (v. 7a).
8. Reciprocal—"The hearts of the saints have been refreshed
   through you, brother" (v. 7b).
9. Gentle—"I have great boldness in Christ . . . I appeal to you,
   instead, on the basis of love" (vv. 8-9).
10. Exhortive—"[I] appeal to you for my son, Onesimus" (v. 10a).
11. Evangelistic—"I became his father while I was in chains"
    (v. 10b).
12. Perceptive—"He was useless to you, but now he is useful both to
    you and to me" (v. 11).
13. Tender—"I am sending him back to you—I am sending my very
    own heart" (v. 12).
14. Honest—"I wanted to keep him with me" (v. 13).
15. Righteous—"I didn't want to do anything without your con-
    sent" (v. 14).

16. Tactful—"For perhaps . . . he was separated from you for a brief time" (v. 15a).
17. Hopeful—"That you might get him back permanently . . . as a dearly loved brother" (vv. 15b-16b).
18. Gracious—"If you consider me a partner, welcome him as you would me" (v. 17).
19. Generous—"If he has wronged you, or owes you anything, charge that to my account" (v. 18).
20. Humorous—"I will repay it—not to mention you owe me even your very self" (v. 19).
21. Uplifting—"I am confident of your obedience" (v. 21a).
22. Expectant—"Knowing that you will do even more than I say" (v. 21b).
23. Hospitable—"Prepare a guest room" (v. 22a).
24. Supportive—"Since I hope that through your prayers I will be restored to you" (v. 22b). (Rae, "Love Is," 21; slightly adapted)

We Honor God by Our Faith in His Son

Paul uses the present tense when he says he hears of Philemon's "love for all the saints" and his "faith . . . in the Lord Jesus" (v. 5). He continually hears these good reports (Moo, *The Letters*, 387). Philemon loved his brothers and sisters in Christ. I have no doubt such love was grounded in and flowed from the faith he had in the Lord Jesus. The gospel of the Lord Jesus received by faith in Christ's perfect atoning work cannot help but work itself out in tangible acts of love toward others. God-given faith is active, dynamic; it does things! David Garland is right on target when he says,

> Faith in Christ is the impetus for love for others, and together they make one a Christian. Missing either faith in Christ or love for others renders any claim to be Christian a deadly lie (see 1 John 3:10). Paul notes that Philemon's love is directed to all the saints. He does not discriminate, which suggests that he would not exclude from his love slaves who are in Christ. (*Colossians and Philemon*, 319)

We should work hard at giving authentic praise to our brothers and sisters for the good things we see God doing in their lives. It will bless and encourage them—something we all need. It will also inspire and motivate them to keep on keeping on.

Ask God to Help Them Grow in the Knowledge of All We Have in Christ
PHILEMON 6

I think we all must admit that the prayers we too often hear in our churches do not sound a whole lot like the prayers we read in the Bible. It is not that our prayers are bad or wrong, but they may lack the substance we see in Scripture. Paul has thanked God for the way Philemon loves his brothers and sisters. He has praised God for the faith Philemon has in the Lord Jesus. Now he asks God to give him something more, something the ESV calls "full knowledge" (Gk *epignosis*). Though the specifics of the verse are a bit tricky (Moo says, "This verse is universally recognized as the most difficult in Philemon"; *The Letters*, 389), the general thrust is clear, and the practical wisdom we find is extremely helpful.

We Grow as We Participate in Our Common Faith

Paul moves from the thanksgiving component of prayer in verse 5 to the intercessory component in verse 6. Actually, the words "I pray" are not in verse 6 in the Greek text, "but [are] supplied from verse 4 to show that this verse is dependent on verse 4, not verse 5" (Garland, *Colossians and Philemon*, 319). His prayer is that Philemon's "participation [ESV, "sharing"; NASB, "fellowship"] in the faith may become effective through knowing [ESV, "for the full knowledge of"] every good thing that is in us."

I think Paul's point is something like this: as those who share fellowship (*koinonia*), common life in the blessings of the gospel, we should pray that our faith will be effective in this context. It will actually work and produce the fruit ("every good thing") that is the natural result and outgrowth of the gospel lived out in community. Moo puts it well: "When people believe in Christ, they become identified with one another in an intimate association and incur both the benefits and responsibilities of that communion" (*The Letters*, 392).

The Onesimus affair is going to stretch Philemon—there is no doubt about it. This is going to be an uncomfortable situation for him and his church family. This is unchartered territory for this small congregation, and Paul prays that their common bond and the knowledge of all they have in Christ will be their guide. He prays that their shared life in the gospel will be that which energizes the manner in which they handle this issue—that their common faith will be the fuel that guides the heart and enlightens the mind of this spiritual family as they conduct God's business.

We Grow as We Do Good Things for Christ

Knowledge without action is useless. It might be harmful. "Faith without works," James tells us, "is dead" (Jas 2:26). To truly "know" in the biblical sense "is both to possess and to perform" (Lightfoot, *St. Paul's Epistle*, 336); it is to understand and act. Paul wants Philemon to act on his knowledge of our common life in Christ and do something, that which he calls "every good thing." Of course, every good thing is about to become a specific good thing for Philemon! If Philemon is committed to every good thing, and Paul is confident he is, he will respond well to Onesimus "for the glory of Christ."

Moo paraphrases well the gist of Paul's argument:

> Philemon, I am praying that the mutual participation that arises from your faith in Christ might become effective in leading you to understand and put into practice all the good that God wills for us and that is found in our community, and do all this for the sake of Christ. (*The Letters*, 394)

Richard Melick spells out clearly what is on Paul's heart and what is at stake with the request that will soon come in verse 10:

> Paul prayed that Philemon would use this knowledge to work out the implications of his faith in the matter with Onesimus. The "good thing" he knew to do was to forgive an erring and repentant brother who sinned before his salvation. Such a reconciliation would have far-reaching implications in the whole church. It watched this test case with great interest. If Christianity could work in such tension-filled relationships, it could work anywhere. Paul, Philemon, Onesimus, the church, and all of Christianity had much at stake in Philemon's response. Paul prayed that Philemon would make the correct choice. (*Philippians, Colossians, Philemon*, 355)

Rejoice in Their Acts of Love that Bless Others
PHILEMON 7

Church life is not about entertaining others; it is about serving others. Entertainment is usually about the host. Hospitality, on the other hand, is always about the guest. Entertainment is easily seduced by the shallow and superficial. It is only surface deep. Hospitality, rooted in our

common fellowship in Christ, has authenticity and depth and significance that are truly meaningful and long-lasting.

This mindset was evident in the life of Philemon. Paul had heard
about it, and the church at Colossae had seen it on full display. This
servant mindset would soon be tested; but because of what Paul already
knew (the blessing that Philemon was to others), he was confident it
would be extended to Onesimus as well.

Three things are highlighted in Paul's prayer concerning how
Philemon was a blessing to others. How wonderful it would be if the
same things were said about each of us.

Be a Source of Joy

Paul tells Philemon he has "great (ESV, "much") joy" from his love. The
word "for" ties verse 7 back to verse 4, where the theme of love was introduced. Paul's great joy derives from Philemon's love for "all the saints"
(v. 5). This joy overflows.

Paul hopes to be encouraged by this brother again by the way he
receives and treats another brother, one he describes as nothing less
than "dearly loved" (v. 16). Philemon has brought joy to Paul in the past
and in the present. Is future joy just around the corner?

Be a Source of Encouragement

Paul's great joy in Philemon is accompanied by great encouragement
(ESV, "comfort"). D. Edmond Hiebert says,

> The news of Philemon's love had animated the apostle. . . . It
> had sent a beam of happiness into his dreary imprisonment
> and had given him encouragement in his bondage." (*Titus and
> Philemon*, 88)

In a time of his life when he could easily have given in to disappointment, discouragement, and even depression, Paul's spirits were lifted
and his heart was allowed to sing with joy because of this godly servant.

Be a Source of Refreshment

Paul concludes this short but important prayer by telling his dear friend
Philemon he has refreshed the hearts of the saints, the holy and set
apart ones who follow Christ. Two words are important for our reflection: "hearts" and "refreshed."

Paul uses the word "heart" eight times in his letters, with three of those occurrences appearing in this short letter (vv. 7,12,20). The Bible often uses the word *heart* to describe not the physical organ beating in your chest but the real you, who you are on the inside. Here it has that meaning, addressing the "seat of the emotions," the "total personality at the deepest level" (Moo, *The Letters*, 397). All of a person's behavior, emotions, feelings, and speech—everything you really are—flows from the heart.

Sometimes I will say, "I love my wife Charlotte with all my heart!" I mean that I love her with all that I am. That captures something of what Paul meant. Philemon had refreshed the totality of the saints.

"Refreshed" is an interesting word and one that Paul strategically uses two times in this letter (vv. 7,20). It is a verb in the perfect tense, indicating that the hearts of the saints have been and are still being refreshed (Harris, *Colossians and Philemon*, 219). John MacArthur says "refreshed" is "a military term that speaks of an army resting from a march. Philemon brought troubled people rest and renewal; he was a peacemaker" (*Colossians and Philemon*, 215). Philemon's servant heart had served the hearts of others and encouraged them. His influence and ministry went deep and made an impact.

Paul ends the prayer by again using the word "brother" (cf. vv. 1,7,16,20), perhaps as a point of emphasis. In all matters Philemon had again and again shown himself to be a true brother. His past performance had been stellar. However, his greatest test is about to unfold. The Lord had been preparing him, as he does us, for that moment.

Conclusion

The International Justice Ministry (IJM) is a wonderful organization that seeks to help the hurting and disenfranchised around the world. They are particularly active in confronting the evil world of the sex slave trade.[1] Concerning their vital work, the ministry says, "The first work of justice is the work of prayer." Isn't that amazing? Among the many good things they do, that which they deem to be the most important is the work of prayer. I suspect they got this from the Bible and learned it in the fiery furnace of experience.

---

[1] Their website is www.ijm.org.

Prayerlessness gives evidence of our belief in our own self-sufficiency. Prayer gives evidence of our need of divine dependency. Courageous humility will flow from a life of communion with our heavenly Father as we hear his heart and then do his work. This is the example of Jesus. This is the example of Paul. I say, under much conviction, these are footprints we should, we must, seek to follow.

I once heard Adrian Rogers, a wonderful pastor now in heaven, say, "God gave you his unlisted phone number and invites you to get in touch with him anytime." What a wonderful truth to know. What a wonderful truth to put into practice.

Reflect and Discuss

1. Why is prayer the appropriate starting point for any major decision or conversation? What role has prayer played in your decision making and reconciliation efforts?
2. What does Paul's prayer teach us about what it means to pray without ceasing?
3. What is the connection between love for the church and faith in Christ? Do these two always go together?
4. What characteristics of love (as seen in Paul's letter to Philemon) are most difficult for you to show?
5. Why do you think the prayers in our churches lack much of the substance that marked Paul's prayers for his brothers and sisters?
6. What are some of the benefits we gain in communion with the body of Christ? What are some of the responsibilities?
7. How does the fact that you share a common faith with other Christians affect the way you approach conflict and other awkward situations?
8. How is Philemon 6 connected to James 2? What do both passages tell us about how faith leads to action?
9. How can we bring joy, encouragement, and refreshment to our brothers and sisters in Christ?
10. What ministry has God called you to, and how can you follow Paul's example by leading out in prayer?

How to Resolve Conflicts in the Family of God

PHILEMON 8-16

Main Idea: Not only can the power of the gospel change our broken relationships with God; it can also change and heal our broken relationships with one another.

I. **Remember the Gospel Principle of Humility (8-9).**
   A. Do not pull rank (8).
   B. Do not neglect love (9).
II. **Remember the Gospel Principle of Sensitivity (10-11).**
   A. Make a hopeful appeal (10).
   B. Make an honest appeal (11).
III. **Remember the Gospel Principle of Integrity (12-13).**
   A. Share your heart (12).
   B. State the facts (13).
IV. **Remember the Gospel Principle of Accountability (14).**
   A. Know who is responsible.
   B. Know what is right.
V. **Remember the Gospel Principle of Sovereignty (15-16).**
   A. God's goals are eternal, not temporal (15).
   B. God's goals are spiritual, not carnal (16).

In ministry, and in life for that matter, few things are more important, more valuable, than knowing how to say the right thing. I will often remind my students that we need to learn how to say the right *thing*, in the right *way*, at the right *time*, and to the right *person*. Each component is essential, and the absence of any can often cause disappointment and failure.

The Bible underscores the importance of this issue and repeatedly addresses it. Just note a few examples:

- Proverbs 10:32: "The lips of the righteous know what is appropriate, but the mouth of the wicked, only what is perverse."
- Proverbs 12:18: "There is one who speaks rashly, like a piercing sword; but the tongue of the wise brings healing."

- Proverbs 15:1: "A gentle answer turns away anger, but a harsh word stirs up wrath."
- Proverbs 15:23: "A person takes joy in giving an answer; and a timely word—how good that is!"
- Proverbs 15:29: "The Lord is far from the wicked, but he hears the prayer of the righteous."
- Proverbs 16:21: "Anyone with a wise heart is called discerning, and pleasant speech increases learning."
- Proverbs 16:24: "Pleasant words are a honeycomb: sweet to the taste and health to the body."
- Proverbs 25:11: "A word spoken at the right time is like gold apples in silver settings."

We have come to the moment of truth in the Philemon and Onesimus affair. After setting things up as best he can, Paul is prepared to ask this slave owner to forgive his runaway slave and receive him back, "no longer as a slave, but more than a slave—as a dearly loved brother" (Phlm 16). Paul is a model of tact as he makes his appeal. He is also convinced that the power of the gospel is real and that it works. Not only can it change our broken relationships with God; it can also change and heal our broken relationships with one another.

A delicate situation needs to be handled in a delicate manner. What we see in Philemon 8-16 are some of the wisest principles we can employ when attempting to reconcile estranged parties. There is even wisdom here for sharing the gospel and doing missions. They are especially helpful in showing us how to address the wounded party and also the one in the position of power and authority—the one in the position of advantage. My friend Rick Warren says, "The purpose of influence is to speak up for those who have no influence" ("How to Be a Good Steward"). Here we see Paul go to work and do that very thing.

Remember the Gospel Principle of Humility
PHILEMON 8-9

It is never right to be rude. It is never right for those who follow Jesus to be arrogant, abrasive, or uncouth. To be called "obnoxious for Jesus" is not a badge of honor, even if you may be in the right. Our evangelism would be more effective if we would remember this. So would our marriages and family life. Paul will now make his appeal to Philemon on behalf of Onesimus. His use of tact is amazing, and not surprisingly, he begins with a spirit of humility. A good definition of *tact* may go something like this: it is a skill that, without any sacrifice of honesty or truth, enables a person to say the right word at the right time in the right way and to do the right thing in the right way in any given situation. Now this is a skill we should all greatly desire! It is a skill beautifully put on display by Paul. As Paul begins his humble appeal, he makes sure to avoid two things: he does not pull rank, and he does not neglect to express his love.

Do Not Pull Rank (8)

Paul now moves into the body of his letter and his main point, signaled by the phrase, "For this reason" (ESV, "Accordingly"; NASB, "Therefore"). Looking back to Philemon's "love for all the saints" (v. 5), Paul will ground his appeal in love (v. 9). Further, he will not take advantage of his position as an apostle and pull rank. He does have "great boldness in Christ" and could "command [Philemon] to do what is right," but that would be coercive, and coerced love is a contradiction.

Paul wants Philemon to do the right thing for the right reason. He is concerned about what motivates his decision, his heart. He is also concerned about how all this will affect the covenant community. Moo provides helpful insight at this point:

> The contrast is between Paul's apostolic authority and what we might call the "moral" authority arising from the *koinōnia* that exists between Paul and Philemon (v. 6). Our relationships to one another in Christ create expectations and impose obligations that cannot be ignored and that often go far beyond what any "law" might impose. Love is foundational to Christian ethics (e.g., Rom. 13:8-10; Gal. 5:13-15) and makes Christian ethics something that is open-ended, incalculable (as Jesus' Parable of the Good Samaritan illustrates). (*The Letters*, 401)

So Paul will appeal instead of command. He will plead and not demand. His approach is both gracious and humble.

Do Not Neglect Love (9)

Love is indeed foundational to Christian ethics. It dictates how we treat one another. So Paul is clear in his request: "I appeal to you . . . on the basis of love." Interestingly, "Philemon's name meant 'the loving one.' Paul was asking him to live up to his name and show the same loving attitude toward Onesimus that he had shown in the past to others" (Hawkins, *Tearing Down Walls*, 80).

Paul figuratively walks up to Philemon, gives him a big hug, and puts his arm around him. The love they share with each other because of Christ is the basis on which he will encourage Philemon to do the right thing.

Paul then twists the arm of Philemon a bit! And though it is the first time, it will not be the last. He reminds him that he (Paul) is an old man ("an elderly man") and "a prisoner of Christ Jesus." This puts additional pressure on Philemon. Paul is trying to make an emotional connection and impact. This is not intended to be manipulative, but it is certainly intended to be effective. Paul is twice helpless! He needs Philemon to show him some love. He also needs Philemon to show someone else some love.

Remember the Gospel Principle of Sensitivity
PHILEMON 10-11

The gospel gives us a completely new status before God. Once alienated from his love, dead spiritually, and a slave to sin, I am now his child, spiritually alive, and no longer in bondage. The gospel radically changes us on the *inside*. This has to do with how I look to God. However, the gospel also changes us on the *outside*. This has to do with how we look to others.

The gospel, then, changes us inwardly and outwardly. Paul had seen this transformation in Onesimus, but now he wants Philemon to hear about it and to see it. He is almost certain that the sound of Onesimus's name will strike a negative chord in Philemon's heart. Emotions will likely flood over him, and they will not be positive. Paul, therefore, moves with great care and sensitivity. Just because he believes Onesimus has changed does not mean Philemon will believe it. For the first and only time in the book, the name of Onesimus will appear. And in the Greek text it is placed as the final word in verse 10. This was a wise and rhetorically effective strategy. It was a sensitive move to ease the impact of Philemon hearing his name. What does Paul do to ensure a positive, gospel-centered response?

Make a Hopeful Appeal (10)

For the second time in two verses, Paul uses the word "appeal" (Gk *parakalo*). And the one for whom he is making his plea is his spiritual son whom he brought to Christ (fathered) while imprisoned. Paul saw God's hand all over this, of that I am certain. His hope is that Philemon will see it too!

Up to this point Paul has not specifically identified the one for whom he is speaking. Now the bomb is dropped: it is Philemon's runaway slave Onesimus! I've often wondered if it was only at this point in Philemon's reading of the letter that Onesimus stepped forward to make his presence known. No doubt things would have been tense. Yet by his return Onesimus indicates he is as hopeful for reconciliation as Paul. He had by divine providence (see v. 15) met Paul and been saved. He is not the same man who ran away. He hoped Philemon believed this. Paul certainly did, as seen by the next verse.

Make an Honest Appeal (11)

Paul uses a play on words related to Onesimus's name, which means "useful." With complete honesty, remaining sensitive to the volatility of the situation, Paul says plainly that BC (before Christ) Onesimus was "useless" to Philemon. He was *achrēstos*. However, the gospel has transformed him; he is now a new creation in Christ (2 Cor 5:17). He is now "useful" (Gk *euchrēstos*). From useless to useful, from unprofitable to profitable, this man is now helpful and valuable to Philemon but also to Paul!

Some see Paul setting the stage to ask Philemon to return Onesimus to him (see also v. 13). This is certainly possible. As William Hendriksen says, "The apostle obviously has planned this statement with great care" (*Exposition*, 217). Whatever the case, we see Paul providing a helpful model for seeking to restore broken relationships. He makes his appeal on the basis of a new family relationship. He makes his appeal on the basis of the transformation brought about by new life in Christ through the gospel. God has done a work in Onesimus. Certainly Philemon can give thanks for that. Hopefully that will help him in his reunion with Onesimus. Here is the beauty of the gospel doing its work.

Remember the Gospel Principle of Integrity
PHILEMON 12-13

Many times, too many times to be honest, people deceive themselves in thinking, *The end justifies the means.* If things end well, it doesn't matter how we get there. This is especially tragic when done by those who call themselves Christians. Scripture is clear that God is concerned with both the means and the end. We must be committed to doing the right thing in the right way for the right reasons.

There is no question that Paul believed this. He knew how he hoped the Onesimus affair would end. However, he was committed to absolute integrity in how he handled the situation. As a leader in the new covenant community, he was determined to be "above reproach" (1 Tim 3:2). How desperate we are for Christian leaders like this in our day!

Share Your Heart (12)

Paul is simple and straightforward: "I am sending him back to you—I am sending my very own heart." Paul's words are filled with emotions and feelings. Sending Onesimus was not an easy decision for the apostle to make. It hurt!

That Paul was sending him back, though, in no way implies that Onesimus was unwilling to return. When he left Paul, he could have chosen to run away again. Instead, he trusted Paul, a man willing to expose his own heart and lay bare his soul. Wendell Grout says, "Paul was making an appeal for Onesimus, but he was basing that request on love, not apostolic muscle" (*Colossians and Philemon*, 156).

It is not always easy to expose our hearts and make ourselves vulnerable. It can be frightening, even threatening, because if we are honest, there is a risk! However, God will use it when done as an act of integrity and not manipulation. Our homes and our churches, in particular, would be so much healthier if we would follow Paul's example. When you are faced with the choice between protecting yourself from potential hurt or seeking gospel reconciliation, run the risk! It is well worth it.

State the Facts (13)

Paul's honesty is once more a model for all of us. He straightforwardly says to Philemon, "I wanted to keep him with me." Why? Making the only explicit reference to the gospel in this letter, Paul explains: "That in my imprisonment for the gospel he might serve me in your place."

The one who is now useful because of the gospel could be useful to Paul, as he suffers for the gospel. He could serve as Philemon's substitute, and Paul could certainly use him.

Paul wants to keep him because he sees him as a son. He wants to keep him because he needs help. He wants to keep him to advance the gospel and the mission of the church. These clearly are the facts. Paul is self-interested, but he is not selfish. Paul has sacrificed. He is imprisoned, and he has sent away a valuable helper. He hated doing it, but he believed it was the right thing to do. These are the facts. Now what?

Remember the Gospel Principle of Accountability
PHILEMON 14

All of this has been well said:

> The wrong action at the wrong time leads to disaster.
> The right action at the wrong time brings resistance.
> The wrong action at the right time is a mistake.
> The right action at the right time results in success.

Truth and timing are twin essentials in resolving conflict. In the case of Onesimus, Paul knew who was ultimately responsible at this point (Philemon) as well as what the right thing to do was (set Onesimus free and send him back). So he puts the ball in Philemon's court. Just as Paul is trying to do the right thing in the right way, Philemon needs to have the opportunity to do the same. Note how Paul reveals this twofold challenge.

Know Who Is Responsible

Paul knew that ultimately Philemon had to make the call. This was true legally as well as spiritually. Paul's admission that he "didn't want to do anything without [Philemon's] consent" again reveals Paul's heart. Paul will neither presume on their friendship, nor will he usurp Philemon's rightful authority in the world in which they lived. He knew Philemon and Onesimus needed to have a face-to-face meeting. Philemon still owned Onesimus. In the evil world that allowed for slavery, there was an owner and a slave who was his legal (though not rightful) property.

Whenever we seek to resolve conflicts, we must identify where the responsibility lies. Further, those who are responsible must take responsibility. We may need to lead them to that place, but they must go there.

Know What Is Right

The goal of this reconciliation is to do the right thing out of proper motivation. God is just as concerned, if not more so, with the *heart* as with the *act*. Thus Paul says to Philemon, I want "your good deed" to be done not "out of obligation, but of your own free will." Paul will not demand or force Philemon to do the right thing. He wishes to shepherd his heart in this difficult and trying situation. He wants his "participation in the faith [to] become effective" (v. 6). He wants God to do a work in Onesimus, Philemon, and the fledgling community meeting in Philemon's home. An obedient but unwilling Philemon will only lead to contempt and bitterness. But doing the right thing because he wants to will truly glorify God and be good for the community as they watch the gospel put on full display for all to see.

Remember the Gospel Principle of Sovereignty
PHILEMON 15-16

Theologically, *sovereignty* means "God's lordship extends over all that exists." Nothing is beyond his authority, power, and rule. Providence is an aspect of his sovereignty; it is the outworking of all his decrees. As my pastor and missionary friend Jim Wilson says,

> It is the hand of God molding all events and directing the
> progress of all things to suit his purpose. It is God controlling
> all circumstances to bring about what He wants to be brought
> about. It is the opposite of chance. Nothing sneaks up on God,
> He is in control of everything that happens in the universe.
> ("What God Can Do")

Nothing sneaks up on God. Nothing is left to chance. There are no accidents or coincidences with God. Paul certainly embraced such a theology. There was no "process theology" for Paul. "Open theism" would not do for this apostle. We see this clearly as Paul closes out this portion of his argument. The words are simple, but the theology is strong. Just as the Allstate Insurance Company tries to reassure customers with the slogan, "You're in good hands with Allstate," Paul knows that he is in the great hands of the Lord who is sovereign over all (ibid.).

God's Goals Are Eternal, Not Temporal (15)

Paul is humble ("perhaps this is why") and admits we cannot know the divine mind and plan except that which he has chosen to reveal to us. John MacArthur says,

> He says **perhaps** because no man can see the secret providence of God at work. But it is surely reasonable to assume that God had this in mind when Onesimus left. Paul suggests to Philemon that God was using the evil to produce good (Gen 50:20; Rom 8:28). God triumphs over sin through His providential power and grace. He takes the myriad contingencies of human actions and uses them to accomplish His own purposes. (*Colossians and Philemon*, 223)

So Philemon lost him temporarily, but now he is getting him back forever ("permanently"). He lost him as a slave, but now he gets him back "as a dearly loved brother."

Paul challenges Philemon to see the big picture. He wants him to understand the big story, not simply the little one. I like Moo's insight on this verse when he writes,

> Paul's suggestion about the divine intention behind Onesimus' separation from Philemon (vv. 15-16) might be a kind of "commentary" on the events he has narrated in vv. 8-14. (*The Letters*, 418)

Only by seeing God's purpose in all of this does the flight of Onesimus make sense. It is good that they are back together now. It is so much better that they will be together forever—not as master and slave but as brothers!

God's Goals Are Spiritual, Not Carnal (16)

C. S. Lewis says,

> There are no ordinary people. You have never talked to a mere mortal. Nations, cultures, arts, civilizations—these are mortal, and their life is to ours as the life of a gnat. It is immortals whom we joke with, work with, marry, snub, and exploit. (*The Weight of Glory*, 46)

Likewise, Martin Luther King Jr. says,

The founding fathers were really influenced by the Bible. The whole concept of the *imago Dei* . . . is the idea that all men have something within them that God injected. Not that they have substantial unity with God, but that every man has a capacity to have fellowship with God. And this gives him uniqueness. . . . There are no gradations in the image of God. *Every man from a treble white to a bass black is significant on God's keyboard,* precisely *because every man is made in the image of God.* One day we will learn that. We will know one day that God made us to live together as brothers and to respect the dignity and worth of every man. This is why we must fight segregation with all of our non-violent might. ("The American Dream"; emphasis added)

Paul, I believe, would agree with both of these men. The Roman Empire saw Onesimus as a slave. It saw only with the eyes of the flesh. Paul, in stark contrast, saw Onesimus as "a dearly loved brother." He was now part of a special family—God's family. For Paul this was "especially" precious because he saw Onesimus as not only a brother but as his spiritual son (v. 10). Now for Philemon, this new spiritual status of Onesimus should be "much more" special. He is getting Onesimus back on both an earthly and a spiritual plane. Yes, he is returning as your slave. But even better than that, you are getting him back as a brother!

Now Philemon can see the providence of God in all of this. What the evil one meant for evil, God had worked for good—the greatest good of all—Onesimus's salvation. Philemon had to see this. He had to rejoice in this. Only the eyes of faith, a faith in One crucified like a slave himself, could enable Philemon to see things as they truly were.

Conclusion

Paul, through the power of Christ and the gospel, had learned the value of saying the right thing, in the right way, at the right time, and to the right person. I think he understood well what an anonymous author penned:

A careless word may kindle strife;
A cruel word may wreck a life.
A bitter word may smite and kill;
A brutal word may do more still.

A gracious word may smooth the way;
A joyous word may brighten the day.
A timely word may lessen stress;
A loving word may heal and bless.

Paul was determined to do all he could to bless Philemon, Onesimus, and the church that met in their home. He believed the God who had reconciled sinners to himself through His Son, the Lord Jesus, could also reconcile a master and a slave who had become brothers! This is the beauty and power of the gospel at work in people's lives. It is a glorious thing to put on display for a watching world to see.

Reflect and Discuss

1. Discuss the importance of saying "the right thing, in the right way, at the right time, and to the right person." Which is most difficult for you to practice?
2. Why are those in authority tempted simply to pull rank in times of conflict? How does Jesus show us a better way?
3. Why is love the commanding ethic for the Christian? What other passages reinforce the love Paul asks for from Philemon (v. 9)?
4. Consider the gospel changing us on the inside and changing us on the outside. How are they connected? How are they similar? How are they different?
5. An honest appeal seems like obvious counsel, but how does Paul's example differ from ways we often pursue reconciliation? How can our tactics undermine the power of the gospel?
6. Why is the saying "the ends justify the means" not always true? What passages of Scripture show this philosophy to be false?
7. What does it mean for someone to be above reproach? Why is this character quality especially necessary for leaders?
8. Can you think of a time when you had to choose between protecting yourself from potential hurt and seeking gospel reconciliation? If so, which did you choose? How did it end?
9. Why is obedience from an unwilling heart an insufficient goal for reconciliation? What effects does this have on a community?
10. Why is radical reconciliation in the Christian community so foreign to the world? How is it different from worldly attempts at reconciliation?

How the Gospel Works in Real Life

PHILEMON 17-25

Main Idea: As followers of Jesus, we must bring the gospel to bear on every aspect of life and anticipate its transforming power in the lives of other believers.

I. **Practice the Basics of the Gospel (17-20).**
   A. Remember the principle of substitution (17).
   B. Remember the principle of satisfaction (18-19).
   C. Remember the principle of reconciliation (20).
II. **Express Your Confidence in the Gospel's Work in Others (21-22).**
   A. Express your confidence in their obedience and more (21).
   B. Express your confidence in their affection and prayers (22).
III. **Covenant with Gospel Witnesses You Trust (23-25).**
   A. Call on faithful human witnesses (23-24).
   B. Call for divine enablement (25).

The apostle Paul was a gospel-saturated man. Students of Paul's life and ministry would no doubt agree, but it might seem strange to make such a statement when studying a letter where the word "gospel" appears only once in the entire book (v. 13)! Some have even said if Philemon were not in the Bible, our loss would be minimal, especially in terms of theology. I was once guilty of such a position, and I was wrong. The fact is the gospel of King Jesus oozes out of this letter for those with ears to hear and eyes to see.

W. A. Criswell, who pastored First Baptist Church Dallas for many years and was widely regarded as a powerful preacher, saw this clearly. He saw that what Paul pledged to do for Onesimus mirrors beautifully what Jesus has done for us. In a 1959 sermon entitled "For Love's Sake," he brought his message to a close with these words:

> [Onesimus] must repay what he owes, but how? He doesn't
> have anything to pay with; he's a slave. He has nothing. And,
> restitution has to be made, and how? Onesimus holds in his
> hand the letter: "Accept him as you would me. And if he has
> wronged you in any way, or owes you anything, charge that to

my account. I, Paul, write this with my own hand: I will repay it." Does that remind you of anything else? Does that remind you of you? Does it?

Does that remind you of our Lord, our Savior, standing before God? We owe to God how many instances where we've fallen short. Our debt to God; and the Lord seeks payment, and we have nothing wherewithal to pay. How would you remunerate God? How would you repay God what you owe the Lord? How would you do it? Fallen short, fallen short, in a thousand ways, in a thousand days, how would you repay? How would you pay?

"Lord, I have nothing with which to pay. My righteousness is as filthy rags [Isa 64:6]. All of the goodness of my life is as a stained garment. I have nothing wherewithal to pay my debt to God, what I owe the Lord." And our Lord says, "If he hath wronged thee, or oweth thee aught, put that on Mine account; I will pay it." And when we stand before the Lord, and the Lord would mete out to us the penalty of our sins—what is that? "The wages of sin is death [Rom 6:23] . . . And the soul that sins shall die" [Ezek 18:20]. And we stand before the Lord, and the Lord looks into your face, and asks you, "Are you guilty? Have you ever sinned?"

"Guilty."

"Did you do this wrong?"

"Guilty."

"Do you owe this debt?"

"Guilty." And we stand in the presence of Him who searches the soul and who knows the heart. "Lord, You know I am guilty." Like the cry of Job, "I have sinned; what shall I do unto Thee, O thou preserver of men?" [Job 7:20] Guilty; and the penalty is death. "And the wages of sin is death." And our great Savior says, "If he hath wronged thee, or oweth thee aught, put that on Mine account; I will pay it." And that death of our Lord was a substitutionary death; it was for you, it was for us. He died in our stead. He took our place. He paid our debt. He paid the debt, He washed us in His own blood, and He died in our stead, and we have life, and freedom, and glory, and forgiveness all because He paid it all. "If he hath wronged thee, or oweth thee aught, put that on mine account; I Paul have written it with mine own hand, I will repay it." And that's the gospel message that we preach. (Criswell, "For Love's Sake")

In the final verses of Philemon, we indeed see the gospel working in real life. Both by analogy and by application to life, we see Paul mirror the gospel and apply the gospel. There is no allegory in what follows. We simply honor, as we always should, a historical-grammatical-theological hermeneutic that rightly exalts Christ in all of Scripture. Three marvelous principles emerge to guide our study.

Practice the Basics of the Gospel
PHILEMON 17-20

All of us who live under the lordship of King Jesus must never forget who we once were. All of us were once like Onesimus, runaway slaves (sinners) from our rightful owner (God). But someone stepped in on our behalf, pled our cases, and even offered to pay our debts. Paul never forgot this, and so he puts the basic principles of the gospel into practice in the Onesimus-Philemon issue—principles of substitution, satisfaction, and reconciliation.

Paul's argument is a masterpiece. Until this point in the letter, there has not been a single imperative. Now he peppers the letter with three in rapid-fire succession: "welcome" (v. 17), "charge" (v. 18), and "refresh" (v. 20). A fourth imperative appears in verse 22 ("prepare"). The rhetorical strategy is stellar and intended for maximum impact. After setting up his plea with encouragement and thanksgiving, "Paul comes out in the open and makes a direct request of Philemon" (Moo, *The Letters*, 425).

Remember the Principle of Substitution (17)

Paul begins with the conditional clause, "So if you consider me a partner," (Gk *koinōnos*)—a condition Philemon is sure to accept—to set up his first request: "welcome him as you would me." Paul's words are astonishing, even breathtaking. To paraphrase, "Give to your slave Onesimus the same acceptance and welcome you would give to me. When you see him, see me! The same reaction you would have if I had knocked at your door, I want you to give to this slave, one who is now 'a dearly loved brother'" (v. 16).

Warren Wiersbe, for many years a faithful pastor at The Moody Church in Chicago, sees what is going down in this request:

> This is to me an illustration of what Jesus Christ has done for us as believers. God's people are so identified with Jesus Christ that God receives them as He receives His Son! We are "accepted in the Beloved" (Eph. 1:6) and clothed in His righteousness (2 Cor 5:21). We certainly cannot approach God with any merit of our own, but God must receive us when we come to Him "in Jesus Christ." The word *receive* in verse 17 means "to receive into one's family circle." Imagine a slave entering his master's family! But imagine a guilty sinner entering God's family! (*Be Faithful*, 199)

Remember the Principle of Satisfaction (18-19)

Paul carries his request to a second step and says, "And if he has wronged you in any way"—something Onesimus almost certainly had done—"or owes you anything, charge that to my account. I, Paul, . . . will repay it." In other words, Paul says, "Don't worry; I will make satisfaction for any debt owed to you by Philemon."

"I, Paul, write this with my own hand" indicates he takes the pen, for a moment, from his secretary to whom he is dictating the letter (probably Timothy). One commentator observes that in doing so, "He gave Philemon his personal handwritten I.O.U." (Polhill, *Paul and His Letters*, 347). The words "charge" and "repay" come from the world of commerce or finances. The idea behind their use here is, "I will take on his indebtedness. I will make good on any damages you have suffered. I will satisfy the demands of the law and the wounded party."

What is going on here is a reflection of what theologians call the doctrine of penal satisfaction or imputation. Wiersbe is again simple but helpful in his brief comments:

> Theologians call this "the doctrine of imputation." (To "impute" means "to put it on account.") When Jesus Christ died on the cross, my sins were put on His account; and He was treated the way I should have been treated. When I trusted Him as my Savior, His righteousness was put on my account; and now God accepts me in Jesus Christ. Jesus said to the

Father, "He no longer owes You a debt because I paid it fully on the cross. Receive him as You would receive Me. Let him come into the family circle!" (*Be Faithful*, 200)

Paul then does what can only be considered a sly thing! He turns up the heat with a not-so-gentle reminder: I won't mention to you that you owe me even your very self (i.e., your own soul)! With a rhetorical knockout punch, Paul reminds Philemon that he is in debt to Paul for his eternal soul. Onesimus's debt appears pretty small in comparison. Paul says he won't bring it up, but in saying that, he brings it up! Still, this should not be the deciding factor in Philemon's decision because Paul wants him to act out of his "own free will" (v. 14).

Remember the Principle of Reconciliation (20)

Paul once again uses a pun on Onesimus's name in verse 20. The word translated "benefit" is the same as the word translated "useful" in verse 11 (Polhill, *Paul and His Letters*, 347). "Yes, brother" reaffirms both Paul's confidence that Philemon will do the right thing and their warm, affectionate relationship (cf. v. 7). Paul exhorts Philemon to be useful, to be a blessing to him "in the Lord," and to "refresh [his] heart in Christ." Of course, the way he could refresh Paul's heart was to be reconciled with his slave Onesimus. Paul wants Philemon to do "what he is apparently good at doing for everyone else, 'refreshing people's heart.'"[1]

By forgiving and reconciling with Onesimus, Philemon would refresh Paul, build unity in the house church he was a part of, and extend to Onesimus the same kind of grace he had received when he trusted Christ.

Those who have been reconciled to God through Christ (2 Cor 5:20-21) should be ever ready to do the same for others who have offended or wounded them. It may initially sting, but joy will surely follow. Perhaps Ephesians 4:32 underscores this best. There Paul writes, "And be kind and compassionate to one another, forgiving one another, just as God

---

[1] Melick, *Philippians, Colossians, Philemon*, 367; citing N. T. Wright, *The Epistles of Paul to the Colossians and Philemon: An Introduction and Commentary* (Grand Rapids, MI: InterVarsity Press, 1986), 189.

also forgave you in Christ." We must never forget this: we will never forgive anyone as much as God in Christ has already forgiven us.

Express Your Confidence in the Gospel's Work in Others
PHILEMON 21-22

These two verses provide valuable lessons in terms of practical theology. They show us how to encourage and motivate (v. 21) and how to prompt hospitality (v. 22). Paul encourages Philemon to do the right thing, confident that he will. He also expresses his optimism in the gracious providence of God that he will be released and able to visit Philemon and the church at Colossae.

Paul has seen evidences of God's grace in the past in Philemon's life (v. 7). He is confident that grace will be evident again, which is revealed in how he treats Onesimus (vv. 20-21). He is also certain that same work of grace will appear in the future upon his own hoped-for arrival (v. 22). Few things are more of a blessing than having good friends, good brothers and sisters, whom you can count on. Knowing they have got your back and will be there for you is a precious gift from God.

Express Your Confidence in Their Obedience and More (21)

Once more Paul expresses his confidence in his "dear friend and coworker" (v. 1). "Since I am confident of your obedience" speaks of Paul's confidence not in Philemon's obedient response to him but rather in his obedient response to God and the gospel, what Moo calls "the gospel imperative" (*The Letters*, 434). Philemon's obedience ultimately is to Christ, not Paul.

Paul goes on to tell Philemon that he knows "[Philemon] will do even more than [Paul says]." *The Message* paraphrases it like this: "I know you well enough. . . . You'll probably go far beyond what I've written." Exactly what he has in mind he does not say. The fact is, it does not matter. Some have speculated that he hoped Philemon would free Onesimus. Perhaps. Others believe he wished Philemon would send him back to Paul to help the apostle in his time of need. This is also possible. Regardless, Paul believes Philemon can be counted on. If Philemon surprises us at all, it will be because he exceeds what most people would do in a similar situation. If any law was at work in Philemon's heart, the apostle Paul was confident it was the law of love (see Rom 13:10).

Express Your Confidence in Their Affection and Prayers (22)

Sometimes the most spiritual thing we can do is to give someone something to drink and eat and a place to stay. And as a former colleague of
mine says, "What good are friends unless you use them?" Of course, he
has in mind using friends in only a good way.

Paul is optimistic—something all Christians should be because of
Jesus's ultimate authority (see Matt 28:18)—that he will be released
from his Roman imprisonment. MacArthur says it well:

> Because he knew the case against him was very weak, Paul
> expected to be released from this first imprisonment (cf.
> Phil 2:23-24). He now believes his release to be imminent,
> perhaps because a date for his hearing before the imperial
> court had been set. Accordingly, he asks Philemon to prepare
> [him] a lodging [CSB, "a guest room"] where he can stay
> when he visits Colossae. (*Colossians and Philemon*, 228–29)

"Prepare" is the fourth and final imperative in Philemon, which I
believe takes the actual form of a "polite request" (Rogers and Rogers,
New Linguistic and Exegetical Key, 515). Paul is asking for future aid that
he will only need once their current prayers are answered.

Paul understood that his fate ultimately was in the hands of God.
He also believed that in the economy of God's ways, the prayers of his
brothers and sisters made a difference. He says the same thing at greater
length in 2 Corinthians 1:10-11. The compatibility of divine sovereignty and human responsibility was something Paul gladly embraced.
Thus he can say to Philemon, "I hope that through your prayers"—
human responsibility—"I will be restored to you"—divine sovereignty
(it is implied that God is the one restoring him). I agree with John
MacArthur, who says, "Prayers are the nerves that move the muscles of
omnipotence" (*Colossians and Philemon*, 229).

Covenant with Gospel Witnesses You Trust
PHILEMON 23-25

God saves us individually, one at a time. However, he did not save us to
be islands unto ourselves. He saved us for community. He saved us for
mutual accountability, encouragement, and life. He gave us a spiritual
family to which our connection is thicker than blood ties. They help

us grow in grace as we are more and more conformed to his image (Rom 8:29-30; 2 Cor 3:18).

Paul concludes his letter by calling on human witnesses and divine enablement to assist Philemon as he decides what to do about Onesimus. This is additional subtle arm-twisting, to be sure. I think Paul believed Philemon would do the right thing. The fact that this book made its way into the canon of Scripture would support the idea that he did. Philemon had a difficult decision to make, and receiving a little help from his friends could not hurt. Perhaps God used them to seal the deal for reconciliation between these men who are now brothers (v. 16).

Call on Faithful Human Witnesses (23-24)

Paul mentions five men in these verses, calling them "my coworkers." He notes one of them, Epaphras, is "my fellow prisoner." D. Edmond Hiebert points out,

> The list is identical to those sending greetings in the epistle
> to the Colossians except that Jesus Justus is here omitted. This
> seems to imply that those here named were personally known
> to Philemon. (*Titus and Philemon*, 124)

Garland adds, "Presumably, each of these persons would vouch for Onesimus and concur with Paul's request on his behalf" (*Colossians and Philemon*, 341).

A brief description of each man is instructive at this point.

Epaphras was from Colossae and certainly well known to Philemon (Col 1:7-8; 4:12-13), but now he is imprisoned alongside Paul in Rome. Paul sees Epaphras as he sees himself: not as a prisoner of the empire but as a prisoner "in Christ Jesus." He is where he is because he is captive to Christ.

Mark is John Mark, author of our second Gospel. Formerly, like Onesimus, he had been useless (Acts 15:38), but now he is useful both to Paul and to the Lord (see especially 2 Tim 4:11).

Aristarchus was a close associate of Paul and was possibly from Macedonia (Acts 19:29; 20:4). He had traveled with Paul to Rome (Acts 27:2). Colossians 4:10 calls him Paul's "fellow prisoner." Tradition says he was martyred in Rome during the persecution under Nero (MacArthur, *Colossians and Philemon*, 230).

Demas is honorably mentioned here and in Colossians 4:14. However, 2 Timothy 4:10 informs us that he deserted Paul, "since he loved this present world."

Luke is "the dearly loved physician" (Col 4:14) who penned the two-volume work Luke-Acts. Some believe he may also have written Hebrews. He traveled with Paul, helped care for him, and became a dear and faithful friend. He would be the only person with Paul in the last days of his second Roman imprisonment as he awaited execution (2 Tim 4:11).

These men, then, stood with Paul on behalf of Onesimus. Paul knew they were faithful and trustworthy, and so did Philemon. Their "vote" in favor of Onesimus would have carried significant weight.

Call for Divine Enablement (25)

Paul ends this letter in the same way he began: with Jesus. In fact he begins and ends using our Savior's full majestic title, "the Lord Jesus Christ" (vv. 3,25). And as he began with a prayer following his greeting (vv. 1-3), he ends with a prayer of a single sentence of eleven words in our English text. He prays gospel grace, which is ours abundantly in the "Lord" (emphasizing his deity) "Jesus" (his humanity) "Christ" (his office). Murray Harris insightfully notes that the personal pronoun "your" is plural. Thus Paul's final words might be paraphrased, "May the grace given by the Lord Jesus Christ be with you Philemon, your household, and the whole church, sanctifying the spirit of each of you" (*Colossians and Philemon*, 224). Grace flooding their spirits would be key in dealing with the Onesimus affair. Paul, I believe, was confident it would lead Philemon to the right decision.

Conclusion

In an article titled "How Paul Worked to Overcome Slavery," John Piper provides an excellent summary of the letter to Philemon. In the process he shows us specifically how the gospel works in real life by reconciling brothers and sowing the seeds of the destruction of an evil and sinful institution. He makes eleven observations:

1. Paul draws attention to Philemon's love for all the saints (v. 5), putting Philemon's relation with Onesimus (now one of the saints) under the banner of love, not just commerce.
2. Paul models for Philemon the superiority of appeals over commands when it comes to relationships governed by love (vv. 8-9).

3. Paul heightens the sense of Onesimus being in the family of God by calling him his child (v. 10).
4. Paul raises the stakes again by saying that Onesimus has become entwined around his own deep affections (v. 12).
5. Paul again emphasizes that he wants to avoid force or coercion in his relationship with Philemon (vv. 13-14).
6. Paul raises the intensity of the relationship again with the word "forever" (v. 15; CSB, "permanently"). In other words, Onesimus is not coming back into any ordinary, secular relationship.
7. Paul says that Philemon's relationship can no longer be the usual master-slave relationship (v. 16). Whether he lets Onesimus go back free to serve Paul, or keeps him in his service, things cannot remain as they were.
8. In the same verse (v. 16), Paul refers to Onesimus as Philemon's beloved brother, replacing the old master-slave relationship with a more fundamental and spiritual one.
9. Paul makes clear that Onesimus is with Philemon in the Lord. Onesimus's identity is now the same as Philemon's.
10. Paul tells Philemon to receive Onesimus the way he would receive Paul.
11. Paul says to Philemon that he will cover all of Onesimus's debts. Philemon would no doubt be shamed by this, if he had any thoughts of demanding repayment from his new brother.

Piper concludes,

> The upshot of all this is that, without explicitly prohibiting slavery, Paul has pointed the church away from slavery because it is an institution which is incompatible with the way the gospel works in people's lives. Whether the slavery is economic, racial, sexual, mild, or brutal, Paul's way of dealing with Philemon works to undermine the institution across its various manifestations. To walk "in step with the truth of the gospel" (Galatians 2:14) is to walk away from slavery. ("How Paul Worked to Overcome Slavery")

These are wise words with which to conclude a wonderful little book in the Bible—too often abused, too often neglected. We ignore it at our great loss.

Reflect and Discuss

1. How do we see the gospel played out in the message of Philemon?
2. In what ways are all of us like Onesimus?
3. What are some basic ways we can apply the essentials of the gospel to everyday life? In what areas of your life do you need to begin applying the gospel?
4. How does Christ provide satisfaction for our debt? To whom does he pay the debt?
5. How does Paul want Philemon to refresh his heart? What are some ways you can be refreshing to brothers and sisters in your local church?
6. How does Paul know Philemon will do even more than Paul asks? What does this show about Philemon's faith?
7. Why is Paul confident about his future well-being? Should Christians always be confident they will be delivered from their circumstances?
8. How can prayer be effective if God is sovereign?
9. Why does Paul end his letter with a prayer? What did Philemon need most to be able to make the right decision?
10. How does Paul's letter to Philemon undermine the institution of slavery, rather than uphold it?

WORKS CITED

Akin, Daniel L., and R. Scott Pace. *Pastoral Theology: Who a Pastor Is and What He Does.* Nashville, TN: B&H Academic, 2017.

Aristides. "The Apology of Aristides the Philosopher." Translated by D. M. Kay. *Early Christian Writings.* Accessed October 22, 2020. http://www.earlychristianwritings.com/text/aristides-kay.html.

Beale, G. K. *Colossians and Philemon.* Baker Exegetical Commentary on the New Testament. Grand Rapids, MI: Baker, 2019.

Bratt, James D., editor. *Abraham Kuyper: A Centennial Reader.* Grand Rapids: Eerdmans, 1998.

"The Bystander Effect." *UKRI.* Economic and Social Research Council. Accessed March 1, 2020. https://esrc.ukri.org/about-us/50-years-of-esrc/50-achievements/the-bystander-effect.

Calvin, John. *Commentaries on the Epistles to the Galatians . . . Philemon.* Translated by John Pringle and William Pringle. Calvin's Commentaries, vol. XXI. Grand Rapids, MI: Baker, 1979.

Campbell, Douglas A. "Unraveling Colossians 3:11b." *New Testament Studies* 42 (1996), 120–32.

Criswell, W. A. "For Love's Sake," February 1, 1959. *W. A. Criswell Sermon Library.* Accessed October 22, 2020. https://www.wacriswell.com/sermons/1959/for-love-s-sake.

Garland, David E. *Colossians and Philemon,* The NIV Application Commentary. Grand Rapids, MI: Zondervan, 1998.

Grout, Wendell K. *Colossians and Philemon: The Supremacy of Christ.* Deeper Life Pulpit Commentary. Camp Hill, PA: Christian Publications, 2001.

Harris, Murray J. *Colossians and Philemon.* Exegetical Guide to the Greek New Testament. Grand Rapids, MI: Eerdmans, 1991.

Hawkins, O. S. *Tearing Down Walls and Building Bridges.* Nashville, TN: Nelson, 1995.

Hendriksen, William. *Exposition of Colossians and Philemon*. Baker New Testament Commentary. Grand Rapids, MI: Baker Book House, 1964.

Hiebert, D. Edmond. *Titus and Philemon*. Everyman's Bible Commentary. Chicago, IL: Moody, 1985.

Keller, Timothy. *Center Church: Doing Balanced, Gospel-Centered Ministry in Your City*. Grand Rapids, MI: Zondervan, 2012.

King, Martin Luther, Jr. "'The American Dream,' Sermon Delivered at Ebenezer Baptist Church on 4 July 1965." Accessed June 1, 2020. https://kinginstitute.stanford.edu/king-papers/documents/american-dream-sermon-delivered-ebenezer-baptist-church.

Lewis, C. S. *The Weight of Glory and Other Addresses*. San Francisco, CA: HarperSanFrancisco, 2000.

Lightfoot, J. B. *St. Paul's Epistle to the Colossians and to Philemon*. Repr. ed. Grand Rapids, MI: Zondervan, 1959.

MacArthur, John. *Colossians and Philemon*. MacArthur New Testament Commentary. Chicago, IL: Moody Press, 1992.

McFadden, Robert D. "A Model's Dying Screams Are Ignored at the Site of Kitty Genovese's Murder." *New York Times*. December 27, 1974. Accessed March 1, 2020. https://www.nytimes.com/1974/12/27/archives/a-models-dying-screams-are-ignored-at-the-site-of-kitty-genoveses.html.

Melick, Richard R., Jr. *Philippians, Colossians, Philemon*. New American Commentary, vol. 32. Nashville, TN: B&H, 1991.

Moo, Douglas J. *The Letters to the Colossians and to Philemon*. Pillar New Testament Commentary. Grand Rapids, MI: Eerdmans, 2008.

Moule, C. F. D. *The Epistles of Paul the Apostle to the Colossians and Philemon*, The Cambridge Greek Testament Commentary. Cambridge, MA: University Press, 1962.

O'Brien, P. T. *Colossians, Philemon*. Word Bible Commentary. Waco, TX: Word, 1982.

Pao, David W. *Colossians and Philemon*. Exegetical Commentary on the New Testament, vol. 12. Grand Rapids, MI: Zondervan, 2012.

Piper, John. "How Paul Worked to Overcome Slavery." *Desiring God*. Last modified September 3, 2009. Accessed October 22, 2020. http://www.desiringgod.org/articles/how-paul-worked-to-overcome-slavery.

Polhill, John B. *Paul and His Letters*. Nashville, TN: B&H, 1999.

Rae, Allen. "Love Is . . . : Practical Manifestations of Love from the Epistle to Philemon." *Uplook*. September 1998, 21.

Robinson, Haddon. *Biblical Preaching: The Development and Delivery of Expository Messages.* 2nd ed. Grand Rapids, MI: Baker, 2001.

Rogers, Cleon L., Jr., and Cleon L. Rogers III. *The New Linguistic and Exegetical Key to the Greek New Testament.* Grand Rapids, MI: Zondervan, 1998.

Slater, Thomas B. "Translating ἅγιος in Col 1,2 and Eph 1,1." *Biblica* 87 (2006), 52–54.

"37 Who Saw Murder Didn't Call the Police; Apathy at Stabbing of Queens Woman Shocks Inspector." *New York Times.* March 3, 1964. Accessed March 1, 2020. https://www.nytimes.com/1964/03/27/archives/37-who-saw-murder-didnt-call-the-police-apathy-at-stabbing-of.html.

Warren, Rick. "How to Be a Good Steward of Your Influence." pastors.com. Accessed August 3, 2020. https://pastors.com/good-steward-influence.

Wiersbe, Warren W. *Be Faithful: It's Always Too Soon to Quit!: 1 & 2 Timothy, Titus, Philemon.* Colorado Springs, CO: David C. Cook, 2009.

Wilson, Jim. "What God Can Do: Philemon 8–16." Unpublished sermon.

SCRIPTURE INDEX

.